I0754547

We then follow her in a stormy voyage across the Atlantic, in which she was shipwrecked, when two little brothers were washed overboard; one was rescued, but "the other was lost." She then naïvely sketches the history of her school-day joys and sorrows, ending with an elopement and a precocious marriage. All the details, both tragic and comic, are given with the most amusing, often affecting particularity; and the sympathetic reader is involuntarily led to make her joys and sorrows his own. Like every true chapter of checkered human life, the lights and shadows are nearly equally, often fitfully blended, and we are alternately moved to tears and laughter. — *New York Mirror.*

One of the few books which it is difficult to lay down till every page is read is the "Autobiography of Mrs. Mowatt." I have actually stolen the time which ought to have been appropriated to certain special demands, to look through the pages of this strange volume. To look at any chapter of contents is sure to send you to the text; and to start with the text is to rivet your attention, in spite of every extraneous call. Mrs Mowatt's Autobiography will have a permanent place in American literature. Edition after edition will come from the press. It will be the exciting theme of book notices, and even of labored reviews. — *New Covenant.*

These personal memoirs are replete with romantic interest. The life of Mrs. Mowatt has been an eventful one, beyond that even of most actresses; and it is not alone her personal friends who will find this volume full of interest. Every one who has witnessed the impersonations of the talented actress, and who has heard something of her romantic story, will eagerly avail themselves of this opportunity to learn more of one whose life has been one of singular vicissitudes, and whose experience must, of necessity, be rich in personal reminiscence. The book has the interest of a novel from beginning to end. The tone is high and unaffectedly religious; and while the author vindicates the profession which she is about to quit, she mingles words of counsel with her farewell, which cannot fail to benefit those for whom they are intended.—*Dollar Newspaper.*

Mrs. Mowatt is certainly one of the cleverest women living. In all that she undertakes she succeeds, and this not so much by force of genius as by her womanly tact, and a degree of energy that could scarcely be expected in so slight and delicate a frame as hers. She has written good poetry; good magazine sketches; the best of modern American comedies (Fashion); a capital poetical drama (Armand); has taken high rank as an actress, and now she has given to the world the pleasantest bit of autobiography that we have seen for a long time. It is a frank, simple narrative, with little affectation, and no more egotism than is always unavoidable where the narrator is the heroine. Her school-days, her courtship and elopement, her domestic habits, her reverses, her career as a public reader and actress, at home and abroad, her widowhood, and everything in her recent history, except her second courtship, which is to take her from public life, are admirably told. Anecdotes abound in the volume; and there is not a page that does not exhibit the traits of a truly "smart" woman. We shall not be surprised if this book takes the lead of all others in popularity this season.—*Philadelphia Mail.*

* * * We have been looking for this volume with some interest, and now that it has at length reached us, we give it the cordial welcome due to its intellectual writer, who is one of the most accomplished females that has ever graced the American boards. The Autobiography makes a handsome volume of four hundred and forty-eight duodecimo pages, well printed and bound. The scenes, incidents, and characters, so graphically presented, are distributed through various portions of this country and Europe, and give the details of a most varied and interesting life, passed among vicissitudes of exceedingly bright and darkly adverse fortune. It has much the air of romance, and portions possess a truly dramatic and effective interest. The portrait that adorns the frontispiece looks full of truthful earnestness, and almost speaks the author's bright and sparkling

thoughts, the emotions flashing in the exuberance of flowing spirits and expressive animation, which wreathe the whole countenance in smiles. — *Saturday Courier.*

It is with the greatest simplicity and candor of thought and expression, with the modesty and true refinement which made her so beloved in private life, and respected in her successful career. There is so much naturalness and kindly spirit in every page, that we think no one can rise from its perusal without feeling they have made the acquisition of a very charming friend, whom they will delight to meet again in her own person. There is a good deal of playfulness in her temper, which has fine scope amid the various people and scenes among which her profession led her. Her passing notice of cotemporary celebrities is always interesting and to the purpose. Miss Martineau and mesmerism, in their connection, are very fully and boldly handled. Her defence of the stage is sustained by a good deal of research and good sense. There were portions of her domestic relations and personal narrative that are very touching; but we leave our readers to receive their sweetness and sadness from the book itself. The laurels are still new, and fresh, and green, on her brow. Those who have seen her beautiful embodiment of the most lovely and powerful characters will ever remember these occasions as among the most interesting in their experience; and those who have but this opportunity, and who, in her withdrawal from the stage, can never hope to be moved by her personations, will repent more than ever their loss. — *New Bedford Mercury.*

THE PROMPTER'S DAUGHTER.

MIMIC LIFE;

OR,

BEFORE AND BEHIND THE CURTAIN.

A SERIES OF NARRATIVES,

BY

ANNA CORA RITCHIE

(FORMERLY MRS. MOWATT),

AUTHOR OF "AUTOBIOGRAPHY OF AN ACTRESS," "ARMAND," "FASHION," ETC.

He who feels contempt
For any living thing, hath faculties
Which he has never used; and thought with him
Is in its infancy.
WORDSWORTH.

BOSTON:

TICKNOR AND FIELDS.

M DCCC LVI.

STEREOTYPED BY
HOBART & ROBBINS,
New England Type and Stereotype Foundery,
BOSTON.

Affectionately Dedicated

TO

SAMUEL G. OGDEN.

MY FATHER:

Whose name but yours could I inscribe upon this volume, commenced in my southern home, but two thirds written at the very desk over which your own honored form has bowed for more than half a century; — written in this sunny little chamber, which is hallowed to me by such a host of old associations? All harmonious influences have combined to render my labor light, and full of love. The very pine-trees, tossing their familiar plumes at the window, have aided in sending back my thoughts

"Along the pebbled shore of memory,"

that I might gather up the shells life's surges cast at my wandering feet; for my task has consisted in *remembering*, not inventing.

What this book will be to the world I cannot judge; to you, my beloved father, be it a remembrance of the brief months that, beneath your hospitable roof, have fled so happily for

Your daughter,

ANNA CORA RITCHIE.

RAVENSWOOD, *October 27th*, 1855.

PREFACE.

To record the singular incidents that occurred around me, and sketch the striking histories which awakened my interest, was a favorite employment during a professional career of nine years. Out of the many-colored webs of life thus collected the narratives that compose this volume are woven. Fiction has lent but few embellishing touches. Truth is left to proclaim her own *strangeness.* Should this work achieve the object contemplated, its readers will receive a more correct impression of some unlaurelled laborers for the public amusement than is generally entertained. Between them and the every-day world the curtain of prejudice has fallen in impenetrable folds. From its fatal shadow those alone who climb to the highest pinnacles of fame emerge. Yet among the most lowly of the proscribed band there are many whose lives bear witness that Heaven plants its flowers and scatters its pearls in unexpected places. Look for them, you who judge rashly, before you pronounce that they have no existence there !

ANNA CORA RITCHIE.

Ravenswood, October 27th, 1855.

CONTENTS.

STELLA.

CHAPTER I.

CHAPTER II.

CHAPTER III.

CHAPTER IV.

CHAPTER V.

CHAPTER VI.

CHAPTER VII.

CHAPTER VIII.

CHAPTER IX.

THE PROMPTER'S DAUGHTER.

CHAPTER I.

CHAPTER II.

CHAPTER III.

CHAPTER IV.

CHAPTER V.

CHAPTER VI.

CHAPTER VII.

THE UNKNOWN TRAGEDIAN.

CHAPTER I.

CHAPTER II.

CHAPTER III.

CHAPTER IV.

CHAPTER V.

CHAPTER VI.

CHAPTER VII.

STELLA.

We know what we are, but we know not what we may be.

OPHELIA.

STELLA.

We know what we are, but we know not what we may be.
OPHELIA.

CHAPTER I.

A Sheriff's Sale. — Faithful Mattie. — Stella. — The Sudden Project. — Ernest Rosenvelt, the Tragedian. — A Mourner without Hope. — Stella's Startling Disclosure to Mrs. Rosenvelt. — Apathy of the Mother, and Fixed Resolution of the Daughter. — Mr. and Mrs. Oakland. — Stella's Visit to their Cottage. — Mr. Oakland's Repugnance to the Theatrical Profession. — Futile Endeavors to discourage his Impetuous Pupil. — A Reluctant Consent. — The Study of Juliet. — The First Lesson. — Effects upon Stella's Highly-wrought Imagination. — The Widowed Mother's Alarm. — Losing one's Identity. — The Expected Letter. — Disappointment. — Enthusiasm that Runs Riot. — Genius and Mediocrity.

"MUST you hang that red rag from the drawing-room window? Could n't you choose any other?"

Mattie ventured to touch the elbow of the man whom she thus querulously addressed. He was in the act of securing the pole that suspended a scarlet flag in front of a stately mansion in one of the most fashionable localities in Boston.

"It 's a sheriff's sale!" was the *brusque* reply.

"All the world knows that, without your red-dragon token!" sighed Mattie. She looked disconsolately around the spacious apartment, in which the costly appliances of wealth were ranged, not in their customary order, but as best fitted their display for an auction.

Thirty years before the period alluded to, Mr. Rosenvelt, an American merchant, visited London with his youthful wife. Mattie chanced to be employed by the lady as assistant dress-maker. The English girl became a widow one year after her marriage, and a few months before the book of her teens was closed. She had never contemplated entering service, but soon conceived a warm attachment for Mrs. Rosenvelt, and was induced to accept the situation of lady's maid. A year afterwards, the devoted attendant accompanied her master and mistress to America. Very great was her astonishment when she was first thrown in contact with the Boston "helps," who are so horrified at the word "servant" that they would gladly have the expression "thy man-servant and thy maid-servant" erased from the decalogue. Mattie was puzzled to comprehend how honest servitude could be considered a degradation.

"Must not some rule, and some serve?" she would say. "It is my lot to serve, and I take pride in serving faithfully. If I begin to think myself too good to serve my mistress, I shall soon think myself too good to serve my God."

The policy of leaving a tried situation for one more profitable — an idea of peculiarly American growth — never found its way into her simple, uncalculating mind. She deemed herself grafted upon the family which she first entered; their interests were hers, their sorrows hers, their welfare hers; she was their helpful friend as well as their domestic. The much-enduring Mattie never talked of too much trouble, or too much fatigue; she always undertook more than any one mortal could possibly accomplish; and, though her inclination constantly outstripped her strength, she was never wholly baffled. Her hands were ever tendered to lift other people's burdens; her sympathies ever ready

> "——— to fly east or west, whichever
> Way besought them."

Her existence was completely merged in that of others.

A crowd of curious idlers, or intended purchasers, now made their way into the apartment. Mattie noticed the rude manner with which they examined the objects of *vertu* which had been so highly valued by their owners — the gifts, perchance, of dear friends, the prized mementos of happy hours. She brushed away a troublesome tear, and hurried up the stairs, looking first into this room, then into that, evidently in search of some one. At last she opened the door of a large but totally dismantled chamber; it was once the favorite apartment of the master of the house, the room from which his corpse had been borne out.

There a young girl was rapidly walking up and down, her eyes fixed on the ground, her small hands clasped tightly over her head, lost in deep thought.

To paint an odor or an atmosphere, the melting

hues of a rainbow, the soft effulgence of a moonlight lamp, would be a more promising attempt than to portray by language the intangible attribute which compelled those who gazed upon her to pronounce Stella beautiful. The charm dwelt not in any one feature, for none was faultless. The perfect harmony that blended the whole countenance, the rapid transitions of expression, the flashing soul shining through its transparent covering as through a crystal casement — these constituted the elements of her loveliness.

Her eyes were neither very large nor very small. At one time they appeared to be brilliantly black; at another, they seemed a lustrous blue. They were, in reality, of a grayish hue, mingled with light hazel, which possesses the peculiarity of changing its color with varying emotions.

Her abundant hair exhibited that rare tint which the French call *chatain doré* — chestnut, streaked with gold. It partook of the chameleon property of her eyes: when the air was clear, and radiant with sunshine, her tresses were almost golden; in a humid atmosphere, the shining yellow was extinguished, and replaced by a soft brown.

Her flexible lips disclosed immaculate teeth, and, in repose, the mouth seemed to curve itself spontaneously into a smile. Her figure was slightly above the medium height, with the slender, *spanable* waist, undeveloped proportions, and not very erect bearing, which characterize the American maiden at eighteen; the precise opposite of the swelling form, the rounded arms, dimpled shoulders, and firm carriage, that distinguish an English girl at the same age.

"There 's a crowd pouring in below, Miss Stella, dear. Had we not better come away home ?" asked Mattie, tenderly.

"Home ! — O, Mattie !"

"Well, I did n't mean to vex you. I know well enough you never knew any home but this, and can't get accustomed to think of the shabbyish rooms at the boarding-place as home. But your mother 's there, and she 's wanting us, perhaps."

"Yes — I 'll go, Mattie. My mother may want us. But first let me tell you of what I am thinking. Only don't start, and remonstrate, and be horrified with me,— I could n't bear that now. I have just been told by our lawyer that the sale of this house and our furniture — all we have — will not more than meet my father's liabilities. My dear mother and I are left without provision, solely dependent on my brother. You know how noble Ernest is ; how willingly he would share his last farthing with us ; but his salary at the theatre as yet is small — not sufficient to furnish him with the expensive wardrobe that is requisite in his profession."

"True enough, dear. Yet he wrote that he would manage to spare sufficient to take care of his mother and of you ; and are we not all sure that he will do it gladly ?"

"So he would. But he cannot possibly secure to my mother the comforts, the luxuries, to which she has been accustomed, which her feeble health demands. And we shall be as a huge millstone around the neck of Ernest ; we shall prevent his climbing the ladder of fame; we shall keep him always on the lowest round. No! I tell you it must not be!—it shall not be! I am as fitted to work as he. Why should not I exert myself? Why should I

> "——— dully sluggardized at home,
> Wear out my youth with shapeless idleness"?

"You, child!—*you!* What could you do?"

"Not teach, perhaps;—I have thought of that—the compensation is too pitiful; not give music-lessons, though that would be more profitable; not become an artist—I have not talent for that; those walks are all closed to me;—but there is one open—*the stage.*

"O, Miss Stella! I shall think you demented!"

"So people said of my brother, when my father took him into his counting-house, and Ernest grew weary and listless, and one day declared that he had no turn for commerce; that he preferred a profession; that there was one profession alone for which he had decided abilities—that of an actor. My father was angry enough at first, and my mother wept and talked of disgrace. But Ernest was so fixed in his resolution, he proved himself so upright, so persevering, that he won them over. Don't you remember, Mattie, when he engaged as 'second walking gentleman' in a country theatre at a miserable salary, how we all remonstrated? But he studied incessantly; he rose rapidly; he soon received an offer to appear here at the Tremont. My father saw him perform, pronounced that he had genius for his vocation, and, after that, was content. It was just one year before my dear father died, and now Ernest is engaged as leading man in one of the largest theatres in New York. To be sure, he shares the business with an older actor, which is unfortunate. But who doubts that he will become one of the most renowned tragedians of the day? Not I!"

"The Lord love him! I always said he was cut out for the pattern of a great man, and it's coming true."

"Why did n't you make a prophecy about me at the same time, Mattie? for there are laurels springing somewhere about this earth which I hope to wear. I am tired of this aimless existence. You remember Mr. Oakland, with whom my brother read, and who was also my teacher of elocution? I once heard him say that my powers of personation were not inferior to those of Ernest. Hundreds of times that remark has come back to me, for Mr. Oakland is no idle flatterer. My brother must procure me an engagement in the theatre where he acts; we shall perform together; — he will instruct me and protect me; — I will use my talents as well as he!"

"It 's not for me to presume upon advising; and I know nothing of theatres except what I 've heard from Mr. Ernest. But this I know,— *I 'm* always happiest with *my hands full,* and so, perhaps, will you be. But how will you get your mother's consent?"

"She has never seemed to care for anything since my father's death. She will hardly rouse herself to refuse,— I think I can persuade her. Let us go —" ("home," she was about to say, but she checked herself) — "back to the boarding-house."

Stella found her mother sitting in the attitude of

listless despair, which had become habitual to her since the death of her husband. She was clad in the deepest mourning, her hair smoothed from her brow, and covered with a close widow's cap, which, to her morbid mind, seemed one of grief's needful expressions. Her wan face, grown prematurely old, rested on her thin hand; her whole mien betokened the most perfect apathy. She could not occupy herself; she could not converse, or even think; she wholly surrendered her spirit to the dominion of a sorrow that paralyzed all her faculties. Grief filled every chamber of her heart, and left no room for comfort to enter in. Yet she was what is styled a "church-going woman," and scrupulously strict in all pious observances. No hypocrite, though a misconstruer of the great ends of religion — it never occurred to her that there is impiety in yielding to hopeless despondency; that there is sin in everything that obstructs, or even partially curtails, our usefulness; that the eyes of living Faith are never rivetted downwards on the grave, but upraised to the heaven beyond.

Mr. Rosenvelt died suddenly. His affairs were left to the settlement of lawyers. In a few months it was announced to the helpless widow that she was penniless, — that she must leave her luxurious home, forego her customary habits, and look to her son for future support. The second shock had been so much transcended by the first, that this new blow was scarcely felt. She removed to a comfortless boarding-house without betraying any unusual emotion. She wept much, but silently. She seemed to think that "taking up a place in the world" was all that now remained for her in life; and day by day her mental torpor increased.

Mrs. Rosenvelt scarcely looked up as her daughter entered the room. Stella knelt down by her mother's side, and caressingly took the hand that lay in her lap.

"Mother, I want to talk to you, if you have strength to hear me. May I?"

"Yes," was the languidly-uttered reply.

"But I shall perhaps startle you by a project that I have at heart. I want you to be prepared, dearest mother."

There was no answer, but a heart-sore sigh, which seemed to say that nothing in life could startle or grieve her more.

"May I go on, mother, dear?"

"Yes."

Then Stella courageously repeated the hopes and schemes that she had confided to Mattie, warming with her subject, as though she thought to inspire her mother with her own ardor. Her cheeks glowed and her eyes flashed, as she paused, panting for a reply.

Mrs. Rosenvelt shook her head. "It is one of your wild dreams, child; it will never be,—you cannot accomplish it."

"Mother, I *can*, and *will*, with Heaven's help and your permission! Have I that?"

It cost Mrs. Rosenvelt a great effort to rouse herself sufficiently to utter a few commonplace objections, such as her daughter easily combated. The will of the former, opposed to that of the latter, bowed as a reed before a strong blast—was borne onward as a straw on a rushing tide. But the facile mother could not be lured into an argument.

"At least, may I write to my brother, and see what he will say and do?"

"Yes."

"Thank you, mother; now all will be well. I am sure of it! If I could only see you smile!"

"Stella! Stella!" and Mrs Rosenvelt burst into an agony of tears. The possibility of smiling seemed to her almost sacrilege.

Stella's caresses only increased the violence of her mother's grief, and the young girl silently waited for the paroxysm to subside. She could not weep herself; she had too much to plan, too much to accomplish. Strenuous action and the luxury of tears are incompatible.

When at last the sobs died away, Stella arose and disappeared in the closet-like apartment which served as her chamber. The letter to her brother was written at once, and Mattie despatched with it to the post.

This much effected, Stella grew restless to achieve something more. She took it for granted that her brother's answer must be favorable. Her next step was to visit her former tutor and ever-dear friend, Mr. Oakland. A few minutes' walk brought her to the garden gate of his bower-like cottage. Without, as within, this unpretending abode, a presence of tasteful simplicity, an evident love and cultivation of the beautiful, proclaimed the refined tone of its inmates.

Mr. Oakland was by birth an Englishman of sterling family. In his first manhood, Prosperity, with lavish hands, scattered her good gifts about his path. He might have aptly styled himself "the very button on Fortune's cap." Scarcely had she launched him on a brilliant-seeming commercial career, than her smiles were capriciously withdrawn. Then came the struggles so bitter to a proud and sensitive nature. We pass over his youthful contest with life. At the period of which we write, his day of wrestling with adversity had nearly closed. For some years he had been recognized as an eminent master of elocution, and his talents found ample exercise in colleges, institutes, literary coteries, and the public lecture-room. The world made him tardy compensation for early buffets.

In intellect, as in appearance, he preserved the freshness and vigor which belong to manhood's prime. There was a singular mingling of reserve and frankness in his manners. Too courteous to be positively blunt, he notwithstanding often spoke truths to his best friends that lacked gentleness. Beneath the dignified reticence, which was sometimes mistaken for coldness or pride, there flowed a current of warm geniality. The thin icy barrier was but a mere coating on the external surface, which quickly melted before the sunshine of appreciation.

To Mr. Oakland's instruction and advice Ernest Rosenvelt had been greatly indebted for his first success upon the stage. Out of this fact sprang Stella's determination to apply to her former tutor. Mr. Oakland, while he enjoyed to the highest degree the displays of dramatic genius,—while the performances of Siddons and O'Neill, Kemble and Cook, were engraven as on tablets of steel, and treasured in his memory,—yet entertained a deep-rooted repugnance for the theatrical profession itself. Stella was aware of this antipathy, and felt sure that he would attempt to dissuade her from her purpose; but the wayward girl was too strongly armed in her self-will to believe that she could be conquered.

When she reached his residence Mr. Oakland was engaged; he might not be at leisure for some time. Stella inquired for Mrs. Oakland, and was soon admitted to her presence. Subdued in manners, mild and ladylike in person, Mrs. Oakland exemplified the beauty of that most lovable and womanly trait, the power of appreciating others — of drawing forth their finest qualities, without the desire to shine herself. She never originated, but always reflected back brilliancy. Her quick apprehension and ready sympathy were even more conducive to delightful social intercourse than the display of sparkling intellectual gifts. She possessed the gracious faculty of rendering her guests pleased with themselves; consequently they were always charmed with her.

Stella made a failing attempt to talk on indifferent subjects; then broke off abruptly, and dashed at once into a full relation of her scheme. She had risen from her seat, and was discoursing so enthusiastically upon her future career that she did not hear the door open. The expression of her auditor's countenance caused her to turn. Mr. Oakland stood behind her, intently listening.

"Then you know what I am talking about? You have heard my project?" was her eager greeting.

"Yes; and what am I to think of you?"

"Think? Think that I am, in the words of Portia,

'An unlessoned girl, unschooled, unpractised!
Happy in this, she is not yet so old
But she *may learn*; happier than this,
She is not bred so *dull* but she *can* learn;
Happiest of all is, that her gentle spirit
Commits itself to you to be instructed!'

Why do you smile?"

"I was reflecting that, if you could carry that earnestness and naturalness of manner to the stage, instruction would almost be an act of supererogation. But you do not know the difficulty of *representing* in public that which is easy to feel, or to simulate, in private. A thousand obstacles —"

Stella interrupted him impatiently: "Do not talk to me of difficulties and obstacles! Every pursuit in life has its difficulties and obstacles. Leave *me* to wage war with those! Will you help me? Will you fit me for what I am about to undertake? Do not refuse! I should only make the attempt without you, and then I *might* fail!"

"If you really persist in venturing, let me caution you —"

"Now, do not damp my ardor with wet-blanket cautions! I dare say I shall encounter remonstrances enough; so I make my declaration of independence at once, and give you fair warning that I shall listen to no one, since my mother has yielded her opposition."

Mr. Oakland saw that it was useless to check the headstrong girl. If she had strength and ability equal to her perseverance, she possessed the chief elements of success.

"What shall I study first? In what character shall I make my débût?"

"You must inform me first in what theatre you expect to appear, and with what privileges."

"O! of course in New York, with my brother, and with all sorts of privileges, — no fear about that!"

"But there *is* fear. It may not be so easy to procure an engagement. You do not know the difficulties —"

"There! You will fill my ears with *difficulties* again! Do make him stop, Mrs. Oakland; and ask him to advise me what I shall study."

"Well, then, young Impetuosity, I should advise Shakspeare's heroines. At least, let your school be high. You can study Imogen, and Desdemona, and Ophelia, and Beatrice, and Rosalind, and Portia, and Viola, and Juliet, and Cordelia, at once. Will that satisfy you?"

"It delights me; I shall begin immediately!"

"What! to study them *all together?* What a theatrical prodigy you intend to be! And with a memory as capacious as Garagantua's mouth!"

"Now, don't laugh at me! I mean I'll begin with one, — Juliet, I think. I should delight to personate Juliet. We will select that for my débût, and Ernest will enact Romeo. There! that's settled. Now for the rest: when may I begin to read with you?"

"Had you not better wait to hear what your brother advises?"

"No, no! Wait! — that's impossible! His answer will make no difference. Is he not an actor himself? Does he not openly profess to honor the stage? How can he object to my becoming an actress? Tell me when I may commence! Why not now — this very moment? Here is a Shakspeare temptingly ready!" And she commenced turning over the leaves in search of Romeo and Juliet.

Mr. Oakland laughed as he took the volume from her hand.

"Not so fast, my dear little histrionic candidate! You quite take away my breath with your impetuous spirit. We can't build up this theatrical Rome of yours in a day. I expect a young clerical pupil in a few moments. Shakspeare must give way to the Episcopal service, which I am to read with him."

"Then, when shall I commence? Shall it be to-morrow?"

"Yes; to-morrow, at this hour."

"Thank you a thousand times, my kind friend! You may be sure I shall be punctual. Day after to-morrow I will bring you my brother's letter, and we shall know everything. I may truly say, with Juliet, ''t is twenty years till then.' And so good-by, — good-by, Mrs. Oakland! 'Parting is such sweet sorrow,' etc. etc."

Stella returned home, elated by her interview. Shakspeare's Juliet engrossed her entire thoughts for the remainder of that day. She dwelt in wonder over the affluent imagery, the luxuriance of metaphor, with which Juliet's language teems. But it was not merely the text of the peerless bard that she studied. Her mind grappled with his conception of the enamored maiden, whose whole being is made captive by a passion as sudden and pure as it must have proved constant. Stella pondered upon the depth and rich variety of Juliet's attributes; the girlish simplicity, the fiery impulsiveness, the heroism born of suffering, the rapid transition, through "the inly touch of love," from unexpanded girlhood to perfect womanhood. All these revelations of character she grasped intuitively; but could she portray them? Could she compel an audience to exclaim, "This is no counterfeit presentment, but a living portrait of Shakspeare's unrivalled creation"?

She would gladly have passed the night in her fascinating occupation, but this attempt the prudent Mattie successfully opposed. Sleep touched the young girl's eyelids but lightly, and in brief and broken visits.

When she appeared at breakfast, her manner was so abstracted that even her unobservant mother's attention was aroused. Stella hardly tasted the food before her; her eyes were fixed as though upon some far-off object, and now and then she muttered a few indistinct words, or involuntarily uttered them aloud.

"My dear Stella, I am afraid you are ill!"

"O no, mother! I am only studying a part, and it interests me so much, I cannot think of anything else."

"Is that all?" returned her mother, languidly.

The appointed hour was just striking, when Stella passed through the garden entrance to Mr. Oakland's residence. The greeting of her tutor was brief and grave. Reflection had only added to the unwillingness with which he yielded to her request. But her absorbed attention as she listened to his analysis of Juliet's complex traits, her rapid seizure of his ideas when he pointed out a line of demarcation between the graceful embodiment that would be charming in a drawing-room and the strongly-marked lights and shadows requisite in the wide arena of a theatre, the Protean changes of her speaking countenance, her concentration of mind, and total self-forgetfulness, perforce dispelled his reluctance.

When she began to read, her crude but striking conception startled him into a sensation very closely akin to enthusiasm.

"Her talent vindicates her determination!" he ejaculated mentally. "This diamond needs but polish to proclaim its true water!"

But no such language passed his lips. He was no spendthrift of his praises.

Stella was still reading when Mrs. Oakland gently opened the door.

"Surely, the hour is not out?" exclaimed the young girl.

"Yes, and another hour has gone with it, and a third is beginning to follow them." Mrs. Oakland affectionately saluted her, and then added, "I knew how completely absorbed you must be; and I would not have interrupted you, but a class has been waiting for some time."

"Two hours gone! Is it possible?" said Mr. Oakland, rising. "I must bid you a hasty good-morning."

"May I come to-morrow, at the same hour?"

"I suppose I shall be compelled to say yes."

"I should not listen to 'no,'" replied Stella, playfully. "To-morrow I will bring my brother's letter."

She returned home, and instantly resumed her studies. She had now reached the "potion scene."

The thronging horrors of Juliet's tomb — her awakening among the dead, the "bloody Tybalt festering in his shroud," the gliding spirits, Juliet's frenzy of terror, her mad playing with her ancestors' bones — were so vividly conjured up by Stella's excited imagination, that she suddenly leaped from her seat, with arm uplifted, exclaiming, wildly,

> "With some great kinsman's bone, as with a club,
> *Dash out my desperate brains!*"

Her mother uttered a feeble shriek, and drew back affrighted. Mattie's quick ears caught the sound, and she ran into the room.

Stella looked confusedly about her. She saw her mother's pale consternation and Mattie's look of alarm, and tried to collect her scattered thoughts. She swept back the long tresses, that had broken their bands and fell in dishevelled clusters around her face, wiped the cold dew from her forehead, and tried to force a smile, as she said, "It 's nothing, mother; I was only studying a part."

"Studying a part, my dear, with that fearful outcry? You terrify me! What is coming over you, Stella? Your eyes look as wild as though you were losing your senses!"

"No, no, mother; only losing my identity in Juliet's. Pray, don't be discomposed; it 's nothing."

She laid aside her book, and seated herself by her mother's side. It was some time since Mrs. Rosenvelt had been so completely roused. She even asked her daughter a few questions concerning the character she was studying. Mrs. Rosenvelt had seen Juliet enacted years ago. She spoke of her impressions, but they brought back some painful memory. Her eyes gradually filled, and she relapsed into silence.

Stella looked wistfully at her book, but feared to disturb her mother if she stole back to the sofa where it was lying.

The usual hour for retiring was near. She rejoiced when she found herself alone in her little chamber — alone with the shadowy Juliet, who seemed to exist within her and beside her. They were not parted in dreams. Stella awoke from her fitful slumbers, vehemently crying out

"*Dash out my desperate brains!*"

Those words haunted her. Numberless times during the night they broke involuntarily from her lips. And when the sun

"Peered forth the golden window of the east,"

she found herself repeating them still

While she was making her toilet, she caught sight of her own countenance reflected in the mirror just as she again unconsciously uttered that frantic ejaculation. She gazed in wonder at the haggard, terrified expression, and then laughed to see the look change to one of surprise. It seemed to her as if she were scanning the face of another. She was indeed "losing her own identity."

At the earliest hour that the mail could possibly arrive, Mattie was hurried to the post-office. Stella awaited her brother's answer with feverish expectation. She stationed herself at the window to watch.

The instant her messenger came in sight, before she could reach the porch, the door was thrown open.

"The letter! the letter! Give me my brother's letter!"

"There was no letter, miss."

"No letter? Impossible! Has the post come in?"

"I inquired, and the clerk said it was in, and the morning mail distributed."

"O, Mattie! you have made some mistake; do go back again! The clerks have overlooked the letter! I know there is one! Make them find it!"

Mattie was only too ready to gratify the whims of her beloved young lady. She trudged back to the post-office, and duly tormented the clerk with her positive assurance that he had mislaid the letter, and must look again. He looked — there was no letter.

Stella's impatient temperament did not help her to bear this disappointment; but she had no alternative. She returned to the study of Juliet, and soon even her brother's missing epistle was forgotten.

Stella's second lesson with her tutor differed from the first. In the fine development of her sentient faculties, her reflective powers, Mr. Oakland discovered germs of highest promise. But he found that her enthusiasm fairly ran riot. He devoted himself to the difficult task of curbing its exuberance, toning down her too strong coloring, and illustrating the danger of extravagance, even though it be true to nature. A refined audience invariably feel the disenchanting effect of exaggeration. They unavoidably take that one, fatal step which lies between the sublime and the absurd. But Mr. Oakland's faith in his pupil's success was undiminished. He knew that it was easier to rein in enthusiasm than to inspirit tameness. The one is the hand-maiden of genius; the other, the never-failing companion of mediocrity.

CHAPTER II.

Ernest's Letter to his Sister. — His Views of the Stage. — Unperilled Chastity. — A Brother's Entreaties. — Stella's Unaltered Resolve. — Self-Will. — Application to Managers. — An Anxious Interval. — Mr. Oakland's Disregarded Warning. — A Self-reliant Nature. — A Venture. — The Stage Door. — First Entrance behind the Scenes. — Sudden Intrusion upon a Lugubrious Manager. — Mr. Grimshaw's Mysterious Inquiries. — Stella's Confusion. — Request to Read. — Recital of Portia's Address to Shylock. — The Unexpected Interruption. — Insolence of an Actress. — Stella and Mattie's Retreat from the Manager's Office. — Disconcerted, not Conquered. — An Inspiring Paragraph. — Obituary of the Young Actress, Lydia Talbot. — A Mantle for Shoulders yet Unfound. — Mr. Belton's Advertisement for a "Leading Lady." — "Eureka!"

STELLA'S first thought, the next morning, was of the anticipated letter. The ever-willing Mattie was despatched to the post-office long before it was possible for the mail to be delivered. During her absence, Stella's restless spirit lengthened the minutes to hours, through its tormenting disquietude. At last her straining eyes caught sight of Mattie in the distance. She carried something white in her hand, and walked at a rapid pace. But that quick tread was slow to the expectant girl. She darted out of the room, and returned in an instant, exultingly holding up the letter.

"It has come, mother! My brother's letter! Now all is right! — all is arranged!"

"Read it aloud, dear, will you?" replied her mother, in a more animated tone than usual.

Stella had already torn open the seal, destroying a portion of the writing. Her eyes glanced rapidly over the page; the paper shook in her hands. Gradually her countenance changed; the mantling blood flew back from her cheeks, the delighted expression died out of her eyes. She read silently on and on to the close, and then the letter fell from her nerveless grasp.

"What ails you? What does your brother say?"

Stella drew herself up with a look of resolution, almost of defiance, and exclaimed: "Why should it matter? It shall *not* matter! Nothing now shall turn me from my purpose! Ernest should have known me better!"

She gave the letter to her mother, and paced the room with an agitated step; her hands clasped over her head — her favorite attitude — in deep meditation.

Mrs. Rosenvelt, with great deliberation, as though she had been called upon to make some overpowering effort, turned to her son's letter, and read:

"*New York, March* —, 18—.

"SWEETEST SISTER IN THE WORLD:

"I took a day to reflect upon your letter, and the delay has not altered my first conviction. Stella, you well know that I reverence the profession which I adopted from choice. I toil in it with delight; I glory in the rough road over which, step by step, I may climb to eminence. You also know that I look upon none of the world's baseless prejudices as more false, more *vulgar,* than that which presupposes that a woman who enters this profession hazards her spotless character, or is even subjected to more than ordinary temptations. If the lode-star of purity dwell in her heart, it attracts to itself only that which is pure. If light thoughts inhabit there, and evil passions convulse her breast, then may the stage prove perilous. What place is safe to such infected blood?

"Many unfortunates have brought their frailties here, and thus desecrated our temples of art; but I do not believe *that through the consequences of the profession one chaste woman ever fell!* For you, my sister, whose mind has been precept-strengthened, whose spirit is

'In strong proof of chastity well armed,'

I should have no fears of shoals and quicksands. But, to launch you upon this life of turmoil, contention, perpetual struggling!—you, my delicately-nurtured, sensitive, excitable sister!—Heaven forbid! To bid you, who have been environed, from your cradle, with the appliances of ease and opulence, exist upon the capricious breath, the uncertain suffrages, of the public?—never! To throw you, with a nervous system so highly strung that its chords can be played upon by every chance breeze, into this whirlwind of excitement?—never! I implore you to abandon all thoughts of the stage as a profession. Your talents may qualify you for its adoption; your temperament and education do not.

The sense of fitness produced by the former is neutralized by the latter.

"To procure you an engagement here would not be possible. The only two positions you could hold are permanently occupied.

"And now, dear sister, let me ask, Why should you trouble your unarithmetical brain with calculations about the cost of existence? True, my salary is limited at this moment; but it will provide, in a moderate way, for you and my mother. You may be forced to encounter a few privations; but the future is rich in promise, and they will not be of long duration.

"You will trust to your brother's judgment? You will heed his warning? Will you not? Say 'Yes,' and that you pardon him for gainsaying the beloved being whose wishes he never before thwarted. My love to our dear mother. Take tender care of her, for your own sake, and for that of

"Your devoted brother,

"ERNEST ROSENVELT."

As Mrs. Rosenvelt finished the letter, she gazed with a troubled expression at her daughter, who was still pacing the room, her hands tightly clasped, her pale lips compressed, her whole soul evidently in tumult.

"Stella, what Ernest says is so reasonable, so *right!*"

"Right for him, mother; but wrong for me, should I heed him. Why should I sit with folded hands, growing weary of my own purposeless existence, while he strains every nerve in the exercise of his faculties? To what end has Heaven gifted me with equal talents, if I am not to use them? Ask Mr. Oakland whether or not I possess them! Sensitive, excitable, and unaccustomed to hardships, I may be, as he says; but what I *am* is not what I may *become* through fitting discipline!"

"Pray be calm, Stella! It distresses me to hear you talk in that wild tone. What, then, do you propose to do?"

"Not to discuss the matter with my brother — my arguments will not move him, nor have his moved me. But, unless you forbid it, mother, — and I pray you not to do so, — I must still obey the dictates of this strong impulse within me. I must become an actress!"

"How is it possible without your brother's assistance?"

"I must *make it possible!* Only tell me that you do not oppose the attempt."

"No — not exactly — if there is no other way of contenting you. But — "

"Thank you, mother; and let me crush in the bud all *buts*. Now I must consult Mr. Oakland."

We pass over Stella's interview with her tutor.

He took sides with her brother, and refused either to advise or assist her in obtaining an engagement. Stella was disconcerted, not conquered. Her self-reliant nature was not dependent upon extraneous support.

That very afternoon, she addressed letters to the managers of three theatres in Boston, earnestly requesting an immediate reply. She also wrote to her brother, and apprised him of her unaltered determination.

A week passed. Her letters to managers brought no answers. The reply from her brother showed that he counted upon the difficulty of obtaining an engagement, and looked forward to her discouragement and final abandonment of the project.

During this week Stella paid daily visits to Mr. Oakland, and her studies were prosecuted as energetically as though every arrangement for her débût was concluded.

Mr. Oakland imagined that her fervor would be damped by neglect on the part of managers, and opposition on that of her brother. He might as well have hoped to see a fire quenched by the adverse blowing of the wind, which only makes it blaze the higher.

"Is it not strange that I receive no reply?" she inquired of her tutor.

"Not very," was his dry answer. "Managers are not apt to notice letters which may emanate from pretenders of all sorts. They are generally looked upon as the effusions of stage-struck misses, who place an estimate upon their own abilities and attractions which the public is not likely to have the complaisance to endorse."

"And what shall I do to convince them that I do not belong to this class?"

"I have already said that I would have no agency in this matter, that I would not even advise you."

"True, my dear, unconquerable Mentor! I know you are as obstinate — as obstinate — as obstinate as I am myself! If managers will not notice my letters, and if I cannot persuade any one to intercede for me, there is but one alternative left. I must essay the eloquence of my own tongue; I must plead in person; that is what I intend to do next."

"Don't be too sure of success, even then," remarked Mr. Oakland, oracularly.

"At all events, I echo the words of my country's hero, and pin my faith to his colors—'*I'll try!*' So, good-morning."

"Had you not better wait? had you not better reflect a while?" urged Mr. Oakland, detaining her. "There is no truer admonition than the old friar's:

'*Too swift* arrives as tardy as too slow.'"

"I am no more inclined to heed him than was the impetuous youth upon whom his warning was wasted. '*They stumble who run fast*' may be true enough, when the pulses beat sluggishly; but the rapid strokes of mine sound the alarm for instant action. So, bestow upon me one *benedicite*, good *Friar Lawrence*, and let me be gone."

The next morning, accompanied by the faithful Mattie, Stella presented herself at the front entrance of a theatrical establishment which, in those days, held the highest rank in Boston. She drew back to escape notice, and desired Mattie to inquire at the box-office if Mr. Grimshaw could be seen.

"How many tickets?—what circle?" asked a gruff voice.

"None, thank you. A lady wishes to see the manager."

"This is not the place to inquire."

"And which is the place?" questioned Mattie, prompted by Stella's whisper.

"Make way there, my good woman! You are preventing people from coming up for their tickets, — get out, will you?"

Mattie was retiring, but Stella whispered to her again.

"It 's on business, sir; we would be obliged to you for informing us where we should inquire."

"Private entrance — round the corner — make way there, I say!"

Stella was glad to retreat. The crowd of ticket-purchasers gathering around the box-office surveyed her with impertinent glances.

The private entrance! She and Mattie sought for it in vain. They went "round the corner," according to direction; trying the nearest corner, and then inspecting the furthest corner, and then the first corner again. They expected to discover a place of admission resembling the ladies' entrance to some fashionable hotel.

"Ask that boy," said Stella, designating a well-dressed youth who was intently perusing a play-bill.

Mattie made the inquiry.

The stripling hardly raised his eyes from the promised dramatic feast, as he gave vent to a careless "Don't bother me!"

Stella accosted him herself.

He looked up at the sound of her musical voice. Evidently mistaking her, from the nature of her question, for some young actress recently engaged, he bowed, and said, in a tone of sudden interest, "Allow me to show you."

He pointed out a small, rough-looking door, which opened into a narrow alley. Stella was disconcerted at the uninviting locality. She pressed close to Mattie, and grasped her dress with a vague fear, as they entered. The young girl took a step or two; then hesitated, and stopped.

"Which way must we go to see the manager?"

"You will find a door at the end of this passage, which opens into the theatre; but, as you appear to be strangers, permit me to lead the way."

They followed him through the close, and by no means odoriferous or cleanly alley. There was a door at the end, upon which the youth loudly knocked. It was opened by an individual with a rubicund face, and heavy, bloodshot eyes.

"Show this lady to Mr. Grimshaw's office," said the boy, with an authoritative air. It conveyed the impression that the lady in question was expected by Mr. Grimshaw, and had the right to enter.

Stella gracefully thanked her escort, and, with Mattie, followed the sleepy door-keeper.

At first they appeared to be in almost total darkness. She could not imagine into what part of the theatre they had been ushered. What was that Mattie struck against?

"Keep clear of the wings!" drawled out their slumberous guide.

They were behind the scenes, then, — that mysterious haunt of Melpomene, Euterpe, Terpsichore, into which she had so often longed to intrude! Behind the scenes of a theatre! An indefinite, wondering awe began to steal over her, but hardly of that kind which cries out, "Put the shoes from off thy feet!"

Through winding nooks, and passages crowded with scenery, hardly visible in the dim light, they followed their conductor, trying to peer into the gloom, and fathom some of the supposed marvels of the theatrical labyrinth.

He knocked at a door.

"Enter!" sounded from within, in such a deep, sepulchral tone, it might have appropriately issued from a tomb (a stage tomb), or been uttered by the ghost of Hamlet.

"A lady for you, sir!" The man threw open the door, and retraced his steps along the "untrodden ways" which Stella had just threaded for the first time.

Seated at a table which was covered with play-bills and manuscripts, was a grim-looking man, in a would-be heroic attitude. His long, shaggy hair fell around a cadaverous visage; his dark eyes were studiously fierce; his attire had a melodramatic air, from the tie of the cravat to the cut of the coat.

Mr. Grimshaw was an actor as well as a manager. He belonged to that numerous class of Thespians who never cease personating some favorite character, — to whom the world is as much a stage as the actual "boards."

Stella's courage began sensibly to ooze away. How fervently she wished herself out of the dramatic lion's den!

"Mr. Grimshaw, I believe," she murmured timidly.

"Even so!" replied the unearthly voice.

"I think you received a letter, signed Stella Rosenvelt, about a week ago."

"*Pro*-ceed!" Stella fancied his tone had sunk a portentous octave lower.

"I am Stella Rosenvelt." She seated herself unbidden; Mattie had offered a chair.

"*Pro*-ceed!"

"I—I am desirous—I am seeking—that is, it is my wish to obtain an engagement in some theatre: this one, if possible."

"What line?" still with tragic intonation.

"I beg pardon, sir—what did you say?"

"What line?"

"I do not understand."

"What business?"

"My business I have just told you, sir."

"What line of business?" The words were thundered out with a touch of regal wrath.

"The stage, sir, as I said before."

The manager rolled his eyes at the marvellous unsophistication of this person to whom he condescended to give audience.

"What have you acted?"

"Nothing, as yet, sir."

"Novice? Ah!"

"Yes, sir."

"Want situation?"

"Yes, sir."

"What line?"

"Sir?"

"Tragedy? comedy? walking lady? singing chambermaid? What line? 'Wind up the watch of your wit, and strike!'"

"O!" exclaimed Stella, comprehending at last, "such characters as Juliet, and Desdemona, and Portia."

"Juvenile tragedy! My favorite business. 'Give us a taste of your quality!'" waving his hand majestically.

"Sir?"

"Anything — don't matter what — a touch of the tragic, if you like. But—'suit the action to the word, the word to the action, with this special observance, that you o'erstep not the modesty of nature; for anything so overdone is from the purpose of playing, whose end, both at the first and now, was, and is, to hold, as 't were, the mirror up to nature; to show Virtue her own features, Scorn her own image, and the very age and body of the time his form and pressure!'" This memorable injunction was delivered by Mr. Grimshaw with a stilted declamation that admirably illustrated the old saying, "Do as I preach, not as I do."

Stella trembled from head to foot, as she falteringly asked, "Shall I recite Portia's address to Shylock?"

"*Pro*-ceed!"

After a moment's hesitation she rose — paused — then, in an uncertain, husky tone, commenced:

"The quality of mercy is not strained;
It droppeth as the gentle dew from heaven
Upon the place beneath. It is twice blessed:
It blesseth him that gives, and him that takes.
'T is mightiest in the mightiest; it becomes
The throned monarch better than his crown.
His sceptre shows the force of temporal power,

The attribute to awe and majesty,
Wherein doth sit the fear and dread of kings:
But mercy is above the sceptred sway;
It is enthronéd in the hearts — "

The door opened. Stella ceased. A bold-visaged but handsome female, in showy attire, entered the room.

"Hearts!" echoed she, contemptuously; "hearts! Really, 'I hope I don't intrude,' as Paul Pry says."

"Silence!" ejaculated Mr. Grimshaw. "Note you not that this young person

——— 'hath into bondage
Brought my too diligent ear'?"

"Only diligent when there 's mischief brewing!" retorted the lady, glancing rudely at Stella.

Mr. Grimshaw gave her a ferocious look, then turned to the frightened girl, and, in a stentorian voice, cried out, "*Pro*-ceed!"

"The hearts — the hearts of kings — "

continued Stella.

"It is enthronéd in the hearts of kings."

She paused. The scornful eyes of her new auditor took away her voice, and dimmed her memory.

"*Pro*-ceed!" repeated Mr. Grimshaw.

But Stella was unable to comply; she dropped silently into her seat.

"Very entertaining, really!" was the sarcastic feminine comment. "I ought to apologize for interrupting your private theatricals!"

Stella turned haughtily to the manager.

"Did I understand you, sir, that you might possibly give me an engagement?"

"An engagement!" almost shrieked the lady. "You ventured — you *dared* to promise her an engagement in this theatre, when the leading parts, such as I presume she has the impertinence to aspire to, from what I heard her spouting, all belong to *me!*"

"Madam!" exclaimed the manager, pleasurably excited at the prospect of a scene in real life; "Madam," and he thrust his long fingers through his tangled hair, "doubt me not, but listen!"

"I have listened, and —"

"'Hear me for my cause, and be silent that you may hear!'"

Stella could endure this contest no longer. She rose, with dignity, and said, "I have evidently misunderstood you, sir; I must bid you good-morning. May I beg that you will order some one to show me the way out?"

"Show you the way out?" repeated the lady, with an insolent laugh. "Nothing we 'll do with more pleasure, and you need n't remember your road back!"

"Nick," called out Mr. Grimshaw to a boy who was passing the door with a basket on his shoulder, "show these ladies through the front entrance."

"Nick 's the guide you generally give your pupils; but your paths are usually the back ways!"

Stella and Mattie could not avoid hearing this coarse remark, as the door was slammed to behind them. Descending a stair, they soon found themselves in the box-office, and a moment afterwards in the street.

Stella checked her attendant's affectionate volubility with, "It 's too dreadful! I can't talk of it, Mattie; let us hasten home; my head is whirling!"

She had not abandoned her scheme, but her resolution had received a shock. Leaving Mattie to give her own account of their adventure to Mrs. Rosenvelt, Stella retired to her chamber, deeply mortified, and inclined to chide "every breather living." With her mercurial temperament, this mood could not last. She was too buoyant, too sanguine, too full of resources. She resolved to implore her brother to furnish her with a letter of introduction to some manager of standing. That would smooth her way; she would deliver it in person, and doubtless procure the desired engagement.

A morning paper was lying before her. Of late she had read all the theatrical intelligence; other public news possessed little interest. Her eyes rested upon an eulogistic obituary of Miss Lydia Talbot, a young actress, whose loss the dramatic community were loudly lamenting. As the "stock star" of a popular theatre, in Boston, she had shone several years in the dramatic firmament. The writer remarked "that no actress yet had been found upon whose shoulders her mantle could worthily fall." A crowd of hopes rushed, with headlong impetuosity, into Stella's quick-suggesting brain. They filled the atmosphere with rainbow tints, and lifted her up on soaring wings. She glanced at the next column, and every hope assumed form and substance, and stood before her—a reality!

The manager of the theatre to which Miss Talbot formerly belonged advertised that the situation of "leading lady," in his theatre, was vacant. He invited immediate applications from gifted members of the profession. The hours between ten and three of that day were appointed for the personal reception of candidates.

"Eureka!" cried Stella, internally. She turned to the clock; it wanted a quarter of ten. Before the hour sounded she and Mattie were on their way to the theatre.

CHAPTER III.

Light in which Mr. Belton regarded his Company and his Audience. — A Conscientious Manager. — An Inexplicable but very General Hallucination. — Stella's Interview with Mr. Belton. — A Wished-for Result. — Explanations and Stipulations. — An Important Item forgotten by the Dramatic Candidate. — Prosaic Business Arrangements. — An Engagement. — The Contract. — Ten Days before the Début. — Cabalistic Words of the First "Call." — Stella's Irresistible Entreaties to her Tutor. — The Novice's First Rehearsal. — Aspect behind the Scenes. — Illusions Dissolved. — Mr. Allsop, the Prompter. — Fisk, the Call-Boy. — Fantasticalities of Fisk. — Stella's Perturbation. — Formal Introductions. — Virginius Rehearsed. — Sensations of the Novice. — The Manager's Command. — Derision of Actors. — Wavering. — The Alternative. — Decision before it is too Late. — A New and Convenient Style of Declamation. — Romance Dethroned. — The Nimble-tongued Icilius. — Dentatus on Crutches. — A High-spirited Girl Metamorphosed into a Conscious Automaton. — Mrs. Fairfax. — Heavenly Music of Sympathy. — Theatrical Formalities at an End. — Fisk's Oracular Decision. — The Novice Disheartened. — "Feathers of Lead."

Mr. Belton was not a manager of ordinary stamp. The mania of speculation, with which the larger numbers of his confrères were afflicted, had not lured him into becoming the autocrat of a theatre. A genuine passion for the profession, a desire to promote its interests, combined, perhaps, with a natural love of rule, rendered him a theatrical lessee. He looked upon the members of his company as an incongruous family circle, of which he was the all-potent head. He regarded his audiences as a bevy of captious friends, whom he condescended to amuse and instruct. He took pleasure in noticing the same well-known faces nightly scattered through his boxes. One cluster of venerable *habitués*, who congregated in the stage-box, he invariably watched. Through their approval of or dissent to a performance, his judgments were silently swayed. He comprehended and revered the social influence of the drama. He was conscientious, and never intentionally ministered to a meretricious or vitiated taste.

In his disbursements Mr. Belton was strictly economical, but as rigidly just. The salaries he allowed were not large, but they were always certain. His company was, perhaps, too limited, but its members labored amicably and indefatigably. Some of the subordinates rejoiced in two sets of cognomens on the bills, and were adepts in doubling characters; but it was the unanimous opinion that double duty, under Mr. Belton's management, was lighter than single duty in more pretentious establishments, where less system and justice reigned.

It was almost a misfortune for Mr. Belton that he was endowed with histrionic talent. In common with the generality of actors, he mistook his own forte As a comedian he would have shone preëminent. His rotund figure, jolly face, the merry twinkle of his eye, the *bonhommie* of his whole manner, peculiarly fitted him for humorous personations. But Mr. Belton detested comedy. High tragedy was his aspiration. He would rather have been hissed as Lear than applauded as Dogberry.

As he was sole arbitrator in his theatre, no one could remonstrate against his assumption of the tragic heroes; that is to say, no one but the audience, and they now and then availed themselves of the privilege. When the sound of merriment greeted his ears, instead of an expected burst of applause, Mr. Belton gravely asked "what the people *could* be laughing at."

"Ah, well!" he would console himself by saying, "we must educate our audiences until they comprehend us; nothing like elevating an audience to one's own standard. Besides, they have been so much accustomed to laugh when I intended to be funny, that they never understand me when I show them how high tragedy ought to be acted."

The decease of Miss Talbot had left in the theatre a vacancy difficult to be filled. Mr. Belton was sitting in his office, searching the morning papers for favorable notices, when he was informed that several ladies had called in answer to his advertisement.

"Show them up, one at a time; first come first served, remember; — a fair chance for all." Then, as the messenger left the room, he added, "There 'll be no contenting the public, no matter whom I engage. They 'll be sure to say she can't step into the shoes of poor Lydia."

Three young dramatic aspirants, in turn, obtained an interview. All three passed out of the theatre with downcast countenances. Stella, accompanied as usual by her attendant, was now ushered into the presence of Mr. Belton. She was prepared to encounter a second edition of Mr. Grimshaw. Mr. Belton's courteous reception and gentlemanlike bearing quickly placed her at ease. She briefly made known her wishes. Mr. Belton listened with an air of interest. He requested her to read. With prompt self-possession she delivered the animated dialogue which takes place from Juliet's moon-lighted balcony, between the lovers of Verona.

Mr. Belton's countenance expressed more than he framed into language. Managerial policy is chary of praise. He allowed her to resume her seat in silence. His internal ejaculation was, "How fortunate! She has unquestionable talent — grace, freshness, beauty; she may perhaps replace our Lydia!"

"You have probably no idea, Miss Rosenvelt, of the arduous duties incumbent upon every member of this profession. Histrionic eminence is not compatible with a life of ease and pleasure."

"I know something of the mode of life, sir; my brother is an actor."

"Still it is better that we should understand each other. My company say that they work harder than any other; — perhaps they do. If you engage with me, I shall expect your energies to be at my command. You may be disheartened, at first, at the amount of study requisite. Then I cast all plays myself, and allow no dictation, though I endeavor to be just. I permit no refusing of parts, — no contention about the manner in which the names shall appear upon the bills. The interests of my company are *my* interests, and that must content them."

"I think there will be no difficulty, sir."

"Then I will make you the offer of a trial engagement. Mr. Tennent commences with me on Monday next. Miss Talbot was to have supported him. You can occupy her place. But I warn you that the public will demand a great deal from any successor of hers. Your name shall appear second to Mr. Tennent's at the head of the bills. If you succeed, you can keep it there. If you make a *great hit,* and *sustain it* by after performances, your name, in time, will be placed first. Your line of business will, of course, be juvenile tragedy and comedy. Occasionally you may be called upon to attempt heavy tragedy; — that depends upon the plays which Mr. Tennent selects. I will keep you out of afterpieces for a while; but you must prepare yourself to appear in them when you are a little more familiar with the stage."

Stella could with difficulty conceal a rush of tumultuous emotions as she asked, "In what character am I to make my débût?"

Mr. Belton referred to Mr. Tennent's last letter. "'First night, Virginius; second night, Othello.' Good,—you will make your débût in Virginia, and the next night appear in Desdemona. That will do admirably. Your powers will not be too severely taxed. You will not be *overweighted* at the first start. You will gradually become accustomed to the footlights. Perhaps you are not aware of their terrifying effect upon novices?"

"I scarcely think I shall feel alarmed," said Stella, confidently. "Could you favor me with a list of the other characters which I shall be required to study?"

"Mr. Tennent has only selected his plays for the two first nights. He acts with me for one fortnight.

Probably the plays will not be settled upon, until he arrives."

"But what time should I then have even to memorize my parts?"

"The same time that the other ladies have," returned Mr. Belton, carelessly. "Here is a list of all the dramas which Mr. Tennent acted when he was here last. He will repeat most of them. If you choose, you can study hap-hazard, so as to be 'up' in as many pieces as possible."

"I will study all," thought Stella, nothing daunted. Without examination, she folded up the list.

"When will there be a — a — a rehearsal?"

Well might she hesitate; that word brought so forcibly to mind all that was before her.

"Let me see; — Mr. Tennent will not be here before Monday morning; but, as you are a débûtante, I will call a rehearsal, with the company, for you, on Saturday. On Monday you will rehearse with Mr. Tennent. You must manage with two rehearsals; — they are not enough, I admit."

"O, quite enough, I dare say;" and Stella rose to depart. She was impatient to return home, that the pent-up sensations which agitated her breast might find vent.

"You have forgotten one very important part of the business,— one of which actors are not usually oblivious. The small item of *salary*. Hamlet says, 'The lover shall not sigh gratis.'"

"O, yes! I *did* forget; but I leave that to you; of course it will be all right."

"Rather a loose way of doing business,— not after my style at all. Pray be seated for another moment.

I shall not pretend to offer you the salary that I gave Miss Talbot; you must first render yourself so valuable to my establishment that you can command the same remuneration. Five years ago, in this very room, — yes, in that very arm-chair where you are now sitting,— she signed her first contract with me. Poor Lydia!"

Mr. Belton paused and hemmed, and turned over the play-bills hastily, as though he were fearful of betraying an emotion in the presence of this young girl, which, before the foot-lights and the eyes of the public, he would not have thought of repressing.

After a moment, he cleared from his throat a telltale huskiness, and resumed.

"Her salary — her salary at that time was thirty dollars per week. I offer you the same terms for your two first weeks; after that, there may be an increase. Are you satisfied?"

"Perfectly," and again Stella rose to depart.

"Be seated — pray be seated; — words are not bonds."

Stella sat down, evidently chafing at the delay, and rendered uncomfortable by prosaic business details, to which she was wholly unused.

Mr. Belton drew up two contracts, and, signing them himself, requested Miss Rosenvelt's signature. He then presented her with one, and carefully placed the other in his desk. For the third time Stella started up, and Mr. Belton now conducted her to the door.

She could not return home without communicating her success to Mr. Oakland. He was engaged with a class when she called at his residence; but she petitioned for a moment's interview. When he came to the door she recounted, in a scarcely coherent manner, her morning's adventure, and, without waiting for his deliberate reply, hastened home, and roused her apathetic mother with her startling story.

It wanted but ten days of the evening fixed for her dêbût,—and how much remained to be accomplished! Parts to be studied, materials for dresses to be selected, costumes to be decided upon, and fashioned after historical authority.

Stella was guided by Mrs. Oakland's chaste and refined taste, in the choice of her stage attire. They agreed that the external draping and adorning should be a manifestation of the character assumed. Mr. Oakland advocated the severest simplicity. He detested the tawdry ostentation of stage heroines in general, and argued that prodigality of ornament oftener concealed than set forth real charms.

Mattie and a nimble-fingered assistant sat plying their needles in Mrs. Rosenvelt's chamber, from daylight until midnight. Even Mrs. Rosenvelt herself now and then ran a seam or bound on a trimming. She found the bustling, occupied manner of every one around her irresistibly contagious.

On Friday evening Stella received a note which rendered her already perturbed brain giddy with agitation. The epistle contained but these cabalistic words:

"Virginius — rehearsed, ten o'clock, Saturday morning, April —, ——.

"TOBIAS ALLSOP, Prompter.

"*Call.*"

It was her first "call" to the theatre. Until now she had seemed to herself to be moving through some exciting dream; but this bit of tangible paper, which she could touch and gaze upon, suddenly made all real. Could she venture to a rehearsal, a first rehearsal, alone, or only accompanied by Mattie? Impossible! True, she felt confident of receiving the utmost courtesy from the actors, — Mr. Belton was so kind himself, — yet the presence of a friend would sustain her. Mr. Oakland must be pressed into service.

That gentleman received her request with undisguised coldness. His scruples were not easily combated. He had wielded the critic's pen at one period of his life, and unsparingly pointed out the shortcomings of certain members of the profession; he looked for resentment from those who were not wise enough to kiss the rod. He essayed to convince Stella that his presence could not serve her within the circuit of any Boston theatre. She still pleaded earnestly, unanswerably; and at last wrung from him a slow consent.

The hand of time was on the stroke of ten when Mr. Oakland, the next morning, conducted her through the private entrance of the theatre to the dimly-lighted stage. From many theatres the outer light is wholly excluded, even in the day-time, and gas usurps the place of sunshine. But in this the sunbeams struggled through distant windows, often intercepted by detached wings of scenery, but shedding light sufficient to lift the gloom out of positive darkness. Gas was dispensed with, except when the sky was wholly overcast.

Stella glanced wonderingly at the bare stage, intersected by tawdry scenes, on which dust and paint were amicably united; the mechanical stage auxiliaries; the dark-looking pit; the tiers of empty boxes, fronted with dingy devices. What glamour could transform this dismal region to the realm of enchantment which it had ever appeared to her young eyes? What magical touch could invest these terrene, prosaic surroundings with poetic grace and witchery? How many illusions melted away as she stood, transfixed, mutely gazing on the unsightly objects that environed her!

The stage was unoccupied when they entered. A slender, sallow-faced young man now appeared, bearing a table. He placed it on the right, close to the foot-lights (or rather to the semi-circular range which would become foot-lights at night). This individual bestowed upon Mr. Oakland and his pupil a few furtive glances, but no salutation. He laid upon the table pens, ink, paper, play-bills, prompt-books, and then took his seat, and was soon busily employed in writing.

"Is there nobody here?" whispered Stella, in a tone not wholly free from awe.

"It has just struck ten, and actors are allowed ten minutes' grace," replied Mr. Oakland. "I believe they generally avail themselves of the extra moments. Come and walk with me up and down the stage, before they arrive; you must get accustomed to its length and breadth."

Stella had never found it so difficult to command her limbs. She half stumbled, and clung to Mr. Oakland's arm for support. Her fancy peopled those vacant boxes with cold, critical eyes, that froze her blood, paralyzed her faculties, metamorphosed her into a dull, insensate clod, the reflex of the glaring *shows* around her.

"You are nervous," said Mr. Oakland, with concern.

"A little — not very — that is, not at all;" and she made a desperate attempt to rally.

The next person that emerged from the darkness behind the scenes was a boy about eleven years old. His consequential bearing, as he trod the stage, betrayed that he already aped the airs of self-important manhood. He deliberately scanned Stella and Mr. Oakland, without removing his cap; then with mock solemnity marched to the prompter's table. As he inspected the long strip of paper which contained his "calls," the words, "Those individuals — novice — wonder if she 's got anything in her?" were uttered in one of those convenient *stage whispers* which are intentionally audible.

Stella's perturbation momentarily increased. She began to feel certain that she would be guilty of some inexcusable *gaucherie.*

"Make your call, Fisk!" sang out Mr. Allsop, the prompter, as loudly as though the boy at his side were stationed at some invisible distance.

Master Fisk recrossed the stage, giving a ludicrous imitation of a high-tragedy gait — a mode of progression which requires one foot to be placed at the greatest possible distance in advance of the other, and the backward foot slowly drawn along to meet its companion, the dragging process being scrupulously repeated at each step. Fisk's voice was then heard shouting lustily at the green-room door: "First act of Virginius — Servius — Cneius — Virginius — all the Roman citizens."

The call-boy then strutted back to his place by the prompter's side, — "Virginius and Titus not come."

At this moment Mr. Belton appeared, accompanied by his stage manager, Mr. Finch. He greeted Stella somewhat stiffly; his manner implied that he had no words to spare — all must be business now.

Mr. Finch was introduced. Stella presented Mr. Oakland.

Mr. Belton bowed without extending his hand. Mr. Oakland did not offer his. All managers, and almost all actors, set their faces against the introduction behind the scenes of persons unconnected with the theatrical profession. Stella's disregard of this prejudice explained Mr. Belton's unusually chilling manner.

Without exchanging another word with Stella, he turned to his prompter. "Don't rehearse the whole play, Allsop. We only want the Virginia scenes for this young lady. Miss Rosenvelt, Mr. Allsop — Mr. Allsop, Miss Rosenvelt."

Mr. Allsop bowed in the briefest manner.

"As Mr. Tennent is not here, read for him," continued the manager. "Now, my dear, your entrance is from that side."

These words were addressed to Stella. The familiar "*my dear*" caused the quick blood to rush to her cheeks. She soon learned that the term is one in such constant use throughout all theatres that it is rendered meaningless by its indiscriminate application.

Mr. Allsop rose, took his position in the centre of the stage, and gave the cue, "Soft! she comes."

Stella grasped the side scene to which Mr. Belton had conducted her; she had lost all other power of motion.

"Come on, if you please, my dear! That 's your cue," called out the manager.

Stella, with a faltering step, advanced towards Mr. Allsop.

"Well, father, what 's your will?" was uttered in a low, quavering tone.

"'A voice soft, gentle and low, an excellent thing in woman,' but *not on the stage*," remarked Mr. Belton. "You 'll have to speak twenty times louder than that at night; better try your voice in the morning. It 's far easier speaking in an empty theatre than a full one. Lift up your head, and throw out your words as though you were talking to the furthest man in the gallery yonder; that 's the rule."

Stella's suffused countenance dropped lower and lower. Several members of the company had gathered around the wings. She thought she read derision in their curious eyes; they were watching her, to detect and ridicule her insufficiencies. Tongue-tied by confusion, she turned with a supplicating look to Mr. Oakland. She had never seen his face wear such a distressed expression.

He bowed to Mr. Belton, and said, "Excuse me for infringing rules;" then approached Stella. "It is not yet too late, Stella; you can withdraw from this ordeal. Do you not feel that you are not qualified to pass through it triumphantly?"

That humiliating doubt recalled the high-spirited

girl to herself. "No!" she answered, with recovered firmness; and then, in a clear, ringing tone, repeated the first words of her part.

"Good!" cried Belton, encouragingly; "that's what we want."

Allsop read the eloquent language placed in the mouth of Virginius as though he were stammering through a primer. Stella replied as Virginia. But, though she delivered every line as set down in the text, she made but a futile attempt to embody the character. The words she articulated lacked expression. The business air with which the manager surveyed her, the prompter's unmeaning reading, the disenchanting locality, hurled Romance from her aërial throne, annihilated all poetic inspiration, and clogged the wings of Fancy with a commonplace, matter-of-fact heaviness. As she varied her position on the stage, and made her exits and entrances, according to Mr. Belton's directions, she seemed to herself a conscious automaton, deprived of reflection or self-guidance. Once she thought she heard a slight titter at the wing, doubtless at her expense.

Mr. Belton called out, in a commanding tone, "Order! order!" and silence was restored.

Dentatus hobbled upon the stage with the assistance of a pair of crutches.

"Miss Rosenvelt, Mr. Martin — Mr. Martin, Miss Rosenvelt," said the manager.

Both parties bowed. When Virginius and Dentatus *exeunt*, Virginia is left alone. Stella found the soliloquy which she was then required to deliver far more difficult of utterance than the brief replies to her father and Dentatus. Mr. Belton, Mr. Finch,

Mr. Allsop, Mr. Oakland, and Fisk, were standing directly in front of her, their eyes all fastened on her countenance. Her memory was at fault; Mr. Allsop gave her the word; that confused her more. She stammered in the endeavor to proceed. He prompted her a second time; and now, instead of the tender, fervent tone, in which she had again and again rehearsed that very passage in her own chamber, she found herself repeating the words after the prompter, with a parrot-like intonation, as though she had never heard them before, and had no comprehension of their sense.

Icilius enters, exclaiming, "Virginia! sweet Virginia!"

"Miss Rosenvelt, Mr. Swain—Mr. Swain, Miss Rosenvelt," interrupted Mr. Belton.

Icilius paused to bow, and then continued: "Sure, I heard my name pronounced, etc. etc."

This gentleman belonged to that numerous class of actors who consider rehearsals a necessary bore. He gabbled with telegraphic speed over the language of Icilius, gliding one word into the other, without attempting to convey any meaning by the enigmatical sounds. Punctuation was wholly ignored in this convenient style of declamation. How could Stella fancy herself the beloved Virginia of such a nimble-tongued, brainless Icilius?

The act ended; but no interval is allowed at rehearsal. In the next scene, Virginius betroths his daughter to Icilius. The poetic principle with which Stella's whole nature was deeply imbued received its severest shock when Allsop droned out the beautiful betrothing speech of Virginius. It produced the same jarring sensation as a succession of false notes on the fine ear of a musician, and drew from her a suppressed groan. The love-making of Icilius, which followed, — Icilius, who declares himself "dissolved, overpowered with the munificence of the auspicious hour," — was positively laughable. Under any other circumstances Stella could not have kept her countenance, when he rattled off at full speed:

> "O, help me to a word will speak my bliss,
> Or I am beggared! No! there is not one!
> There can not be! for never man had bliss
> Like mine to name!"

It was obeying the noble Dane's injunction to "speak the words trippingly on the tongue," with an original fidelity.

Towards the close of the scene, Servia is summoned.

"Miss Rosenvelt, Mrs. Fairfax — Mrs. Fairfax, Miss Rosenvelt," said Mr. Bolton.

Mrs. Fairfax came late, and missed her first scene. At Virginius' charge to Servia to take his daughter in, Mrs. Fairfax encircled Stella's waist with her arm. The touch thrilled through the trembling girl, it was so tender, so gentle. Stella looked into the stranger's face. It was one of the most benign that goodness and intellect ever illumined.

When they reached the wing, Mrs. Fairfax remarked, kindly, "How cold your hands are! Even through your gloves they feel like ice! It must be the effect of nervous excitement. A first rehearsal is *very* trying; but you will soon get accustomed."

What music were those words to the ears of the downcast girl! The heavenly music of sympathy descending into the troubled heart, and charming away its restless throes.

Stella smiled gratefully, but could only answer, "I am a little — a little nervous — and you are very kind!"

Mrs. Fairfax replied by chafing the cold hands, and warming them in her own.

Virginia's next scene is very brief. She crosses in front of the forum with Servia, and meets Numitorius.

"Miss Rosenvelt, Mr. Doran — Mr. Doran, Miss Rosenvelt," said Belton. They bowed.

The next scene is in Act Third. Claudius drags Virginia across the stage. Of course, this "business," as it is theatrically termed, is omitted at rehearsal. Virginia meekly walked by the side of Claudius, having been duly apprised that she would be dragged at night.

"Miss Rosenvelt, Mr. Conklin — Mr. Conklin, Miss Rosenvelt," said the punctilious Mr. Belton, as Virginia and Claudius met. Virginia is supposed to be fainting, and does not speak during this scene.

She next appears in the Roman Forum, as the captive of Appius; then in her uncle's house; and then, for the last time, before the tribunal. There she is stabbed by her father. These scenes were hurried through in a formal, business-like way, and rehearsal ended.

Stella overheard Fisk remarking to the prompter, in an oracular tone, "Can't say it's a bit like it!

Don't think there 's anything in her! No go! *Decidedly*, no go!"

Mr. Belton made no comment on her performance, as he bade Stella good-morning, and honored Mr. Oakland with a distant bow.

"You will receive the call for Monday; Mr. Tennent will, of course, be here," were the manager's parting words.

Stella returned home thought-sick, disheartened, overwhelmed by a mental and bodily lassitude which she had never experienced before. Mr. Oakland made not the slightest attempt to reässure her.

Among the thronging images which rose up like phantoms to torment her, there was but one she could contemplate without a shudder — the mildly-beaming face of Mrs. Fairfax. Was this the commencement of the career which she had pictured to herself as so inspiring, so full of exhilarating triumphs and delights? True, she had encountered but trifles; these were mere *feathers* that weighed thus upon her spirit; but they were "feathers of lead."

CHAPTER IV.

The Morning of the Débût. — Emotions at First Sight of the Placard.—The Second Rehearsal.— Mr. Tennent.—The Great Tragedian's Manifestations of Importance. — Friendly Hints of Mrs. Fairfax. — Mr. Tennent's Disdain of the Novice. — The Crushed Hat. — Unconcern of the Stage-Manager. — The Ballet-Girl and her Brother, the Witless Basket-Carrier. — A Sad History. — The Ballet-Girl's Devotion to a Brutalized Father. — Unrest. — Heart-Sinkings. — Arrival of Perdita and Florizel. — Perdita's Effect upon Stella. — Chilling Gloom of a Theatre at Twilight. — The Star Dressing-Room. — The Officious Mrs. Bunce. — The Dresser's Volunteered Information. — Her Treatment of the Novice. — Virginia's Toilet. — A Discussion. — Tender Care of an Experienced and Compassionate Actress. — Wanderings behind the Scenes. — Comfortless Localities. — The Green-Room. — Mr. Martin, the Rheumatic Martyr. — Wonderful Effects of Excitement upon Physical Ailments. — The Prompter's Seat. — Fisk's Humorous Impertinence. — The Surreptitious Aperture in the Green Curtain. — First Peep at the Audience. — Brief Visit of Mr. Oakland. — First Music. — Second Music. —Third Music. — Increasing Terror of the Novice. — Sudden Diversion of her Thoughts. — Perdita and her Father. —Rising of the Curtain. — Sandalled Feet a Moment Visible. — Fisk's Enjoyment.—Change of Scene. — Actors Pouring from the Green-Room. —The Agonies of Stage Fright. — Darkness in Light. —The Débût. —Churlish Treatment from the Representative of Virginius. — Mechanical Obedience of the Novice. —Spell Broken. —The Soliloquy. — Stella's Performance of Virginia. — The Manager's Cautious Comment. —The Débûtante's Return Home.

It was the morning of Stella's débût. As she drew back the curtains of her window, the sight of her own name, in huge characters, on a placard opposite, sent an electric shock through her frame. The novel sensation could hardly be designated as pain, yet it would be mistermed pleasure. There was too much incertitude, too much thrilling expectancy, too many turbulent thoughts contending in her mind, for the sense of enjoyment to predominate. She had broken the thrall of tyrannous custom, she had triumphed over all opposition; and yet the cankerworm of discontent entered her breast, and blasted the spring blossoms of her youth. The unrelaxed tension of her nerves, her mental unrest, had quenched the sparkle of her effervescing spirits. Her state constantly alternated between high excitement and an oppressive weariness.

As soon as her determination to become an actress was bruited in the public ear, she was, of course, besieged by the remonstrances of friends. But their opinions she set at naught. Her independent tone and resolute manner silenced exhortation. To her mother's presence no one gained admission.

Mr. Oakland declined to accompany his pupil to her second rehearsal. His tenderness towards the unprotected girl had induced him to violate a principle, at her strong entreaty, but he saw no cause to subject himself to further slight without being of essential service to her.

The clock had struck its tenth warning on that eventful day, and the ten minutes' theatrical grace had expired, before Stella, with Mattie at her side, once more entered the theatre. They found the company already assembled, but rehearsal had not commenced. Everybody awaited the appearance of the great tragedian. Punctuality would have been derogatory to the dignity of Mr. Tennent. To cause his co-laborers as much annoyance as possible was to impress them with a due sense of his own importance.

Mr. Belton saluted Stella more cordially than on a previous occasion. He was gratified to find that Mr. Oakland's presence was not considered indispensable. Fisk bestowed on her a familiar nod. The stage-manager and actors curtailed their civilities to the utmost brevity. The profession never pay homage in anticipation. Miss Rosenvelt's assumed position in the theatre as yet lacked the stamp of public recognition. All novices are looked upon as pretenders until success proclaims their legitimacy.

Mr. Belton chanced to be called away. Stella was left standing in the centre of the stage, beside Mattie, looking wretchedly uncomfortable and out of place.

Mrs. Fairfax, who had just entered, joined her at once, and ordered Fisk to bring a chair.

"You will learn the ways of a theatre, little by little, my dear. Every one feels strange at first." She placed the chair beside the manager's table. "You can sit here or in the green-room, just as you please. It is the privilege of stars to take their seat on the stage and watch the rehearsal. The rest of the company are not allowed this liberty. How flushed you look! Will you not be more comfortable if you lay aside your bonnet? You will rehearse better."

Stella willingly removed her hat, for even its light weight seemed to press painfully on her throbbing brain.

Mrs. Fairfax hinted that Mattie had better keep a little more in the background. She might subject herself to reproof from the austere stage-manager. Mattie, at a word, retreated behind the scenes. But her honest, anxious face was constantly visible, peeping round one of the wings, and watching Stella.

After half an hour's delay, Mr. Tennent made a pompous entrance. The stage echoed with his heavy tread. His deep, sonorous voice, as he issued some despotic orders, his imperious bearing, his athletic frame, cast in one of nature's rudest moulds, inspired Stella with a feeling akin to awe.

Mr. Belton presented him.

"Sorry you 've got me a novice! Detest acting with *amateurs!*" was his audible observation, as he eyed the young girl with supercilious scrutiny. "Poor Lydia! we shan't soon see her match again." He turned on his heel without addressing a single syllable to the discomfited novice.

"And *he* is to enact Virginius!" thought Stella to herself. "How will I ever imagine myself his daughter? If he had only spoken one word to me, it would make such a difference!"

Rehearsal commenced. To Stella's great surprise, Mr. Tennent rattled over the language of his rôle in the same senseless manner as the other actors, pausing now and then to explain his particular "business," and ejaculating "Brute!" in an under-tone, every time some unfortunate individual failed to comprehend him.

Stella summoned all her energy, and successfully assumed a bearing which might have been mistaken for composure. She went through her allotted duties without hesitation, and apparently undismayed. Mrs. Fairfax congratulated her on her newly-acquired self-possession. Mr. Tennent occasionally instructed her in "business," but without unbending from his stately demeanor.

As Virginia is seen no more after the fourth act, Stella was at liberty to absent herself before rehearsal concluded. She returned to the chair upon which she had placed her bonnet. Mr. Finch was unconsciously sitting upon both. He laughed unconcernedly, and made a clumsy attempt to pull the hat into shape, but uttered no apology. Then, thrusting it into her extended hand, he said:

"No use of crying over spilled milk! If you don't put your foot in it to-night, and make a failure, you can afford to buy yourself twice as fine a kickshaw as this."

Stella's mind was too much engrossed to dwell upon trifles, but she recoiled from contact with coarse natures. It was less mortification to be forced to wear the damaged hat through the streets than to be treated with such rude indifference.

She was passing out behind the scenes, when Mrs. Fairfax once more joined her.

"Call upon me for any assistance you may need this evening. You will, of course, have the 'star dressing-room.' The luxury of an apartment to one's self is reserved for stars only. The room in which I dress, with four other ladies, adjoins yours. You had better come early, — at least an hour and a half before the curtain rises, — so that you can walk about, after you are dressed, and collect your thoughts. Don't forget that I will assist you with pleasure."

Mrs. Fairfax's partiality for her profession, as well as her native kindness of heart, interested her in a novice who apparently possessed histrionic qualifications of a rare order. The compassionate actress stretched out a loving hand to this young girl, whose uncertain feet were forcing their way within the briery circle which bounded that miniature world, a theatre.

Stella was thanking her new friend with much warmth, when a ballet-girl timidly approached. Her face was grief-worn and sickly, but of touching loveliness. Oppression looked out from her meek eyes. Her coarse and insufficient garb betokened penury. Her attenuated fingers were rapidly knitting lace, and her needles never ceased their motion as she spoke.

"May Floy carry your basket, miss?"

"My basket?"

"The basket with your dresses. Floy carries all the baskets."

Stella looked inquiringly at Mrs. Fairfax.

"You should have a basket for your costumes. A basket is lighter and more convenient than a trunk. This is Floy's sister. He takes charge of all our baskets. Poor fellow! we ought to help him as much as we can." She added, in an under-tone, "The unfortunate boy is half-witted, but very honest."

"Mattie shall purchase me a basket. Let your brother call for it, by all means," said Stella.

"And tell him to be sure to call early, Perdita," added Mrs. Fairfax.

"O, never fear! Thank you, kindly, Miss Rosenvelt." Still knitting as she walked away, Perdita returned to the green-room.

"That poor girl's history is a sad one," said Mrs. Fairfax; "but, alas! there is an abundance of sad histories in all theatres. Her father is now the captain of the supernumeraries. I suppose you hardly know what that means. The captain is a sort of leader who directs and drills the *sups*. His grade in the theatre, as you may imagine, is rather low; yet I remember him a handsome, ambitious, promising actor. But he was unfortunate, or, rather, he imagined himself *unlucky*, and was possessed with the idea that all the world conspired against him. He said that he was always kept down in every theatre where he engaged; that managers never afforded him an opportunity of exhibiting the talents he was confident of possessing. A man of violent passions, he was constantly falling into disgrace by his disputes with his fellow-actors. He was discharged from theatre after theatre. He became dispirited, morose, and finally abandoned himself to the control of the demon Intemperance. Intoxication was nightly 'the prologue to his sleep.' His wife was second walking lady in this theatre; a gentle, inoffensive being, most unfitly mated. She died a few years ago, leaving two children, — Perdita, and Florizel. So the mother called them, after her favorite characters in Shakspeare's 'Winter's Tale.' One day, the father, in a paroxysm of ungovernable rage, locked up little Floy in a dark cellar. The child was left shrieking with terror, while the father lost all remembrance at the neighboring tavern. He returned at midnight, and found poor Perdita sitting outside of the cellar-door, moaning and weeping, and calling to her brother, whom she believed to be dead. The father, suddenly sobered by his alarm, drew the key from his pocket, and opened the door. The boy was discovered sitting on the ground, staring wildly at one corner, his teeth chattering, as he pointed with his fingers, and used frantic gesticulations. Prolonged fear had unsettled his mind. Ever since he has been what people call half-witted.

"Perdita, though she is only four years older, has tended him with all a mother's devotion. Over her father, too, she exerts a more powerful influence than any one else. She belongs to the *corps de ballet* here, but the poor child works night and day with her needle to support the family. The boy has just sense enough to be taught to carry baskets to and fro. At first Perdita always accompanied him, when he received the baskets and delivered them. Not a few weary journeys did that brave girl take daily. By and by, she earned by her knitting, and sewing, and flower-making, sufficient money to buy Floy a wheelbarrow. She has now so thoroughly taught him the way to all the residences of the actors, that he goes for the baskets every night by himself, and takes them home again after the play. He never makes a mistake."

"And is the father still intemperate?" asked Stella.

"Hopelessly so, I fear. That evil spirit, Perdita, angel as she is, cannot exorcise. He is tortured by remorse, and drinks to drown all recollection of the injury he has inflicted on his child. You will see him at night. Perdita is always watching over and helping him. But for her, he would never be ready to go upon the stage at the right moment; he could not be depended upon, and would have been dismissed long ago. But what a time I have spent gossiping over this romance of real life! I must say good-by until to-night. Keep up a brave heart, and success to you!"

"Good-by. I feel more like success than I did on Saturday."

"How much heavier are that poor girl's trials than mine!" mused Stella, as she slowly walked home. "What could have revealed to me the blessedness of my own lot so forcibly as contrast with this greater sufferer!"

The afternoon was one of long expectancy to Stella. The thoughtful Mattie had persuaded her to lie down; but she tossed uneasily on her pillow, finding no repose. Every few minutes she turned to the clock; there was surely some clog upon its hands, they moved so slowly. O, that the night had come and had passed! Then, as the longed-for time drew near, suddenly she grew sick at heart, and was seized with faintness. The thought flashed through her mind that she would fail at the last moment; that she lacked strength to carry the burden which she had lifted upon her own shoulders with such headstrong will.

Half-past seven was the hour at which the curtain must rise. She had been apprised that Mr. Belton enforced the strictest punctuality at night. Even when stars of first magnitude solicited a few moments' delay, it was denied. Mrs. Fairfax had cautioned her to be at the theatre in ample time. It wanted but a quarter of six.

A knock at the door. The pale-faced Perdita stood without. She was accompanied by a tall, ungainly stripling. The extreme sharpness of his countenance reminded Stella of the "profile" shows she had that morning seen scattered about the stage. His large projecting eyes, of faintest blue, seemed starting from their sockets. His nether limbs bore a strong resemblance to a pair of compasses, and his long, lank arms reached below his knees. His mouth remained open with an expression of silly wonder. When he caught Stella's eye, he shook his head, agitating a profusion of straight, tow-colored locks, and chuckled and laughed, as child does with child when they are bent upon some forbidden frolic.

"I have brought my brother," said Perdita, advancing into the room. "He has come for the basket. I show him the way the first time he goes to a strange place. He always remembers it after that."

The serene, sweet face of that humble girl, who had passed calmly through such soul-harrowing trials, who faithfully performed so many difficult duties, had more effect in composing Stella's excited nerves than all the hartshorn and sal-volatile which Mattie solicitously administered.

The basket was already packed. Mattie strapped the cover with leathern girths, and Floy delightedly received his new burden.

Stella's adieu to her mother was very brief. She only trusted herself to say, "I hope I shall bring you good news, mother; and the promise of laurels hereafter, even if I win none to-night."

She was equally surprised and gratified when her mother asked for a copy of Virginius to peruse in her daughter's absence.

Mattie, who was now and then a little tyrannical, had persisted in ordering a carriage, though Stella declared herself quite able to walk. Soon after six, they were driving to the theatre. They presented themselves at the stage-door just as Perdita and Floy arrived with the basket. The door-keeper brusquely questioned Stella as to her identity before he admitted them.

The dreary gloominess of a theatre behind the scenes, when twilight is chasing the out-spent day, must be seen and felt to be fully comprehended. The desolate cheerlessness of the place has struck a chill to the heart of many a novice. The crowded scenery looks rougher and dingier; the painted tenements, groves, gardens, streets, more grotesque; the numberless stage anomalies more glaringly absurd.

The sea-weed floating on the waves in feathery sprays of brilliant red and vivid green, that, seized for closer scanning, turns to an unsightly, shapeless mass, fitly typifies the stage in its resplendent wizard-robe of night enchantment, and its unideal, lugubrious daytime garb.

"Where am I to go?" Stella inquired of Perdita.

"The dresser, Mrs. Bunce, has not come yet, and the gas will not be turned on until half-past six. Mr. Belton only allows it to be lighted for one hour before the curtain rises; but, if you please, I can show you the star dressing-room."

Perdita led the way up a long flight of stairs, then through a narrow entry, or, rather, gallery. On one side appeared a row of small doors, very like those of a bathing-machine. They opened into the rooms of the ladies of the company. A wooden railing extended on the other side. To any one who leaned over this rude balcony the larger portion of the stage became visible. Five or six persons were often crowded into one dressing-room. The apartments were portioned off into set spaces, and every cramped division labelled with a name. The room at the end of the gallery was appropriated solely to the lady "star." The dressing-rooms devoted to the use of gentlemen were located beneath the stage.

Perdita opened the door of this modern "star-chamber." The apartment was very small, the atmosphere suffocatingly close. Mattie at once threw up the tiny, cobweb-draped window. A shelf ran along one side of the wall, after the manner of a kitchen dresser. In front lay a narrow strip of baize; the rest of the floor was bare. On the centre of the shelf stood a cracked mirror. A gas-branch jutted out on either side. Two very rickety chairs, a crazy washstand, a diminutive stove, constituted the furniture of the apartment. In this unseemly chrysalis-shell the butterflies of the stage received their wings. Little did the audience, who greeted some queen-like favorite, sumptuously attired in broidered velvet and glittering with jewels, imagine that such was the palace-bower from which she issued!

The year had just ushered in its most wayward child, smiling, frowning April. Frowns thus far predominated; the unsunned air had all the searching bleakness of March. Mattie threw her own shawl over her shivering charge, and examined the unlighted stove.

"Set down the basket, Floy, and run for a match," said Perdita.

The boy, as he removed the basket from his shoulder, looked at Stella with evident admiration, winked at her, chuckled again, and ran down the stair. He was strongly attracted by this new face. He comprehended that something was going on which principally concerned its possessor; but what it was he could not have defined.

Floy returned with the match, and Mattie was lighting the fire which she found prepared for kindling, when Perdita whispered, "Here comes Mrs. Bunce!" and hurried away with her brother, apparently awed by the approach of some august personage.

Mrs. Bunce, a portly, middle-aged woman, now bustled in. What a voice that Mrs. Bunce had! It was so shrill that, when she spoke, Stella almost fancied her ears were suddenly pierced by a sharp instrument. All Mrs. Bunce's words were darted out with amazing rapidity.

"Here in time, eh? That 's a good sign for a novice. This is the young lady, I suppose," examining Stella. "Quite a stage face. How do you do, my dear? This is your maid, I presume?"

"Her maid, or her nurse, or her costumer, or anything she is pleased to want," replied Mattie, with dignity.

"Ah! that 's well. No doubt a very serviceable person. So you 've set the fire going? That 's a pity! You may be smoked out soon; all the stoves here smoke when the wind 's contrary. Out with the dresses! Hang them up on those nails. Her toilet things go here. Never been on the stage before, miss? It 's a trying thing for beginners. I 've seen hundreds of débûts in my day. Most of the young ones think a deal of themselves until they get before the lights; then they find out what they 're made of. Not one in fifty succeeds. Hope you 're not scared? Don't show it to the audience, or they 'll think it good fun. They always laugh at the fright of novices; you know it makes the poor, simple things look so ridiculously awkward! Here, Jerry," calling over the gallery to the gas-lighter, "if you can't light up that gas yet, give us a candle, will you? The young person is a novice, and I may have trouble dressing her."

"Thank you, Mrs. Bunce," Stella ventured to say; "but Mattie has been accustomed to dress me."

"Yes, that I have, ever since she was that high!" added Mattie, affectionately, and designating with her hand a stature of some few inches.

"Ah! I dare say, but not for the stage. Mr. Belton depends upon me to look after the novices on their first night, and see that they don't disfigure themselves."

Mattie, when her legitimate office was thus peremptorily snatched from her hands, looked like a suppressed thunder-gust; but, considerate even in her wrath, she feared to distress Stella by remonstrating. Not without difficulty, she controlled a strong temptation to forcibly eject Mrs. Bunce from the apartment.

As Mattie opened the basket, Mrs. Bunce seized

upon the contents, and dragged them to light without ceremony.

"White merino: that's right. Has it got a sweep? Not too long, I hope; if she's awkward, she'll trip. Those folds are too small for a Roman dress. She has such a wisp of a figure, she could wear loose folds, which are more correct. Where's your key border?"

"*Key border?*" asked Stella.

"Yes, round the bottom of the dress; it's Roman. We always dress our Virginias with key-border trimming."

"I like the dress better without. Virginia's character is marked by so much girlish simplicity that her attire should be unadorned."

"O, very well! It's no great matter; you are not expected to know much about it as yet."

Mrs. Bunce chattered on without pause, while Stella commenced her toilet. The busy fingers of the dresser made several desperate attempts to assist in the arrangement of the novice's hair; but this Stella would not allow. She folded back the waving, golden-tinted tresses from her pure brow, gathered them in a classic knot, and encircled her head with a white fillet. A stray lock here and there escaped its bonds, and was permitted to curl down her finely-curved throat.

The gas was by this time lighted. Stella was just receiving her dress from the hands of Mattie. Mrs. Bunce snatched it away.

"Wait, wait a bit!" said she. "Where's your paint and your powder?—but you're white enough without powdering—where's your *rouge?*"

"I have none. There is nothing in the poet's description of Virginia to make one suppose that she was particularly ruddy; besides, excitement has given me too much color already."

"Does very well now, but it can't be depended upon like *rouge*. It won't last when you 're frightened out of your wits, that 's the mischief. Better let me borrow some *rouge* from the ladies."

"No, I would rather not. I don't see the necessity."

Mrs. Bunce persisted; Stella refused.

"O, of course you can do just as you please," said the officious dresser, in an irate tone.

"I always do," replied Stella, quietly.

Stella's Roman toilet was completed. Even the critical Mrs. Bunce was forced to confess herself satisfied with the young débûtante's appearance; it was so chastely classic, so befitting the patrician maiden, so indicative of vestal purity.

It wanted more than half an hour of the rising of the curtain. The small stove had been gradually sending out thin wreaths of smoke. The atmosphere was becoming unendurable, as Stella's smarting eyes and irritated lungs began to testify.

"I shall have neither sight nor voice, if I am shut up here any longer," thought she, "and this chattering woman will drive my part quite out of my head."

Then she remembered the kind offer of Mrs. Fairfax, and requested Mrs. Bunce to see if she were dressed. In the Roman matron who returned with the messenger Stella hardly recognized her friend;

the *make up* of the practised actress was so elaborate, so striking, so full of character.

Mrs. Fairfax shook hands, and held the novice at arm's length with a look of unmistakable pleasure; then retouched Stella's dress, disposed a fold here and there with more statuesque grace, and said, affectionately,

"I have seen at last my *beau ideal* of Virginia! I hope you feel quite collected?"

"Tolerably; but this room is so close, the smoke chokes me. Might we not go down?"

"Certainly. Come, and I will show you the green-room, and teach you your way behind the scenes; that will help wear off the newness."

Mattie followed, carefully protecting from contact with the ground Virginia's spotless vesture. To Stella's great relief, Mrs. Bunce remained behind.

"This is the green-room," said Mrs. Fairfax.

Stella looked in curiously. It was a long, narrow apartment. At one end sofas, throne-chairs, and other stately seats for stage use, stood crowded together. On either side of the wall a cushioned bench was secured, the only article of stationary furniture, except the full-length mirror. On this bench lay an actor in Roman apparel. Stella's uninitiated eye failed to detect that he was indebted to art for his white locks and venerable aspect. He appeared to be studying, but every now and then gave vent to an uneasy groan.

"That is Dentatus — Mr. Martin. Don't you recognize him?" inquired Mrs. Fairfax. "He is a martyr to inflammatory rheumatism, and can scarcely stand. He has suffered for years, and finds no relief."

Stella called to mind the gentleman on crutches whom she had seen at rehearsal.

"But how can he act?" she asked.

"That is one of the stage mysteries which it requires some wisdom to solve. You will see him, when he is called, hobble with his crutches to the wing, groaning at every step, and really suffering, there is no doubt about that; but, the instant his cue is spoken, his crutches will very likely be flung at Fisk's head, and, lo! Dentatus walks on the stage, erect and firm as though he had never known an ache. He is a great favorite with the audience, and generally manages to keep them convulsed with laughter, though he never ceases complaining and groaning himself, when he is out of their presence."

Two other Romans were walking up and down the green-room, repeating their parts in a low tone. At the further end, where the sofas and chairs were huddled together, sat a group of girls in Roman costume. Stella recognized Perdita among them. She was knitting lace with a rapidity positively wonderful.

Mrs. Fairfax next conducted Stella to the prompter's nook on the right of the stage. There Mr. Finch sat, arranging his prompt-book, and Fisk was going through a series of ludicrous antics at his side.

The latter nodded to Stella, and inquired, patronizingly, "How d' ye do? How do you feel *now?*"

Mrs. Fairfax checked him by a light box on the ear, and led Stella to the stage. It was covered with green baize; the scene was set for a street in Rome.

"Come and take your first look at the audience," said her cicerone, pointing out a small aperture that had been surreptitiously made in the green curtain. They looked through, and saw the boxes, pit, and gallery, rapidly filling.

At this moment, Floy glided up to Stella, rubbing his bony hands. "Such a house! such a house!" he exclaimed, and then darted away again.

Stella's heart began to leap as though it would bound into her throat, as she caught sight of the thronged audience.

"You won't mind them, when you are once engrossed in your part," said Mrs. Fairfax, noticing her sudden trepidation. "Never think of an audience, if you can help it."

They walked up and down behind the scenes. Stella remarked the broken windows, the open doors through which rushed strong currents of cold air, the dilapidated condition of the walls, and wondered at the comfortlessness of the place.

"It 's the same in all theatres, my dear. I never knew a manager yet who thought it necessary to render the members of his company comfortable behind the scenes. Those windows have been broken all winter. Nobody ever dreams of having them mended. A good many of us have nearly perished in our light clothing. But I dare say we get accustomed to it; and, on the stage, in the excitement of acting, one is not conscious of heat or cold."

The door-keeper came up to them. "There is a gentleman asking to see you, miss. He says you desired him to call. It 's against the rules to admit strangers, and I had to take his name to Mr. Belton to get consent. Mr. Belton said he did n't mind your seeing any one to-night, as you were a novice ; but he wants you to learn the rules, and the sooner the better."

"It 's Mr. Oakland! I begged him to come for one moment. How kind he is!"

Mr. Oakland was standing at the stage-door, somewhat discomposed by the door-keeper's rebuff. Fastidious and sensitive as he was, that he subjected himself to these annoyances, was an eloquent proof of his attachment to the fatherless girl.

"How good you are! The sight of you revives me, and gives me courage!"

"Fair Virginia! Yes — you *are* Virginia in looks — be nothing but Virginia to-night! I must say adieu, for I could not stay here" (and he looked around with an expression of slight disgust) "amongst these dramatic savages. Be natural; do not aim at too much; don't try to act, but to feel; don't *declaim*, but *talk;* remember the good rule: colloquial, but not prosaic; forcible, but not declamatory. Good-by, and Heaven help you!"

Just then, Fisk darted by her, twisting his body into ludicrous contortions as he ran up the stairs, crying, at the top of his piping voice, "First music — ic — ic! First musi — ic — ic — ic!"

Along the gallery, past all the dressing-room doors, he sped, repeating, "First musi — ic — ic!" Down the staircase, beneath the stage, making the circuit of the gentlemen's dressing-rooms, he pursued his rapid flight, still shouting, "First musi — ic — ic!"

"What *is* that strange boy about?" asked Stella of Mrs. Fairfax.

"He is making the *first music call.* It is given a quarter of an hour before the curtain rises."

The musicians could now be heard tuning their instruments. Stella continued promenading up and down with Mrs. Fairfax. After the lapse of five minutes, Fisk was seen rolling himself from side to side, in sailor-like fashion, as he climbed the stairs again, screaming, "Second musi — ic — ic — *ic!* Second musi — ic — ic — *ic!*" He made the same tour, and then rolled back to the prompter's seat.

"Now it wants ten minutes of the time," said Mrs. Fairfax.

Stella was seized with an uncontrollable fit of gasping and trembling. Her head grew giddy; the same sickening faintness which she had experienced at home now nearly overpowered her. Mattie ran for a glass of water. The members of the company, who were on their way to the green-room, stopped to stare at the novice, to nudge each other, and jest at an alarm which most of them had suffered themselves.

"Last musi — ic — ic — *ic!* Last musi — ic — ic — *ic!*" screeched Fisk, with a new variation of his fantasticalities.

The orchestra was playing vociferously.

"Now, my dear, you had better forget everything else, and think over your part. It wants but five minutes of the rising of the curtain."

"O, don't leave me! don't leave me! What would I do without you?" supplicated Stella, for she saw her friend about to mount the stair.

"I will return directly. You don't appear until the second scene. I go on a moment before you, and from the same entrance. I shall be by your side. Now walk about quietly with Mattie, and try to think only of the play."

"I shall fail! I shall fail!" murmured Stella, in an agony of fear. "I shall never be able to articulate a word! O! if Mr. Oakland were here, or my brother, or any one who loved me!"

She was wringing her hands in absolute despair, when Perdita passed her and went up to a man in the garb of a Roman citizen, who was extended on the ground, in one corner. He appeared to be asleep; his head rested on a pile of shields, breastplates, and other warlike accoutrements. Perdita laid her hand gently on his shoulder.

"Father! father, dear! the last music is called; you will be wanted in a moment."

"Get out! get out! don't disturb me; get out, I say!" was the rough reply, accompanied by a motion that somewhat resembled a kick.

"Father, you *must* wake up! The curtain is going to rise! You are on in the first scene! — *do* wake!"

"What is it? Who is it?" asked the man, with a vacant stare. "Perdy, it's you, is it? Always bothering me! no quiet to be found anywhere; no rest!"

"I was forced to wake you, father; for you are called for the stage."

She smoothed his disordered hair, and arranged the tumbled folds of his toga.

He rose unwillingly, shaking himself after the fashion of a huge mastiff. His form was tall and finely proportioned. His countenance must once have been handsome; but the defacing fingers of passion and sensuality had ploughed furrows that destroyed its comeliness. He was not precisely intoxicated, but in that semi-stupid state which habitual intemperance renders second nature.

Stella forgot herself and her approaching trial as she watched the noble girl patiently waiting upon and soothing her brutal father.

"Everybody called for First Act of Virginius!" bellowed Fisk, gambolling up to the green-room door. "Servius, Cneius, Virginius, Titus, and all the Roman citizens!"

"O, where is Mrs. Fairfax?" cried Stella, as she seized Mattie's arm to support herself. "Why don't she come? Do try and find her room, and beg her to come, Mattie! No! no! don't leave me here alone! If she would only come! I go on at that entrance, over there. I must get there quickly."

She was walking across the stage, with Mattie's arm encircling her waist, when the orchestra ceased.

"Clear the stage, ladies and gentlemen," called out Mr. Finch.

The prompter's tinkling bell sounded. Stella's white dress and sandalled feet were visible for a second, as the curtain slowly rose.

The first scene commenced. Where Stella stood, she commanded a full view of the stage. But she saw nothing, heard nothing, — not even the stately Virginius, not the shouts of applause with which his entrance was greeted.

"Courage! courage!" said a kind voice at her side. It was Mrs. Fairfax.

"O, madam, I feel as if I were under water — stifling — drowning!"

"It 's only *stage fright,* my dear; it will pass off by and by. All actors suffer more or less from its paralyzing influence. Even our veterans are not proof against occasional attacks of the monster. Try and collect yourself, and think of what you have to do."

"Virginius — Servia — Virginia," cried Fisk, in a more subdued tone; for, now that the curtain had risen, his former key would have been heard by the audience. Fisk looked saucily in Stella's face, his head on one side, and a sagacious expression upon his countenance, which seemed to ask, "How d' ye like it? Pleasant feeling, is n't it?" And then he repeated almost in her ear, "Vir-gin-ia-a-a call-*alled!*"

"Go away, you young pest!" said Mrs. Fairfax, giving him a shove.

A shrill whistle sounded; it penetrated Stella's very brain. The scene changed to an apartment in the house of Virginius.

"There 's Virginia's broidery," said Fisk, giving Mrs. Fairfax a frame with worsted-work of by no means classic appearance. "There 's your Virginia painting," he added, handing Stella a colored engraving. "That 's the picture of Achilles, which looks so wonderful like your belov*ed* Icilius. An't it fine?"

At the sound of the changing scene all the company poured from the green-room and gathered around the wings, to witness Stella's débût. Actors invariably entertain a sovereign contempt for novices. The stage tremors of youthful aspirants are a fruitful source of mirth. They delight in confusing and tormenting a débûtante.

Virginius enters with Servia. She points out the tell-tale letters L and I twined with a V, in Virginia's embroidery. After a brief dialogue, Servia is despatched for the maiden.

Mrs. Fairfax returned to the place where she had left the panic-stricken Stella, and found her lying in Mattie's arms, breathless with the intensity of her emotion, her face and lips colorless, her eyes half closed.

The actress grasped her by the shoulder with pretended roughness, and shook her, saying, "Rouse yourself, child! rouse yourself! You 've only a second now. You 're not going to make a failure? Think of what a disgrace it would be! Think of the one whom you wish most to please — who is dearest to you — and rouse yourself. Virginius' soliloquy is just over. 'Soft she comes' — that is your cue; go on bravely."

She clasped Stella's icy hand, and with gentle force pressed her forward. Stella was scarcely conscious of what she was doing, as she tottered on the stage and approached Virginius, saying, in a tremulous tone, "Well, father, what 's your will?"

Those foot-lights sent forth a dazzling glare, but Stella was in total darkness. The air grew so thick she could not breathe; her "soul of lead" "staked her to the ground;" she could not move. There was a sound of noisy hands, a prolonged acclamation, but Stella paid no heed to these, as she stood spell-bound before Virginius.

He attempted to speak, but the applause drowned

his voice. As it was bestowed upon another, he would gladly have hushed it down, by proceeding with his part (a favorite trick of actors); but the audience was resolute in obtaining some recognition from the stupefied novice.

Mr. Tennent now churlishly whispered, "Curtsey, curtsey — can't you?" Muttering to himself, "Defend me from novices!"

Stella, thus prompted, turned mechanically to the audience and bended slightly, for her quivering limbs rendered the genuflexion somewhat difficult of accomplishment. The darkness was partially dispelled, but the still misty atmosphere seemed full of floating atoms; her Roman father was enveloped by them. The air was less stifling, but were they not flakes of ice which she inhaled at every breath? Silence was restored, and the dialogue proceeded.

The graceful simplicity of Stella's attire, the changing beauty of her countenance, the refinement of her mien, her rich, well-cadenced voice, made an instantaneous impression on the audience.

Virginius despatches her for her "last task." Mrs. Fairfax had thoughtfully taken the painting from Stella's hand, and was now holding it in readiness. Stella drew one long breath of relief as she passed out of sight of the audience. Only three lines are spoken by Virginius before Virginia reënters. Stella would certainly have forgotten herself but for Mrs. Fairfax. Virginia returns with the painting. Dentatus enters a moment afterwards. There was no trace of the crippled rheumatic in his gait or mien. Dentatus and Virginius retire together.

It was passing strange, but Stella, now that she

was left alone upon the stage, felt as though the freezing influences that begirt her had suddenly melted away. The spell was broken; her lost faculties were restored. Her form dilated, the truant blood rushed back to her cheeks, the lustre to her dimmed eyes, her thoughts concentrated themselves on her part; with an involuntary self-surrender, she became Virginia. Nothing could surpass the girlish naturalness, the earnest sweetness, with which she uttered:

> "How is it with my heart? I feel as one
> That has lost everything, and just before
> Had nothing left to wish for. He will cast
> Icilius off! I never told it yet;
> But take of me, thou gentle air, the secret—
> And ever after breathe more balmy sweet—
> I love Icilius!
> He 'll cast Icilius off! Not if Icilius
> Approve his honor. That he 'll ever do;
> He speaks, and looks, and moves, a thing of honor,
> Or honor never yet spoke, looked, or moved,
> Or was a thing of earth!"

The audience testified their approval. She had taken her first step on the steep, flinty mount. That over, at every tread she gained a securer foothold.

Icilius enters. Virginia has but a few lines to speak in this scene, but the maidenly modesty with which she confessed her love,—

> "My secret 's yours;
> Keep it, and *honor it*, Icilius,—"

her drooping head, the unconscious picturesqueness of her *pose*, drew down a second round of plaudits.

When the act closed, Mrs. Fairfax embraced her

warmly. "You will be an actress. I thought so; now I know it!"

"But what I have suffered, and how much I owe to your sympathy and encouragement!" replied Stella.

By the time that the call-boy's summons for the second act was given, she had entirely regained her self-possession. Every time she appeared, she grew in favor with the audience. There is no field for a striking display of dramatic abilities in the simple character of Virginia, as portrayed by Knowles; but Stella's unaffected, artless delineation left a deep impression.

In the fourth act, as Virginius raises his knife to stab his daughter, Stella gave utterance to an irrepressible shriek, which imparted unusual reality to the scene. Virginius, the instant he had struck the blow, dropped the young girl from his arms upon the ground, and, with upraised knife, rushed towards Claudius, exclaiming:

> "Lo! Appius, with this innocent blood
> I do devote thee to the infernal Gods!"

Stella felt the trampling of the citizens' and soldiers' feet over her dress and on her loosened hair, as they gathered round to form the closing *tableau*; but she lay motionless, inwardly sending up thanks to Heaven that her trial was over. The curtain rapidly descended. Mr. Belton assisted her to rise.

"You have done well, you give promise," were his chary words of commendation.

There was, of course, a "call" for the débûtante. The manager requested Mr. Tennent to be kind enough to lead on Miss Rosenvelt. The pompous tragedian complied somewhat sulkily. As Stella made her obeisance before the foot-lights, every chord of her heart vibrated with a strange, wild delight. It was the first sensation of unalloyed pleasure she had experienced that night.

While she resumed her every-day attire, the tearful congratulations of Mattie drew from her eyes responding tokens of joy.

Floy came for the basket. That he noticed her streaming eyes was obvious. "O! O! O!" he murmured, pityingly; then, when she smiled, he shook his head, rubbed his hands gleefully, and repeated his favorite ejaculation, "Such a house! such a house!"

Half an hour later, the débûtante was sobbing in her mother's arms. "Mother, I have succeeded! Forgive my waywardness!"

CHAPTER V.

The Weight of New Responsibility. — Fate of Public Idols. — Shakspeare at the Toilet. — Mental Aliment. — Rehearsal of Desdemona. — Mr. Oakland's Analytical Criticisms. — The Second Night behind the Scenes. — Floy. — The Ballet-Girl's Request. — Stella's Dreams of Future Power. — Perdita, and her Senatorial Parent. — The Call-Boy's Rebuke of the Novice. — Return of Stage Fright. — A Blustering Othello. — Desdemona's Entrance in the Council-Chamber. — Stella's Conception of the Character. — Evidences of Genius. — Unfortunate Embrace of the Moor and Lady. — Meeting of the Sublime and Absurd. — Stella's Fall from Poetic Heights. — An Awkward Predicament. — Timely Advice of Mrs. Fairfax. — Stella again surrenders herself to the Magic of Personation. — Powers of the Young Actress Unfolded. — Salient Points. — The Spell accidentally dissolved by a Well-meaning Friend. — Fifth Act. — Unanticipated Violence of the Tragedian. — Desdemona's Suffocation. — Kind Assistance of Mrs. Fairfax. — The Picture. — Gradually Increasing Tortures of Desdemona's Position. — Lost Consciousness.

The first perilous ordeal passed, its auguries all auspicious, Stella thought to experience a sense of relief, of serene security, a freedom from the harassing doubts which had tortured her spirit for days. But the weight of a new responsibility that pressed upon her mind soon dispelled these fallacious hopes. She had succeeded; but, alas! how uncertain was the tenure by which that success was held! Are even the smiles of princes as *inconstant* as public favor? What air-blown bubbles are lighter than the empty breath of popular acclamations? What is an actor but a world's puppet, to be to-day extolled to the skies, to-morrow derided and denounced as an egotistic impostor? Has not the veriest caprice, the merest accident, again and again caused an audience to pluck from the brows of their minions the laurels of toilsome years? When the idol is elevated to its throne, and clothed with all imagined perfections, what is left but to tear it down? The existence of the actor, then, must be a daily struggle to maintain the slippery eminence he has won; a constant combat against the uplifted hands ready to pluck him thence; a nightly strife to ascend beyond their reach. And had Stella no prescience of this direful contest? No! The bitter knowledge could only be revealed after she had taken her first irrevocable step.

On the morning succeeding her débût, she forsook her pillow almost before the sun

> "——— began to draw
> The shady curtain from Aurora's bed."

She rose unrefreshed, for Care had taken up his mansion in her breast, and his enemy, Sleep, would not lodge near him. Her limbs ached as she staggered across the room; her heavy eyes could scarcely see. She was compelled to lie down again; and, having selected a volume of Shakspeare, returned to her couch, not to slumber, but to study. She was to enact Desdemona that night, to rehearse Desdemona that morning. The Lady of Lyons was the play selected for the following night; Evadne for the third. In the crowded laboratory of her brain those poetic phantoms must needs receive vitality, and assume shape and substance.

The book remained in her hands until Mattie's summons to breakfast. Nor was it wholly thrown aside as the young actress performed her morning toilet. She fastened the volume to the frame of her mirror, and, while smoothing the rich tangles of her hair, her eyes were fixed on the open pages. More than once her mind became so thoroughly engrossed that the comb dropped from her fingers, her hands involuntarily clasped themselves over her head in their favorite position, and she walked to and fro in the small chamber, rehearsing aloud.

It was long past the usual hour when she joined her mother at breakfast. The latter seemed, for once, inclined to converse; but Stella could not talk, nor could she partake of food. With mental aliment her throbbing brain was overloaded, and labored fruitlessly to digest its too abundant supply.

"I am afraid you are forgetting rehearsal, Miss Stella; we shall hardly be in time," said Mattie; and Stella was quickly roused from her fit of abstraction. The attendant identified herself so completely with her young charge, that the *we* was constantly upon her lips. "*We* play Desdemona to-night." "*We* played Virginia last night."

Mr. Tennent had not arrived when they appeared upon the stage. Other members of the company, calculating upon the great tragedian's habitual dilatoriness, were also absent. The prompter and his flippant juvenile assistant were the only persons at their post. To Stella the interim was not lost time. She seated herself at the manager's table, and diligently resumed her studies. She was totally unconscious of what occurred around her, until Fisk made his call, and rehearsal commenced. Mrs. Fairfax enacted Emilia. Stella had again the encouraging support of the friend to whom she hourly became more attached. Mrs. Fairfax was so helpful, so considerate of the feelings of others, so lenient to their failings, a being to whom all gracious acts seemed so natural, that she was respected and beloved throughout the theatre.

Rehearsal passed off smoothly. It was nearly two o'clock when it ended, and Stella had promised to be at her tutor's residence by one. She had hoped to devote at least two hours to the study of an art, which, still progressing, is never perfected. It was vexatious that her time was thus unexpectedly curtailed; and she could not require Mr. Oakland to abandon other engagements. She prized his instructions, for they pointed out landmarks by means of which she could travel safely on her new pathway. His analytical criticism unfolded the subtlest beauties of the character they were investigating. Stella used to call the process a *"poetic dissection."* The author's most hidden meanings were brought into full light, and often what was the mere outline of an ideal creation was gracefully filled up, and rendered a coherent whole.

Mr. Oakland, though he had been charmed with Stella's personation of the gentle Virginia, was not prodigal of eulogium. He bade her remember that the character was not one in which her powers could be tested. That what she had accomplished was but as a few coruscant sparks compared to a steady, upward-shooting flame, when contrasted with what she must achieve to rank among "earth-treading stars" of first magnitude.

Stella and Mattie reached the theatre nearly an hour later that night than on the previous evening. Fisk had shouted his "Last musi — ic — *ic!*" accompanying his other whimsicalities by "Yankee Doodle" rapped with his knuckles on every door he passed. And Stella had not yet donned her white satin train, and secured her net of pearls over locks which to-night were allowed to escape in struggling ringlets to her waist.

The orchestra had ceased — the curtain rose. Stella's heart, when she descended the staircase, palpitated almost as painfully as on the evening before. She was accompanied only by Mattie, who bore her train. Mrs. Fairfax did not appear until the second act, and her toilet was not completed.

As Stella passed behind the scenes, Floy leaped out from some dark corner, and rushed up to her, whispering, "Such a house! such a house!" then fled again.

Perdita caught sight of her as she passed the green-room door. With a confused mien the young ballet-girl joined her, and placed a long strip of lace in her hand. It was delicately knitted of fine linen thread.

"It is the best I can do. Do you think it pretty?" asked Perdita, timidly.

"Very pretty, indeed. What do you do with it?"

"Sell it, generally, to the ladies of the theatre.

It does almost as well on stage-dresses as real lace. One can't tell the difference from the boxes. Perhaps — perhaps you would like this piece? You may have dresses that need lace trimming."

"I should like it very much. I want five or six yards of lace for the dress. I wear in the Lady of Lyons, to-morrow. But, you have not more than two yards here."

"Let me knit you the rest; it will be such a help to me! You shall have it in time for the dress. I don't mind sitting up all night. Do give me the order, and I won't disappoint you."

"And make you sit up knitting all night? I would not like you to do that."

"I am used to it," replied the girl, tranquilly. "I am only too glad to obtain work. May I knit the lace for you?" she pleaded.

"Yes, certainly; only Mattie must have it at least an hour before we start for the theatre to-morrow."

As Stella listened to the ballet-girl's warm outpouring of gratitude, and watched her flying needles, she thought to herself, "If I am only successful, in the centre of what a field for the performance of kindly offices shall I stand! What a wide sphere of usefulness will be thrown open to me! Why may I not foster this 'violet by the mossy stone' — transplant it, perhaps, to some more fertile soil? It is for such exercise of good my heart has long yearned. Success will be doubly glorious, if her laurels gift me with this power."

Desdemona does not appear until the third scene

of the tragedy. She is then led by Iago into the council-chamber.

Perdita's father represented one of the "most potent, grave, and reverend signiors." Stella noticed that the thoughtful daughter broke off abruptly from conversation, and unfastened a wig of flowing white hair, which she had secured to her waistband. Her father, in senatorial robes, had just emerged from his underground dressing-room. She went up to him, and carefully adjusted the wig on his head, talking to him, the while, in a low, loving tone. This task completed, the knitting-needles flashed backwards and forwards again, as she stood by his side.

"Desdemona call-all-*alled!*" loudly whispered Fisk behind her.

She started, and commenced running towards the entrance from which she was to make her appearance, when Fisk intercepted her, rebukingly:

"Plenty of time! Keep cool — take it easy — don't be in a hurry — two minutes by the watch. My calls always give time enough to prevent ruffling feathers."

The icy tremor, the giddy, choking faintness, were coming back.

She listened to Mr. Tennent's blustering delivery of Othello's memorable speech before the senate. The "course of his wooing," "the witchcraft he had used," were made known through a succession of explosive sounds, accompanied by a series of spasmodic gesticulations. Instead of the modest, exculpatory narration warranted by the text, his manner spoke defiance to the haughty potentates who dared to demand such a history from his august lips.

Stella's agitation was not so great that she failed to make this criticism.

As the Moorish hero announced her presence with

> "Here comes the lady; let her witness it,"

"Your hand, if you please," said the representative of Iago. She had not noticed that he was standing beside her.

Stella gave her hand. Mattie smoothed down and floated the snowy train. Iago led in Desdemona. She curtseyed low to the Duke. The stage was arranged in such a manner that, to face the Senators, her back was necessarily turned to the audience. Its reception passed unnoticed by Stella. Even had she possessed sufficient self-command to turn and acknowledge their greeting by an obeisance, it would have been a breach of good taste. The spectators would at once have lost sight of the

> "Maiden never bold;
> Of spirit so still and quiet that her motion
> Blushed at herself,"

and viewed but the actress, the novice.

When Brabantio addressed his daughter with

> "Come hither, mistress:
> Do you perceive, in all this noble company,
> Where most you owe obedience?"

she bowed her head with an inclination of filial reverence; then, in a tone of modest frankness, her speaking eyes lifted to her father's face, and afterwards turned confidingly upon the Moor, she replied:

> "My noble father,
> I do perceive here a divided duty.
> To you I am bound for life and education;
> My life and education both do learn me
> How to respect you; you are the lord of duty.
> I am hitherto your daughter; but here 's my husband;
> And so much duty as my mother showed
> To *you, preferring you before her father,*
> *So much* I challenge that *I* may profess
> Due to the Moor, *my lord.*"

The audience seldom fail to respond to Desdemona's sentiment, even if its delivery command no approval. But, in this instance, poet and interpreter won equal meed. In a moment the young actress had merged her own individuality into ideal personation. Desdemona's touching softness, the tender pride with which she confesses and defends her devotion to her newly-made husband, were exquisitely illustrated in Stella's glowing recital of the lines:

> "That I did love the Moor to live with him,
> My downright violence and storm of fortunes
> May trumpet to the world; my heart 's subdued,
> Even to the very quality of my lord.
> I saw Othello's visage in his mind,
> And to his honors, and his valiant parts,
> Did I my soul and fortunes consecrate!"

Her pleading to the Duke to be allowed to accompany her husband to the wars; her imploring face as she sank at her father's feet, and clung to his robe, mutely supplicating a blessing; her shudder when he threw her off, exclaiming:

> "Look to her, Moor; have a quick eye to see;
> She hath deceived her father, and may thee!"

her expression of grateful joy when Othello lifts her, with the confident reply,

> "My life upon her faith!"

gave warrant of the fidelity of her conception.

Desdemona next enters with Emilia, Iago, and Roderigo. They have just landed on the island of Cyprus, and are thus poetically welcomed by Cassio:

> "O behold,
> The riches of the ship is come on shore!
> Ye men of Cyprus, let her have your knees.
> Hail to thee, lady! and the grace of Heaven,
> Before, behind thee, and on every hand,
> Enwheel thee round."

Iago's scoffs at womanhood are the leading feature of the brief dialogue that ensues. Desdemona, though she replies merrily to his jests, betrays a secret solicitude in the absence of Othello; not merely by her anxious query, "There 's one gone to the harbor?" and her declaration,

> "I am not merry, but I do beguile
> The thing I am, by seeming otherwise;"

but by her troubled mien, her abstracted looking in the distance, her start of joy, and the sudden lighting up of her countenance at the sound of the trumpet, which Iago pronounces to be that of the Moor.

"Let 's meet him and receive him!" gushed in a burst of rapture from her lips.

There was no hesitation when she rushed into his extended arms, as he greeted her with:

> "O my fair warrior!
> It gives me wonder great as my content
> To see you here before me. O my soul's joy!
> If after every tempest come such calms,
> Let the winds blow till they have wakened death;
> And let the laboring bark climb hills of seas,
> Olympus-high, and duck again as low
> As hell 's from heaven! If it were now to die,
> 'T were now to be most happy; for, I fear,
> My soul hath her content so absolute,
> That not another comfort like to this
> Succeeds in unknown fate!"

Stella never once thought of Mr. Tennent, the supercilious, exacting, self-sufficient tragedian, but of the noble Othello; not of Stella Rosenvelt, the unsophisticated maiden, but of the true-hearted, ingenuous Desdemona, the bride of her Moorish husband. The least undue reserve, the slightest shrinking, would have been an evidence of that painful self-consciousness which is indissolubly allied to mediocrity, but which genius tramples under foot.

Othello had held her off, gazing fondly in her face, but with the last words he suddenly drew her to his heart. The action was unanticipated by the luckless Desdemona. Her face was upraised, her forehead came in contact with his chin. The sublime and the ridiculous embraced at the same moment as the Moor and lady. The reddish-black dye, which gave to Othello's visage its swarthy hue, could be removed by a touch. Stella's forehead had largely received the sombre impression. Not suspecting the untoward accident, she replied, in the same impassioned strain:

> "The heavens forbid
> But that our loves and comforts should increase,
> Even as our days do grow."

Othello rejoins:

> "Amen to that, sweet powers!
> I cannot speak enough of this content;
> It stops me here; it is too much joy;
> And this, and this, the greatest discords be
> That e'er our hearts shall make!"

and while he bent over her, in the *pretence* of suiting the action to the word (stage salutations being generally a very obvious *make-believe*), he whispered:

"Don't turn your face towards the audience, for your life! Your forehead 's as black as the ace of spades!"

Down fell poor Stella from her poetic heights! The black paint, its begriming touch to her own fair forehead, Mr. Tennent's commonplace tone, dissolved the spell; the loving Venetian quickly melted away. The disenchanted girl shrank from Mr. Tennent's encircling arms; she raised her hand to her forehead to hide the stain, but only smeared the inky hue into her eyes; she was strongly inclined to dart from the stage, perhaps would have yielded to the temptation, had not Mrs. Fairfax noticed the mishap, and, approaching her with a step and air that suited Emilia, whispered:

"They won't notice it, my dear! You are off in a few lines. Don't try to rub it away; you are only making it worse, and you will attract the attention of the audience."

As she spoke, she bowed her head deferentially, causing the spectators to suppose that Desdemona's attendant and confidant was merely delivering to her some courteous message.

Stella was at last conducted from the scene by Mr. Tennent. She heard Fisk's peals of laughter as he passed her on his way to make the calls, and the suppressed merriment of the actors. As she removed the disfiguring marks, she resolved to keep at a respectful distance from her grim-visaged lord.

Desdemona, according to the stage version (which omits her during the midnight brawl when Cassio fights with Roderigo), is next discovered conversing with the disgraced Cassio, and pledging herself, with all the generosity of an unsuspicious, inexperienced nature, to restore him to his lost position.

> ——— "before Emilia here,
> I give thee warrant of thy place; assure thee,
> If I do vow a friendship, I 'll perform it
> To the last article. My lord shall never rest;
> I 'll watch him tame, and talk him out of patience;
> I 'll intermingle everything he does
> With Cassio's suit. Therefore be merry, Cassio,
> For thy solicitor shall rather die
> Than give thy cause away."

The promise was uttered with emphatic earnestness; Stella had again surrendered herself to the magic of personation.

Cassio departs. Othello enters. Desdemona at once playfully introduces her suit. When it is denied, she, with bewitching coquetry, chides her lord for being more niggard of his courteous gifts to her than she is to him.

"I wonder in my soul
What *you* could ask *me* that *I* should *deny*,
Or stand so mammering on. What! Michael Cassio,
That came a wooing with you, and many a time,
When I have spoke of you dispraisingly,
Hath ta'en your part; to have so much to do
To bring him in! Trust me, I could do much—
Othello. Prithee, no more; let him come when he will.
I will deny thee nothing.
Desdemona. Why, this is not a *boon;*
'T is as I should entreat you wear your gloves,
Or feed on nourishing dishes, or keep you warm,
Or sue to you to do peculiar profit
To your own person. Nay, when I have a suit
Wherein I mean to touch your love indeed,
It shall be full of poise and difficulty,
And fearful to be granted."

Othello desires her to leave him for a while. She yields to his request; but, not forgetting for a moment her promised advocacy, turns back with an arch taunt:

"Shall *I deny you?* No, farewell, my lord!
* * * * *
Whate'er *you* be, *I* am obedient."

Before Desdemona and Othello meet again, Iago has roused the "green-eyed monster" slumbering in the Moor's breast. But, at the fair Desdemona's approach, the evil spirit vanishes as demons fly the presence of angels. Othello beholds her coming, and, penetrated by the aura of purity that surrounds her, flings away his unworthy doubts, and bursts forth :

> "If *she* be false, O ! then heaven mocks itself !
> I 'll not believe it ! "

The scene is very short. Desdemona summons her husband to join the generous islanders at dinner. With the quick eyes of love, she notices his dejection. He assigns " a pain upon his forehead, here," as the cause ; she would bind the aching brow with her handkerchief; but Othello impatiently puts by her hand, from which the handkerchief drops. It is silently secured by Emilia, who afterwards gives it to Iago.

The following scene finds Desdemona searching for the lost handkerchief, her husband's much-loved gift. Othello unexpectedly breaks in upon her. And now the powers of the young actress unfolded themselves, as she portrayed Desdemona's feminine softness, her unresisting, defenceless nature, her perfect trust in the nobleness of her lord. She greets him tenderly ; and when he asks for her hand, and scans her face with suspicious eyes, rudely telling her that the hand he holds is moist, she replies, with a smile,

> " It yet hath felt no age, nor known no sorrow ! "

Her look of innocent wonder, as Othello warns her that such a hand requires fasting, prayer, exercise devout ; and when he checks himself, and adds, " 'T is a good hand, a frank one," her whole-souled reply,

> " You may indeed say so;
> For 't was that hand that gave away my heart; "

her careless disclaimer of all knowledge that hands

were ever given *without* hearts; her woman-like pertinacity in reverting to her former suit for Cassio's pardon; her almost guilty start when Othello asks for her handkerchief; her equivocation and confusion; her sudden pallor and violent trembling; the quick lights and shadows flitting over her face, when he tells her of the charm that is woven in that handkerchief—the misery it would bring upon her to lose it or give it away; her look of frozen horror, as she gasps out,

"Then, would to heaven that I had never seen it!"

her short, frightened answers to his questioning violence; her hysterical effort to force a laugh and feign composure, as she tries to speak of Cassio again; and, when Othello rushes out, and Emilia, taunting her with former incredulity, coldly asks,

"Is not this man jealous?"

her gazing after him with dilated eyes, and quivering lips, then turning upon Emilia a face all wonder, and slowly answering,

"I ne'er saw this before!"

her subdued greeting of Cassio, who now enters; her mournful communication to him that her "advocation is not now in tune;" her snatching at Cassio's suggestion that something of moment has moved Othello, and her brightening countenance as she persuades herself that it *is* something of state matters which has disturbed him; her extracting comfort from the reflection, that, "in such cases, men's natures wrangle with inferior things, though great ones are their object;" the regretful sigh with which she adds,

> "Nay, we must think men are not gods;
> Nor of them look for such observances
> As fit the bridal —— "

her determination to seek Othello, evidently because she cannot bear his absence, though she bashfully veils her motive under the plea that she must further entreat for Cassio's reïnstatement; — all these changing emotions were delineated with a skill that stamped the youthful actress as one who vindicated her own right to interpret the great master of the drama, by her bold yet delicate, grand yet life-like, embodiment of his conception.

After this, Desdemona seeks Othello's presence, accompanied by her cousin, Lodovico. The latter bears a packet of import to the Moor. She has resumed her wonted smiling serenity; she prattles with Lodovico of Cassio, and the unkind breach between him and her lord; and, even when Othello accosts her in a wrathful tone, she inquires his will with a gentle "My lord?" Nor, as his rage increases, does she seem willing or able to perceive its workings. Once she turns to Lodovico with an incredulous "What, is he angry?" as though she needed confirmation of what was so apparent. Her cousin tells her that doubtless something in the letter he is perusing moves him, and she is satisfied. But when Othello's ire breaks all bounds, and he strikes her with the letter, she utters a low cry, and bursts into tears; looking up, with the mild and touching reproach,

"I have not deserved this!"

Othello orders her from his presence, and she meekly replies,

"I will not stay to offend you!"

In the ensuing scene, the Moor, wrought to frenzy by the conviction that his jealous fears are planted on firm ground, sends Emilia for his wife. Desdemona's whole demeanor is now changed. As she enters, her head droops, her eyes peruse the ground, her limbs quake. She faintly demands,

"My lord, what is your will?"

Othello harshly bids her to let him see her eyes — to look him in the face. She lifts to his a ghastly countenance, and murmurs, with suppressed breathing,

"What horrible fancy 's this?"

A moment after, sinking at his feet, she exclaims,

"Upon my knees, what doth your speech import?
I understand a fury in your words,
But not the words."

When her husband frames his doubts of her fidelity into language, she starts up horror-stricken, and, too much amazed even for indignation, asks,

"Alas! what ignorant sin have I committed?"

But when he unfolds his meaning in plainer and most revolting words, she is stunned by the monstrous accusation, and can scarcely answer,

"By heaven, you do me wrong!"

Othello asks her if this charge be not true; she drops upon her knees, and, lifting up her arms and her beauteous face to heaven, fervently replies,

"No! as I am a Christian!
No! as I shall be saved!"

There was so much reality in the action, — the guileless countenance, the heaven-appealing tone, — that it thrilled the whole audience. The repeated "rounds," that testified their recognition of the true Promethean spark, were followed by a loud, long cheer.

When Othello, in the succeeding speech, applies to his wife a term of worst opprobrium, she falls upon the ground, as though the word had been "shot from the deadly level of a gun," and murdered her. Othello summons Emilia, and leaves his prostrate wife to her care. Emilia raises her friend. Desdemona's mind seems confused by the sorrows which she yet makes a feeble effort to hide. Then, moved by a sudden thought, she bids Emilia call Iago. Desdemona imagines that he may explain Othello's conduct. Iago appears before her; but, when she would repeat to him the insulting epithet used by her husband, her modest tongue refuses its office, — the word cannot pass her pure lips. She weeps in silence, while Emilia descants upon the brutality of the Moor. But the young wife's affection is not shaken; "her love doth so approve him, that even his stubbornness, his checks and frowns, have grace and favor in them." She never dreams of blaming or reproaching him; her whole thoughts are engrossed with plans to win him back. She rushes to Iago in a paroxysm of agony, and cries out,

"O, good Iago!
What shall I do to win my lord again?
Good friend, go to him! for, by this light of heaven,
I know not how I lost him! Here I kneel:
If e'er my will did trespass 'gainst his love,
Either in discourse of thought or actual deed;
Or that mine eyes, mine ears, or any sense,
Delighted them in any other form;
Or, that I do not yet, and ever did,
And ever will, — though he do shake me off
To beggarly divorcement, — love him dearly,
Comfort forswear me! Unkindness may do much;
And his unkindness may defeat my life,
But never taint my love!"

Stella's utterance of these lines was sublime in its pathos. As the kneeling girl was raised by Mrs. Fairfax, at the conclusion of the speech, the latter could not refrain from whispering "Good! good! beautifully given! You are indeed an actress!"

The intention was most kind, but its effect unfortunate. The encomium recalled Stella to herself. It broke the dream; she was Desdemona no longer. She suddenly became constrained and awkward; it was fortunate that the scene drew rapidly to its close.

The exceeding length of the play requires the omission of a most charming dialogue between Emilia and Desdemona, at the conclusion of the fourth act, — one which is essential to the perfect development of Desdemona's character.

In the fifth act, Desdemona is beheld asleep. She is waked by Othello's bending over her to taste

> "The balmy breath that doth almost persuade
> Justice to break her sword."

Her terror, the vehement affirmations of her innocence, her frantic pleadings for a few moments more of life, make up the scene. Stella was not prepared for the violence with which Mr. Tennent thrust the pillow over her face, holding it firmly on either side. Her stifled shrieks might well sound natural to the audience ; she felt as though she were suffocating in reality. But the more she struggled, the more tightly the unreflecting tragedian pressed upon her mouth. It was her duty to lie *still* before he could relinquish his hold. Well was it that Emilia's voice at the chamber door required him to reply. Poor Stella lay with the pillow over her face ; and, being dead, or nearly so, to the audience, she dared not move. In a choking tone, by no means simulated, she groaned out, in advance of her cue, the few words that cause Emilia to fly to her mistress. Mrs. Fairfax not only removed the pillow, but placed the young girl in a more comfortable position.

Stella could now lie still, and listen to the scene. She expected to remain in the same attitude until the curtain fell ; but Othello, when the certainty of Desdemona's innocence was forced upon him, sprang to her side, seized her in his arms, half dragged her from the bed, and sank upon the ground himself, leaving her head hanging over the side of the couch. Her long hair swept the floor ; he wound his fingers in the tresses, and pressed them to his lips, and moaned aloud. The picture was, no doubt, one that Mr. Tennent had well studied, and certainly it was very beautiful, very truthful. Its effect upon the luckless representative of Desdemona was entirely disregarded.

The blood rushed to her head until her brain seemed bursting, crushed by a mountain-load. Her senses were leaving her; it was with the greatest difficulty that she could repress a cry. Every instant appeared an hour; she could no longer distinguish the language declaimed in her very ears; she heard only a confused sound. She could endure no more; she tried to groan, to move, but in vain. When the curtain descended, she was found unconscious.

Mr. Finch was in the act of carrying her to her dressing-room, when remembrance slowly returned. For some time she could neither stand nor speak. She was wholly unable to respond to the summons before the curtain. An apology was made, and her absence accounted for by the plea of indisposition. Mrs. Fairfax had, fortunately, some knowledge of the newly discovered and most efficacious treatment of apoplexy (which the attack resembled); she seized a jug of water, and poured it from a height upon the head of the prostrate girl. Stella gradually revived, and was soon able to reässure the terrified Mattie by a few affectionate words. Soon after, the young girl was conveyed to her home.

CHAPTER VI.

An Energizing Will Conquering Physical Prostration. — The Actor's Private Sufferings set aside. — Rehearsal of Lady of Lyons. — Mystery that enveloped Mrs. Pottle's Straying into the Profession. — Her Peculiar Attainments. — Amusing Eccentricities.— Literal Translation of the Eminent Tragedian's Command. — Merriment of the Actors. — Wrath of Mr. Tennent. — Mrs. Pottle's Efforts to "Back Up." — Fisk's Exuberant Delight. — Company assembled in Green-Room for Reading of New Play. — Murmurs.— The Author's Entrance. — The Reading. — Disrespectful Treatment of Mr. Percy by his Auditors. — Distribution of Parts. — Mrs. Pottle's Queenly Honors. — Mr. Percy's Discomposure. — Disparaging Remarks and Complaints. — Perdita redeems her Promise. — The Young Ballet-Girl's View of Life and Death. — Rainy Evening. — Skyey Influences. — The Fictitious Bouquet. — The Tragedian's Abstraction. — Involuntary Asides of Claude. — Mr. Martin. — Mind over Matter. — Which is Victorious in an Actor's Life. — Stella's Personation of the Lady of Lyons. — Inevitable Shortcomings of a Novice. — The Press Aroused. — Inconstancy of the Public. — A New Idol lifted to Lydia Talbot's Pedestal. — Honeyed Poison. — Ingratitude the Consequence of Sudden Brilliant Success. — Its Cure.

VERY weary were the eyes that Stella unclosed on the morrow. "Another morning! O, that I could rest!" And she turned upon her pillow, yielding for an instant to a delicious drowsiness. But the multitudinous occupations of the day crowded upon her remembrance; her energizing will conquered physical lassitude; she sprang up with a bound. A dull, heavy pain, the consequence of her last night's misadventure, still lingered about her head. But, she was now an *actress!* Private sufferings, private grievances, all private emotions, must be swept aside before the public servitude to which she had enslaved herself.

The Lady of Lyons would be rehearsed at ten o'clock; the reading of a new play was announced to take place in the green-room at twelve, — a drama which was to be performed on Friday, for Mr. Tennent's benefit, and this was Wednesday. The hour for rehearsal arrived only too soon. To Stella's delight, she found that Mrs. Fairfax enacted Madame Deschappelles. Claude's widowed mother was intrusted to the delineation of an odd-looking, shrivelled-up little woman, at whose wiry motions, penny-trumpet voice, and original readings, Stella could hardly repress her mirth.

This singular personage familiarly seized her hand behind the scenes, and glibly accosted her: "How do, my dear? I ought to know you, since you're to be one of us. Made a hit, I hear; — glad of it; — good-looking; — tolerable figure; — fine voice; — passion for the stage, no doubt; — just the case with me; — nothing like it, I say; — can't exist without acting — it's meat and drink. Nobody here to introduce me; — my name's Pottle, — second old woman of the establishment."

How Mrs. Pottle strayed into a profession for which she possessed not a single qualification, was a mystery. Engagements she obtained through her willingness to accept the smallest of salaries, without stipulating about parts. Her most remarkable attainment was a faculty of transmuting, by a species of mental alchemy, sublime sentiments into commonplace absurdities; of unidealizing the most elevated characters by her prosaic personation. She often declared her determination to render herself *intelligible* to her audience. It was not unusual for her to search out in a dictionary the choice words of her rôle, and, for the author's expression, substitute the lexicon definition. If the prompter remonstrated, she indignantly asked *how* the people were to understand what she was talking about, if she adhered to the text; she did not comprehend it herself, — how should they? Her literal mind converted everything into matter of fact; even technical stage directions were all translated *au pied de la lettre*. A rehearsal seldom passed during which her ludicrous idiosyncrasy did not create an uproar of merriment.

She was re-summoned to the stage just as she was addressing Stella. Mrs. Pottle held in great awe the pompous Mr. Tennent. Afraid to approach him too nearly, she frisked about him with timorous movements, and was constantly in his way, barely escaping the wide sweep of his arm, or his huge stride.

"Fall down left," ordered the tragedian, crossing into the right-hand corner. At this command, Mrs. Pottle soberly gathered her garments around her, and gently laid herself down on the left of the stage.

Shouts of laughter resounded on every side. Mr. Tennent's back was turned, but Fisk's caper of delight, as he remarked, "There, she's at it again! An't it fun to have Pottle rehearsing?" caused the actor to look around.

When he marched up to where she meekly lay,

Mrs. Pottle was in mortal dread that he was about to trample upon her; but she dared not move.

"Will you have done with your fooleries, woman? What do you mean by lying there?" he bellowed out.

"You told me to *fall down left*," whined Mrs. Pottle; "it was more convenient *lying down* just for the business in the morning. I'll make you the fall all right at night, never you fear!"

The dignity of Mr. Tennent was in decided peril, but he recovered himself before it was lowered by any mirthful manifestation. "Place yourself on the left hand, towards the corner — that's what I meant."

Mrs. Pottle rose with alacrity, and obeyed. She was strongly tempted to argue with Mr. Tennent about the correctness of his expressions, but he was too august a personage to be taken to task.

A short time afterwards, she stationed herself directly between him and the person whom he was addressing. Mr. Tennent gave her a slight admonitory shove, at the same time saying, "Back up, my good woman! Back up!"

"Back up?" repeated Mrs. Pottle, in a puzzled tone. "Back up! O, dearie me!"

She caught the eye of the mischievous Fisk. He made a pantomimic action in imitation of an indignant Grimalkin.

Mrs. Pottle nodded thankfully, and essayed to copy the feline attitude.

"Didn't you hear me tell you to get out of the way?" repeated Tennent. "What are you doing there?"

"I'm *backing up* the best I can," faltered Mrs. Pottle, vigorously jerking up her shoulders. "Only I have n't quite got the knack of it yet."

Fisk turned a somerset, in the exuberance of his delight.

Mr. Tennent's wrath only augmented Mrs. Pottle's confusion, and increased her vagaries. Claude entertained a most unfilial desire to suppress his mother without ceremony.

When rehearsal was over, the company reluctantly collected in the green-room. Stella was surprised at the discontented tone of their remarks. What *was* the use, they asked, of Mr. Belton's insisting on the old-fashioned idea of a green-room reading? Hundreds of theatres got up new plays without the actors being bothered with anything but their own parts; scarcely any of them had the remotest idea of the plot. "What's the play about?" was a common question, after it had been enacted for a week. And did n't everything go on just as well? Leave the plot to the audience; the actors had enough to do in attending to their own characters.

The new drama required four female representatives, — Stella, Mrs. Fairfax, Mrs. Pottle, and Miss Doran. This was Stella's first introduction into the green-room, though she had once or twice before stood at the threshold. She seated herself beside Mrs. Fairfax. Mrs. Pottle crowded her diminutive person into a small compass on the other side, and drew from her pocket a mammoth woollen stocking, partially knitted. Mrs. Fairfax occupied herself in hemming lace ruffles. Miss Doran scribbled a note. Mr. Martin lay moaning on one sofa; Mr. Doran was stretched at full length on another. Mr. Swain whittled a stick, as he leaned over Miss Doran's chair, and talked to her in whispers. Mr. Concklin practised attitudes before the mirror. Mr. Tennent was forced to absent himself, owing to the severe indisposition of his wife.

Several members of the company were venting their impatience and displeasure in no very measured terms, when Mr. Belton entered, accompanied by the author. Mr. Percy was formally introduced. Mr. Belton drew a table into the centre of the room, and placed a chair for the fluttered dramatist. After he opened his MS., he looked around, as though about to utter a few words, by way of preface; but the intention was crushed in embryo. He bent over his book again, and commenced reading "Love's Triumphs." Not one third of the pages had been turned, when a loud yawn from Mr. Doran was followed by a general titter. Could it have escaped Mr. Percy's ears? He gave no sign of hearing. A second and a third yawn followed. Then Mr. Martin groaned aloud. The author looked up, and looked down again, and paused.

"Do not be disturbed," said Mr. Belton, apologetically. "Mr. Martin is a great sufferer. We are all so accustomed to hear him complain that we hardly notice him."

Mr. Percy proceeded. He had now reached what he considered a magnificent situation in the third act. His delivery became more animated; he was even betrayed into a few gesticulations. Miss Doran giggled. Mr. Percy laid down the book abruptly. The manager considered it prudent to remain oblivious of the interruption, and the author was compelled to continue. He now read in a lower, more subdued tone, and constantly looked up to watch the countenances of his unreceptive auditors. Upon one face alone he perused neither weariness nor contempt; one beautiful face was turned to his in rapt attention. From that moment he no longer heard the moans of Mr. Martin, the yawns of Mr. Doran, the whispered criticisms of the actors. Stella was his entire audience; and, when she lifted her handkerchief to hide a starting tear, the young poet felt his brows wreathed with invisible laurels.

The play was gemmed with noble flashes of eloquence, but it lacked broad dramatic effects. It was fitted for the enactment of poets before an audience of poets.

When the reading was over, the parts were distributed by Mr. Belton. Stella was to personate the heroine; Miss Doran, her rival; Mrs. Fairfax, the mother of the latter; and Mrs. Pottle — Mrs. Pottle, when her part was handed to her, exclaimed, with a puny shriek, "Bless us! if I an't a queen! It will just ruin me to get cotton velvet and foil-paper enough for a robe and crown."

"*You!* have they given Queen Eleanor to YOU?" said the author, greatly discomposed.

Mr. Belton silenced him by a polite "I have cast the play to the best advantage, according to the strength of my company. You have two heroines, and two old women; of the latter, Mrs. Fairfax takes the first, Mrs. Pottle the second."

The company were dismissed, and Mr. Percy was doomed to listen to not a few disparaging remarks and complaints, as they departed. The new play was to be rehearsed after the rehearsal of Evadne, on the ensuing morning.

The author had been presented to Mr. Tennent by an influential editorial friend. The play was accepted chiefly with a view to propitiate a Nestor of the press.

Perdita redeemed her promise; the lace was brought in due time. Mattie, who received it, entreated her to sit down and rest, for she was breathless from the exertion of running. Her wan face and drooping eyelids testified that she had not slept since she received the order.

"What a hard life you do lead!" said Mattie, compassionately.

"Not harder than that of many others, and *it will not last always.* When I am troubled and worn out, I have sweet visions of another life, where rest and peace will be given. My mother has found *that* life, and so shall we, in good time; we have only to wait patiently, and do our best."

"Poor child! is death the best thing you can find in life?"

"My mother believed it to be the best thing in hers; she said so in her dying hour. She gave me counsel that comes back to me when I am sorrowful. I often hear her voice as plainly as though she were near me; I often think she *is* near me.* People

* "Have not *we* too? Yes, we have
Answers, and we know not whence;
Echoes from beyond the grave,
Recognized intelligence.

"Such rebounds our inward ear
Catches sometimes from afar;
Listen, ponder, hold them dear,
For of God—*of God they are!*"
Wordsworth.

laugh, and call me superstitious, and a fool, when I say so; but I am *sure* of her presence. I know that our heavenly Father permits her to watch over her poor orphans. When I do a good action it is my mother's spirit that prompts me. Often I abstain from a wrong one because the eyes of God and my mother are upon me. And God would seem far off, but for my mother, through whom he is near."

"You will almost persuade me that you are happy, in spite of this wretched kind of life."

"I am too busy to be miserable. Let me help you to sew on that lace. It is getting late; you will not have it finished. What a beautiful dress!"

Mattie accepted the offer for the sake of retaining the young girl near her, and conversing with her. This snowy dove, "trooping with crows," bore in her mouth an olive-branch for the great Ark of the Hereafter.

"God for his service needeth not proud work of human skill;
They please him best who labor most in peace to do his will!"

Stella went to the theatre, that night, through a pelting storm. In common with all nervous temperaments, she was subject to *skyey* influences; the atmosphere had a depressing effect on her spirits. The costly attire of the haughty beauty of Lyons was assumed almost in silence. Indeed, there was an unwonted quietude about the whole establishment. Even Fisk shouted his "last musi-ic-*ic!*" in a less hilarious tone than customary.

She did not descend to the stage until summoned, just before the rising of the curtain.

Floy was reconnoitring the audience through the

secret aperture. When he caught sight of Stella, he ran up to her; but his invariable "Such a house! such a house!" was followed by a doleful "O! O! O!" and an expressive wringing of the hands, instead of the usual lively friction.

"Got your *bokette?*" asked Fisk, pertly.

"My bouquet? No, I have none. I quite forgot that Pauline should have one."

"Did n't your beau buy you one? What a sell! Give him his walking-ticket. Well, here 's the beautiful flowers sent by Claude to Miss Pauline. I 'm his messenger. He did n't pay me nothing, though; he left that to you." And he thrust into her hand a soiled, coarsely-made bunch of artificial flowers.

Stella received them with reluctance and vexation, but there was no time for remonstrance. The prompter's warning bell had sounded; she took her seat in Madame Deschapelles' boudoir, and bent over the fictitious nosegay as though it exhaled the most delicious perfume.

The curtain rose. How cheerless looked those rows of half-empty boxes! The play had been worn threadbare: that circumstance, combined with the tempestuous weather, accounted for the meagre audience. Stella was only welcomed by a faint round, which chilled rather than inspirited her. During the first two acts, there was nothing striking in her performance; it was ladylike, but cold.

The acting of Mr. Tennent was unusually tame. His manner was hurried and abstracted. His thoughts were with his suffering wife. In the garden scene, when Claude paints to Pauline the home to which he would lead her, Stella, who should have represented the entranced, enamored listener, was perplexed and distressed by Mr. Tennent's involuntary asides, such as the following:

> *Claude.* "'A palace lifting to eternal summer —
> (*The doctor — the doctor at the wing*) —
> Its marble walls from out a glossy bower
> Of — (*all the medicine don't help her*) —
> Of coolest foliage, musical with birds,
> Whose songs should syllable —'
> (*I wonder if she's worse!*) — thy name!'

What can he want? I must come to cues — don't mind the cutting."

Mr. Tennent's eyes had wandered from Pauline's face to that of the medical gentleman standing at the side scenes. Claude now mangled the author *ad libitum*, and, curtailing his courtship within the narrowest limits, brought the scene to a close, and hurried Pauline from the stage.

As Stella made her exit through the door of Madame Deschappelles' residence, she encountered two carpenters carrying Mr. Martin in a chair. The inclement weather had augmented his rheumatic affection; he appeared to be suffering excruciatingly. The carpenters placed the chair at the entrance he designated.

Fisk stood behind the invalid, making thrusts at imaginary individuals with a pair of foils.

"Lift me up, boys," said Mr. Martin. "Fisk, you young rascal, be ready with those foils!"

The actor was raised to his feet with some difficulty; but, the moment his cue was given, he seized the foils, walked firmly on the stage, and a few minutes afterwards was engaged in an active combat with Claude, who found that he could not disarm him without exerting his utmost skill.

"Well, and what do you think of that?" asked Mrs. Fairfax, who stood beside Stella, watching the combatants.

"Wonderful, most wonderful!"

"Mind over matter! You see which is victorious in an actor's life. Would a single individual in that audience believe, on hearsay, what we have just witnessed? Yet every theatre can afford instances of equal or more marvellous power of will."

The drama of the Lady of Lyons has been so pertinaciously hunted down by critics that there is no temptation to dwell upon its striking situations. The author has planned a series of prominent points, all as unmistakable as sign-posts on a turnpike; a succession of dramatic traps, in which the hands of audiences are invariably taken captive. These Stella could not miss. It was only in the fifth act that she rose above her author, and filled out and perfected his incomplete portraiture. The gorgeous garments with which Pauline had bedecked herself, in the days of her untamed pride, were exchanged for a white muslin robe, fastened with bunches of purple violets, — the emblems of mourning, — and a few of these grief-betokening flowers were scattered among her dishevelled locks.

That Pauline could not recognize her husband, after an absence of two years, because he wore a mustache, was habited in a military dress, and his presence was unanticipated, seemed an improbability which Stella reconciled by never lifting her eyes from the ground, as she addressed him in heartbroken accents. And, when he spoke, her sobs drowned the tones of the loved and well-known voice.

That Pauline's confidential communication could have been made in a room occupied by her father, mother, affianced husband, the notary, etc., is an obvious absurdity when the words of the text are declaimed, according to custom, in an elevated tone. The credulity of the spectators is too largely drawn upon when they are required to believe that only two of the party present are not afflicted with deafness. But every word that Stella uttered was spoken in a whisper which, though distinct to the audience, conveyed the impression that it reached Claude's ear alone. Thus unwonted reality was imparted to a scene which, albeit touching and effective, offends against probability.

Stella's personation of the proud beauty was by no means faultless. It was occasionally marred by too rapid transitions, lacking artistic smoothness, an exuberance of gesticulation, an absence of repose, — the inevitable failings of a novice. Yet her spontaneity, impulsive ardor, flexibility of features and motion, her sculpturesque grace, quickened that weather-dulled audience, and charmed them into forgetfulness of her shortcomings. The sovereignty of genius made its presence felt, and compelled homage even from her unwilling associates.

Stella's débût and second appearance had only been chronicled in the public journals by a few stereotyped phrases, emanating probably from the licensed puffer of the theatre; but now the clarion note of praise was loudly sounded. The press awoke from its apathy; the tide of popular approval bore her aloft on its triumphant waves. The fickle public had already forgotten the worshipped Lydia Talbot, and with ready hands lifted a new idol upon her empty pedestal.

Stella began to taste the intoxicating sweetness of adulation — that honeyed poison, so pernicious to the untried soul, so tasteless to the absorbed intellectual artist, when she becomes truly enamored of her vocation. Complimentary letters, poems, elaborate laudatory notices, daily greeted her eyes. At first she read them with avidity, and treasured them up with proud satisfaction. Of floral gifts she received almost hourly offerings; but her mind was so much engrossed by her professional duties that the flattering testimonials, which for a day enchanted by their novelty, quickly lost all value. Critiques and letters were glanced over, not read; bouquets consigned unexamined to Mattie's care; all flattering demonstrations were treated with strange ingratitude, but it was the ingratitude of a preöccupied mind, which had no *leisure* for *thankfulness* — a dangerous mental state, too surely developed by sudden and brilliant success, but oftentimes corrected by the vicissitudes to which the most favored artist is inevitably subjected, somewhat later in her career.

CHAPTER VII.

Cast of Evadne. — Miss Doran. — Thunder and Pap. — Jealousy. — First Rehearsal of the New Play. — The Youthful Author and Actress. — A Strange Phase of Professional Life. — Pegasus Struggling with the Plough. — Ruthless Suppression of Poetic Gems. — Miss Doran's Comments upon the Neophytes. — First Entrance of Angry Passions into a Gentle Heart. — A Decree of Providence, and its Object. — Representation of Evadne. — Miss Doran's Persecutions of the Novice. — Grand Climax of the Play. — Miss Doran in the Hall of Statues. — Her Cruel Plot. — Bitterness of the Rival Actresses. — The Poem. — Revery of the Young Actress. — Unconscious Betrayal of a Dawning Sentiment. — Night Vigils. — Palms of Honor for the Young Poet from the Hands of the Actress. — Last Rehearsal of New Play. — A Stronger Hope weighed against the Ambition of the Dramatist. — Conspiracy of the Actors. — The Wreath of White Roses. — The New Drama performed. — Action of the Play. — The Author behind the Scenes. — The Play's Success in Peril. — Saved for a Time by Stella and Miss Doran. — Reëndangered by the Troubled Tragedian. — Mrs. Pottle's Representation of Majesty. — Evidence of her Laudable Pursuits in the Green-Room. — Boisterous Merriment of the Audience. — Inquiry of a Wag. — Vagaries of Crestfallen Royalty. — Agonies of the Author. — Mr. Doran's Admonition to his Daughter. — Mrs. Pottle's Conflagration. — Panic and General Confusion. — Queries of the Manager. — A Ludicrous Discovery. — Unfortunate Mrs. Pottle. — The Play's Unanticipated Termination. — A Friend's Advice to the Author. — His Flight. — The Young Actress at her Chamber Window. — A Recognition.

THE cast of Evadne was as follows : Mr. Tennent personated the noble Colonna, brother of Evadne ;

Mr. Swain enacted the lover, Vicentio; Mr. Belton indulged the audience with an amiable and irresistibly comic assumption of the licentious and remorseless villain Ludovico; Mr. Conklin assumed the weak-minded king; Stella was Evadne; Miss Doran embodied Olivia, the false friend, who

> ——— "meanly crept
> Into Evadne's soft and trusting heart,
> And coiled herself around her."

This young lady was bred to the stage, and had been carefully instructed by her father, the "second old man" of the theatre, in all its conventionalities. Her familiarity with traditional "stage business" almost supplied the place of talent. Her acting was bold and melodramatic, but lacked delicacy of conception. She was often boisterous, never intense. The impress of a reflecting mind was wanting throughout all her personations. A caustic critic once designated her performances as "a mingling, in equal portions, of *thunder* and *pap*." Her personal attractions inclined to the Amazonian order, but she possessed in a high degree all the physical elements of beauty. An effective piece of scene-painting contrasted with a finely-executed portrait in oil, would have aptly illustrated the distinctive styles of Stella and Miss Doran.

When the two young girls (they were about the same age) met at rehearsal, the petty envy of a narrow mind betrayed itself in Miss Doran's manner. She treated the "novice" with supreme scorn, seldom deigning to reply to her remarks, and never losing an opportunity of shrugging her shoulders, and indulging in a short, derisive laugh, if Stella appealed to the stage-manager for instruction when the business of the scene chanced to be particularly complicated.

If there were any truth in theatrical reports, Miss Doran was affianced to Mr. Swain. The undisguised jealousy which she evinced when his vocation forced him to enact the lover of another, gave coloring to the rumor.

The rehearsal of Evadne concluded, that of Love's Triumphs commenced. Mr. Percy, as he entered on the stage, silently bowed to the company. He at once singled out Stella. While the prompter was making some necessary arrangements, the young author ventured to address her. Mr. Belton broke up the brief conference by summoning him to his seat at the manager's table; but his eyes still sent her "speechless messages."

The prompter held one copy of the MS., Mr. Percy another. Strange was the phase of theatrical life which now revealed itself to the two neophytes. The presence of the author was wholly ignored by the murmuring actors. After the delivery of a few lines, some *malecontent* made a dubious pause; then came queries of "What does that passage mean?" "What's the sense of that?" followed by unreserved comments upon the absurdity of certain situations. Mr. Percy sat paling and flushing, writhing beneath the sharp thrusts inflicted by these "puny whipsters," and watching Stella's countenance, as though one look of disapprobation there would have annihilated all his hopes. Several times he rose from his chair and endeavored to explain; but the actors were possessed with the idea that they knew what he intended far better than he did himself, and that his meaning was sheer nonsense. He resumed his seat in dumb mortification. Retch's picture of Pegasus struggling with the plough was brought forcibly to his mind. Mr. Finch proposed to "cut" certain speeches. Mr. Percy started up again, and held back the hand armed with its inky weapon; those were the gems of the play, he could not consent to have them suppressed. Mr. Finch looked towards Mr. Belton; then, without attempting to argue with the perturbed author, ruthlessly struck his pen through the lines over which the poet had labored for days, over which he had gloried, which he had pronounced his most felicitous effort. Mr. Percy ground his teeth at this severing of the golden locks of his theatrical offspring.

Stella and Miss Doran were rivals in the new drama, as in Evadne. They were constantly brought on the stage together. Miss Doran divided her talents for tormenting between the hapless novitiates. When not engaged in rehearsing, she stood at the wing, with Mr. Swain, descanting aloud upon the ignorance and egotism of all novices without exception, and the manifest conceit of all play-wrights.

Stella felt her cheeks tingle, and she became conscious of more wrathful sensations than had ever ruffled the smooth current of her life. She had never imagined that so much anger could be excited within her breast. Is it not in accordance with Divine order, a decree of omniscient Providence, that every mortal is thrown into that situation where his hidden evils can be brought forth to his own view, *that he may know them, acknowledge them, struggle against them, and put them away?*

When rehearsal ended, Mr. Percy asked permission to accompany Stella to her home; his request was not denied.

It was quite late before Stella and Mattie left their dwelling for the theatre that night; but Evadne does not appear until the second act. Fisk was standing at the door of the "star dressing-room," with a bouquet in his hand.

"Here 's a nosegay from your *beau*. I thought you 'd catch one, by and by. Who 's your *Claude*, I wonder! There 's a little billy amongst the leaves; don't drop him out."

Stella made a signal to Mattie, who took the flowers. The note was tossed into the dressing-case, unopened.

Stella did not leave her room that evening until she was summoned to the stage. Evadne enters, gazing upon a miniature. Her rapturous reception proved how firmly the youthful actress was established in the good graces of her audience. Again, again, and again, she gracefully bent to their repeated plaudits. Just as she was curtseying for the fourth time, she heard a malicious voice exclaim:

"Only look! she has found out the *catch-applause curtsey* already, and is *begging for more!*"

Stella involuntarily looked around. Miss Doran stood at the wing, ready to appear as Olivia.

The latter enters at the close of Evadne's soliloquy. Most assuredly Miss Doran exhibited her thorough acquaintance with the *catch-applause curtsey*, for, just as one round of clapping subsided, she commenced a new inclination, which brought down another; repeating the wily process as often as the audience could be lured to prolong their greeting. The bewitching salutations over, Miss Doran proceeded, with artistic self-possession, to "back up the stage" so far behind Stella, that the latter was forced to turn her face from the audience whenever she addressed her. Through the whole scene Miss Doran maintained this position. After the exchange of the pictures, Olivia makes her exit, and Vicentio enters. Miss Doran stationed herself at an entrance where she could overlook the entire stage. Her dark eyes flashed with hatred as Evadne accosted Vicentio thus:

> "Are you, then, come at last? — Do I once more
> Behold my bosom's lord, whose tender sight
> Is necessary to my happiness
> As light for heaven? My Lord! Vicentio!
> I blush to speak the transport in my heart,
> But I am rapt to see you."

And when Vicentio gazed on Evadne with a look of unsimulated admiration, and gave significant utterance to the appropriate lines,

> "Let me peruse the face where loveliness
> Stays, like the light after the sun is set.
> Sphered in the stillness of those heaven-blue eyes,
> The soul sits beautiful; the high, white front,
> Smooth as the brow of Pallas, seems a temple
> Sacred to holy thinking; and those lips
> Wear the sweet smile of sleeping infancy,
> They are so innocent!"

Miss Doran bit her own lips until the blood started.

But fruitlessly she attempted to distract Stella's

attention, or force taunting remarks upon her ears. Stella, when she once succeeded in throwing herself into a character, forgot all else.

Miss Doran made a point of following her about behind the scenes, endeavoring to convey, by her manner, an insolent fear that Stella would imagine herself Evadne still, and hold sweet converse with her beloved Vicentio. The novice took refuge in her dressing-room. She did not venture forth again except when required upon the stage. But as often as she appeared before the audience, her eyes invariably encountered the sinister gaze of Miss Doran, at the wing. In spite of this disturbing influence, she achieved a victory far transcending her former triumphs.

Everybody is acquainted with the grand climax of the play, when Evadne rushes to the statue of her father, and, clasping her arms around its neck, bids the king, for whom he died, and who would dishonor his subject's child, to take her thence, *if he dare!* The fifth act, in which this scene occurs, represents a vast hall in Colonna's palace, lined with statues. Moonlight streams through Gothic windows, and falls upon the sculptured forms. Before the curtain rose, Stella stole upon the stage to examine the statues of Evadne's ancestors, which she was about to describe to the king. She desired to assure herself of their locality. As she passed down the aisle, she caught a glimpse of Miss Doran, who was standing upon the pedestal of a statue which supported Evadne's father. The actress leaped down, in obvious confusion. Hastily concealing something in the folds of her dress, she ran towards the green-room.

Stella had cause to remember the circumstance afterwards. There was no time for her minutely to examine the statues before the curtain rose.

Evadne's interview with her brother was enacted with the dignified composure that befitted a being firm of purpose, and sustained by the conscious strength of innocence. At his sister's request, Colonna conducts the king to her presence, and retires. The insulting proffers of the latter are answered by Evadne with a prayer that he will look upon the revered forms surrounding them, "that keep the likeness of her ancestors." She points them out in turn, until she comes to that of her father. There she pauses, and, after gazing reverently upon the beloved image, rises to her full height, as she turns her glowing face upon the king, and proudly asks, "*Who* was my father?"

She describes him, — his services, his death upon the battle-field in shielding his monarch, — then rushes to the statue, and fervently clasps her arms about its neck. The action was made with reckless impetuosity. What was it that caused Stella to start, and stifle a half-shriek, as she drew back? What face was that pressing forward at the wing, with an exulting sardonic expression, which seemed to say, "Her best point is ruined!"

Stella reclasped her half-withdrawn arms; there were drops of blood rolling down the neck of the senseless statue. The arms by which it was encircled had been lacerated by sharp nails, disposed with their points dextrously projecting outwards, to accomplish that cruel office. But the actress never flinched, though they pierced deeper and deeper, as she passionately exclaimed:

"Breathless image!
Although no heart doth beat within that breast,
No blood is in those veins, let me enclasp thee,
And feel thee at my bosom!—Now, sir, I am ready!
Come and unloose these feeble arms, and take me!
Ay, take me from this neck of senseless stone,
And, to reward the father with the meet
And wonted recompense that princes give,
Make me as vile
As guilt and shame can make me!"

The king replies:

"She has smitten
Compunction through my soul!"

"*Evadne.* Approach, my lord!
Come, in the midst of all mine ancestry!
Come, and unloose me *from my father's arms!*
Come, *if you dare!* and in his daughter's shame
Reward him for the last drops of the blood
Shed for his prince's life!
King. Thou hast wrought
A miracle upon thy prince's heart,
And lifted up a vestal lamp, to show
My soul its own deformity!"

The effect produced upon the audience was electrifying. The walls reverberated with prolonged acclamations. Mr. Belton, as the curtain fell, threw off his politic reserve, and warmly commended the young actress. He had noticed her torn and bleeding arms, and now severely reprimanded the property-man who had the statues in charge. Stella made no remark, while the man protested that they contained no nails when he arranged them upon the stage. But, as she triumphantly swept by Miss Doran, to reply to the enthusiastic summons of the audience, she darted at her a look which both comprehended. Could so much scorn flash from Stella's gentle eyes? Could so much bitterness, so much enmity, find room within her loving breast? She was startled at herself, when she found that such fierce passions were developed in her spirit. Look at them, reckless girl, with self-scanning eyes! Admit all their hideousness; marvel that those wolves and tigers could intrude into the lamb-fold of thy heart's tender affections; then pray the Lord for strength to drive them out! So shall thy untried soul leap with its first impulse towards regeneration.

When Stella returned to her room, the note lying in her dressing-case chanced to attract her attention. She sat down, half disrobed, to break the seal. The paper contained a poem of some length. She was tossing it aside, with a careless "I have no time," when the signature, "Edwin Percy," caught her eye. A soft smile, companioned by a blush, threw its radiance over her face as she read. Some lines she appeared to reperuse many times. When she had "sucked the honey of these music-vows," the verses remained lightly clasped between her palms; she neither rose nor spoke. Mattie moved quietly about the room, folding the young girl's stage attire. Everything was in order for their return home. Still Stella remained unconscious of her presence. Presently there came a sound of bustling feet, rushing up and down the stairs. The farce was over; in twenty minutes more, the gas, according to Mr. Belton's strict rules, would be extinguished throughout the establishment.

"I know you are weary, Miss Stella, dear, and it goes against me to disturb you; but it 's getting very late. Won't you put on your dress to go home?"

Stella immediately complied. And the poem? Of course it was restored to her dressing-case? No; it found a fairer receptacle where quick pulses beat against the lines which warmer pulses throbbed in penning.

Mattie had taken up the bouquet, but Stella caught it from her hand. "I will carry those flowers, they are so exquisite! I think this is the most beautiful bouquet that was ever sent me."

"O! no, Miss! Those you received yesterday were a deal more beautiful! I never saw anything equal to them. But, dear me, you hardly looked at them!"

"They did not seem to me so beautiful as these," replied Stella, wholly unconscious of the dawning sentiment that her words betrayed.

When they returned home, Stella could not seek her couch. The new drama had only been imperfectly conned. There was no time for a mellowed conception of her rôle, but the language of the poet must be fixed in her mind. She bathed her burning brows and gas-dazzled eyes, and slowly paced her chamber with the play in her hand. All the house, but Mattie and Stella, had lain their burdens in the lap of sleep. The one plied her needle on a rich brocade designed for the morrow's wear; the other drank in the inspirations of the young poet. As she stored his glowing thoughts in her memory, she dreamed herself the envoy sent with "palms of honor" for his hands. What hour breaks the stillness with its loud strokes? One! Two! Three! Soon the "gray-eyed morn" will "smile upon the frowning night." Three hours, and no more, may Stella's heavy eyelids be folded down.

On the day of the benefit, the well-filled box-sheet, the dense crowd collected around the box-keeper's office, were sure prognostics of an overflowing house. The appointed time for rehearsal had passed by a full hour, and Mr. Tennent was still absent. How anxious and restless the young author must have been! No, not in the least. His seat was on one side of the manager's table; on the other stood two chairs, by theatrical courtesy reserved for the stars; one of them was occupied.

Ardently as Edwin Percy coveted success as a dramatist, that ambition weighed lighter than a butterfly's wing, when balanced against the new, life-absorbing desire, that asserted its supremacy over all other hopes. His thoughts wove themselves closely around Stella, and drew her into the sanctuary where holiest things had residence in his spirit. Her manner towards him was more reserved than it had been on the day previous. The eyes which she now and then lifted to his had taken their softest, bluest hue, but they were not raised long enough for him to peruse their mysterious depths. Her answers were so brief and constrained that one less sanguine than Percy would have deemed her cold.

Mr. Tennent now entered; his wife continued dangerously ill; that apology was readily accepted by all. It was no wonder that the tragedian had only a very vague idea of the author's language. It soon became apparent that he could not the "matter re-word," and, to the horror of Mr. Percy, was compelled to refer to his part. Several of the actors followed his example. The use of parts, at a last rehearsal, is, however, against stage-rules. Stella and Miss Doran were the only two of the company who delivered the words of the play unmutilated. Mr. Doran had bestowed more than usual pains upon his daughter's tuition. He lingered at the wing and watched all her movements, chiding or commending her every time she made her exit. He was resolved that she should compete for laurels with the new favorite.

Mrs. Fairfax had no great affinity for her part; nor was it suited to her style. Had not sweet charity "tempered all her thoughts," she would have wished the play a brief existence.

Mrs. Pottle was perfectly odious in her royal rôle. She converted justice-dispensing majesty into a scolding market-woman.

The actors prophesied the failure of the play. Their tacit conspiracy against its success was well calculated to bring about the prophecy's fulfilment.

Mr. Percy, despite the theatrical torments to which he had been subjected, despite the lashings and buffets and foot-ball treatment which his dramatic offspring had received from the scornful players, was still buoyed up by high expectations. As he made his way that night through the crowd, and secluded himself in a private box, his elaborate toilet betokened that he was prepared to bow from his retreat, in acknowledgment of certain enthusiastic demonstrations; or, perhaps, to appear before the foot-lights and deliver a neat speech, expressive of his overpowering emotions.

Stella found in her dressing-room, at the theatre, a wreath of fresh white roses. The note attached to them contained these words:

"One who would scatter thornless roses in the path of genius prays you to wear this flowery coronal to-night. E. P."

Stella hesitated a while,—she hardly knew why,—and then bound the roses, a fitting symbol, on her pure brow.

The curtain rose. The dialogue commenced between two courtiers, whose duty it was to apprise the audience of the histories of certain individuals, concerning whose welfare they were expected to become solicitous. But this interesting communication was delivered in tones so confidential that the listeners remained in ignorance of the praiseworthy intention. The author only now and then recognized an expression to which he could conscientiously lay claim. Characters of more importance now made their appearance. A mental scuffle for words and ideas ensued. Mr. Percy's box communicated behind the scenes. The author rushed out, and implored the prompter to give the word loudly. Was the audience to suppose that *he* had been guilty of perpetrating such offences against grammar, good taste, common sense, as were committed in the trash just uttered as his? It was distracting! It must not be!

Miss Doran's entrance gave a diversion to his

feelings. She was sumptuously costumed, and looked magnificently beautiful. Stella soon followed; and now the wandering attention of the audience became fixed. Mr. Tennent entered at a critical moment, and the interest increased. But that portion of the dialogue which fell to the share of the troubled actor was supplied by a rapid improvisation. All flowers of poesy and dew-drops of fancy were ruthlessly stripped and shaken from the original stem.

Mrs. Fairfax played languidly; her personation raised up no supporting pillar beneath the tottering dome of the author's dramatic edifice.

Mrs. Pottle next strutted on the stage. Her stunted, shrivelled-up figure was almost concealed in the folds of her far-spreading train, fashioned of flame-colored cotton velvet. She had prodigally adorned her diminutive head with a huge crown, cut out of gilded foil. It was of her own tasteful manufacture, and, being somewhat limp in its construction, shook and rattled at every movement. Such a peal of laughter as broke from the audience when she turned to them her wizened face! Mrs. Pottle had been occupying her leisure moments in the green-room in the laudable pursuit of plain sewing. She chanced, at the moment when Fisk made his call, to be more deeply engrossed by her housewifely avocation than her professional triumphs. The queen had pompously stalked upon the stage without removing the spectacles, which glittered just beneath her gilt-paper crown. The hand which she lifted to give point to her declamation showed one finger armed with a shining brass thimble. The unconscious

Pottle smiled benignantly; and, when the diversion of the audience found vent in mocking applause, she curtseyed in the style in which she thought queens are wont to curtsey. It may be well to state that her conception of royalty was chiefly derived from the right regal dame chronicled in "Mother Goose" as diverting herself in the kitchen with the consumption of bread and honey.

Some individual in the gallery waggishly inquired whether her majesty had quite repaired the aperture in her royal consort's stocking. Mrs. Pottle's attention was consequently attracted to her thimble. She plucked off the tell-tale armor, and hunted for a pocket; but pocket to her newly-made queenly garment there was none. She clutched at her spectacles; they were entangled in her hair, but, after several furious pulls, gave way, dislodging the wonderful crown. It sent forth a tinsel sound, as it lightly dropped on the stage. The merriment of the audience now reached its height. Mrs. Pottle was decidedly *crestfallen.* Her majestic airs melted away; she poignantly felt that, with the loss of her fine topknot feathers, she could no longer pass for a fine bird. Her attempts to scramble the crown on her head, as though it had been a night-cap, were saluted with fresh shouts of hilarity. The little woman, with her crown awry, her frightened face, her long train, presented an object irresistibly ludicrous. The words of her part were all startled out of her so lately *discrowned* head. The second act abruptly concluded, before the audience had received a clue to unravel the tangled plot of the drama.

At the second fall of the curtain Mr. Percy hurried

about behind the scenes, pleading with the prompter, remonstrating with the actors, imploring them to rouse themselves, to have pity upon his feelings. Some laughed in his face; some turned away without a reply; some answered savagely that they comprehended their own business, and should hardly go to him for instruction.

In the third act the tide of disorder suddenly turned; the play progressed intelligibly. Stella and Miss Doran again occupied the stage. Mr. Percy's frost-nipped laurels budded anew.

Mr. Doran stood at the first entrance, watching his daughter, and now and then giving her directions in an under-tone. Stella's spirited performance caused Miss Doran's line-and-metre acting to appear tame. Mr. Doran was determined to arouse her to greater exertion. As she passed close to the spot where he was standing, he exclaimed, in a vehement whisper, "Fire! fire! Malvina, fire!" at the same time working his arms up and down in an excited manner.

Her majesty happened to flit by at that very moment. She heard the terrible words "Fire! fire!" and supposed Mr. Doran was giving his daughter timely warning of a conflagration.

"Fire! fire! fire! The theatre 's on fire!" shrieked the literal Mrs. Pottle, running wildly to the green-room, and then to her dressing-room to make a bundle of her theatrical belongings.

"Fire! fire! fire!" echoed voices on every side; every one following her example, gathering up whatever he could seize, and rushing into the street.

The direful words reached the audience. "Fire!

fire! fire!" resounded from pit to dome. There was a general rush towards the doors. Screams, oaths, mad ejaculations, went up, mingling with hundreds of voices repeating the awful words, "Fire! fire! fire!" Some even fancied they saw the flames, and were becoming stifled with the smoke. The theatre was cleared in front; not a being was left behind the scenes; the fire-bells were ringing vociferously; the engines thronged the streets; the crowd waited without to behold the bursting flames that were every moment expected to dart from the windows of the building. None appeared.

"Where is the fire? Who gave the alarm?" asked Mr. Belton of a shivering group of actors, who, in their fantastical costumes, were huddled together on the sidewalk.

"I heard it from Mr. Finch!"

"I heard it from Mr. Swain!"

"I heard it from Mr. Tennent!"

"Mr. Tennent—where is Mr. Tennent? Whom did you hear it from, sir?"

"Mrs. Pottle was the first person who gave me the alarm," said Mr. Tennent.

"Yes, I started the alarm, that I did! Mr. Doran—I heard it first from Mr. Doran," said Mrs. Pottle, in a self-congratulating tone. "I gave the alarm on the instant. O, I took care to do that! I do believe it's owing to me that you are all saved!"

"You heard it from me, madam?" said Mr. Doran. "Never! I knew nothing of the fire until half the people had rushed from the theatre."

"Yes, yes, I did! You knew it well enough. I

found you shouting out 'Fire! fire! fire!' to your daughter, and trying to warn her first."

Mr. Doran's emphatic but somewhat profane reply may better be imagined than set down on paper. An explanation ensued. Mrs. Pottle was driven about by a whirlwind of reproaches.

The actors returned to the theatre; only a portion of the audience could be lured back again. After a short interval the play proceeded, but its doom was inevitable. The performers were more unfitted than ever to personate their parts; the audience was out of humor. In the fourth act a solitary hiss made itself audible. More appalling was that snaky sound to the young author's ears than the terror-inspiring cry of "Fire! fire!"

The hisses increased. Some of the author's friends tried to drown them with laborious applause, but in vain. The disapprobation became general, and several of the company — unfortunate Mrs. Pottle among the number — were greeted with cries of "Off!" "Off!"

The manager ordered the curtain to be abruptly lowered. The *dénouement* of the play remained in mysterious obscurity.

The mortification of the maltreated author needs no description. A friend, who joined him in his private box, jocosely advised that he should join in the unanimous condemnation, — a practice not unknown to dramatists; but Mr. Percy had not learned worldly lessons sufficient to profit by the sage counsel. As the curtain began to unroll, he made his way out of the theatre, and betook himself to flight.

Two hours later, a wearied young girl, upon whose

brow a wreath of white roses slowly withered, stood for a few moments at her chamber window, before retiring. Whose was the muffled form promenading up and down on the opposite side of the street? Whose the countenance so often turned to that casement? It was too dark for the features to be distinguished. Possibly she was deceived, but a low, sweet voice within her whispered that it was the young author.

CHAPTER VIII.

Second Performance of Virginia. — Jealousy of Miss Doran. — Impertinent Advances of Mr. Swain. — Sabbath. — Stella's First Recognition of its Blessedness. —Accidental Meeting with Mr. Percy. — Kindred Spirits.—The Young Author's Dream. — Rehearsal of Much Ado about Nothing. — Omission of Offensive Lines.— Miss Doran's Consequent Derision.— Stella's Failure in the Personation of the Sparkling Beatrice. — Miss Doran's Triumph as Hero.— A Night of Torment. — The Merciless Critique. — Bitter Reflections of the Novice upon the Life she has entered. — Second Performance of Evadne. — Another Frightful Night. — Rehearsal of Juliet. — Singular Change in Stella's Demeanor. — Alarm of Mrs. Fairfax. — The Friendly Actress determined to snatch Stella from her Perilous Situation. — Sudden Bursts of Hilarity and Fits of Gloom. — Perdita in Grief. — Stella's Thrilling Personation of Juliet. — The Audience and the Ballet-Girl. — Close of the Fourth Act. — A Horrible Accident. — Sudden Death. — The Stage-Manager's Cold-blooded Orders. — Stella's Entire Loss of Self-Control. — The Manager's Visit to Stella's Dressing-Room. — An apparently Inhuman Request. — Juliet's Tomb. — Terror of the Young Actress. — Mrs. Fairfax concealed in the Sepulchral Vault of the Capulets. — A Novel Conclusion of the Tragedy. — The Suffering Actress before the Foot-Lights. — State in which she is taken Home.— Mr. Percy.

One day without a rehearsal! one single welcome day in that toilsome week! Virginius was announced for repetition on Saturday night; and, having once been acted during Mr. Tennent's engagement, no further rehearsal was required.

The brilliant comedy of Much Ado about Nothing was selected for Monday night. The hours usually occupied at rehearsal Stella passed with her tutor.

Her second embodiment of Virginia was a more artistic performance than the first, yet characterized by equal freshness and freedom from mannerism. The evening would have been one of unalloyed exultation, but for the determined persecution of Miss Doran. Though she had no character to personate in the tragedy, she chose to remain behind the scenes, and sought in a hundred trivial ways to annoy the detested novice.

Mr. Swain enacted Icilius, as before. It was very obvious that he entertained a growing admiration for the representative of Virginia. The unfeigned jealousy of Miss Doran gratified his vanity. Stella was surprised and mortified by the preposterous airs that he now assumed, the insinuating tone in which he ventured to address her, his languishing glances and assiduous attentions. These impertinent advances were repelled with the most frigid hauteur. In that short week her character had developed with gigantic growth. Dark shadows were introduced into the picture, before all light, and by their sombre aid its distinguishing features were more strongly revealed.

Sabbath, the blessed Sabbath! Never had this day been so welcome to Stella. When life was but a pastime, existence a holiday, divided between the pursuit of pleasure and a struggle against ennui, she had too often looked upon Sunday as a period of weariness, an interruption to the amusements of the week. The rigid observance of the sacred day in New England grew irksome, and, as she listlessly moved through a round of cold, vitality-lacking formalities, she might have said, with the unrepenting king,

> "My words fly up, my thoughts remain below;
> Words without thoughts never to heaven go!"

But, now that her mind had been chained to the rack, that all her faculties had been summoned into use, that she had experienced fatigue even to exhaustion, the Sabbath was truly a day for rest; a day for devotion; a day for spiritual instruction, such as her heart expanded and craved to receive. For the first time she recognized its holiness, and was penetrated by that calming influence produced by the absence from labor in all around her.

Mattie entered Stella's chamber several times that Sabbath morning, and found her in a refreshing sleep, a smile just parting her lips; no play-book, but a Bible, lying upon the pillow. One delicate finger was closed in the volume, as though she had fallen into a trance-like slumber as she read, and angels were repeating to her, in dreams, the Scriptures' holy promises. She did not rise until the inviting bells had ceased their solemn summons to morning worship. When her mother returned from church, she found her looking calmer and more invigorated than she had appeared for weeks.

The change in Stella's mode of life, and the energy she daily displayed, had wrought a marked effect on Mrs. Rosenvelt. Her apathy had partially disappeared; her mind was no longer wholly absorbed in rebellion against her sorrows. The sluggishness induced by a constant contemplation of *self* was dispelled. Through the daughter's incessant activity, there were healthful mental influences communicated to the mother's spirit. She was forced to think of her child, to take some interest in the stirring events of her theatrical career. Mrs. Rosenvelt even began to hint at a period when she might witness one of her daughter's performances. Her hours were no longer passed in utter idleness. She not unfrequently found Mattie and her assistant so hurried in the preparation of new costumes that even Mrs. Rosenvelt's inefficient aid was gratefully welcomed.

Ernest had written to his sister several times. The instant that he found his remonstrances were unavailing, he encouraged and sustained her by his advice and countenance. But her first marked successes did not alter his original opinion. He still regarded the step she had taken as fearfully hazardous, still looked forward tremblingly to evil results.

Stella accompanied her mother to afternoon service. Never had the anthems sounded so holy; never had her spirit been so lifted up by prayer; never had she been so touched by the exhortation of the preacher. She had sat under his ministry from her childhood, and oftentimes thought him dry and dull; now he appeared inspired. The change was not in him, but in herself. Her perceptions were quickened, her heart softened, her mind became receptive.

As Mrs. Rosenvelt and her daughter returned home, they encountered Mr. Percy. He started, as though some phantom of his thoughts had suddenly risen up before him. The flush that suffused his manly countenance was reflected on Stella's face, as he bowed, hesitated, and then, with a confused, unintelligible apology, joined them. A few steps more brought them to Mrs. Rosenvelt's residence. The door was opened. He lingered, conversing with Stella. Courtesy compelled the mother to invite him to enter. The joyful alacrity with which he complied somewhat shocked her strict ideas of propriety.

Let those who will deny that love is the spontaneous rushing together of two kindred spirits, which belong to each other; which, when united, form a perfect whole; which oftentimes recognize their internal affinity the instant they meet; — the attraction Edwin Percy experienced towards this young girl, from the moment when he first gazed upon her, can be defined by no term but the hackneyed, misapplied, often profaned word, *love*. If Stella's heart throbbed with answering pulsations, she was not conscious of their stroke. In this one instance, the knowledge that flashes upon man penetrates slowly, piercing many a veil and barrier, to woman's recognition.

Percy's unfortunate initiation into a theatre, his brief acquaintance with the discordant elements at war within its walls, added to the failure of his own play through the conspiracy of the actors, created in his mind a strong distaste for the theatrical profession. He could not endure to think that a being, so peerless in her purity and loveliness, should long be exposed to the jarring influences, to the selfishness, the malevolence, the dreary intercourse with inferior natures, she must perforce encounter in the career which she had rashly chosen. His hand would snatch her from such desecration; the myrtle and the orange-blossom would woo her to forget the soul-bewildering laurel; love's tender breathings would fill her ears with richer music than thousand-tongued acclamations. Such was his dream!

They had conversed on many subjects before Stella delicately alluded to the misadventures of Friday night.

"What intolerable mental torture you must have endured!" she remarked, sympathizingly.

The poet's dark eyes were passionately eloquent as he answered,

> "What living man could fear
> The worst of Fortune's malice, wert *thou* near?"

Stella looked confused for an instant; then, with womanly tact, she turned the conversation into commonplace channels.

As the young dramatist walked musingly to his home that night, his failing play appeared the enchanted key to life's dearest triumph.

The morn again brought to the novitiate actress the necessity of study. The sense of oppressive responsibility, of nervous excitement, which had been banished for a day, returned.

The most thorough familiarity with Shakspeare's quaint phraseology is requisite in the personation of Beatrice. Stella appreciated the value of her author's text to the full, but she had been forced to memorize with great rapidity; more than once, at rehearsal, her memory proved treacherous. She had been warned, by Mr. Oakland, against the slipshod habit of gabbling in a senseless manner over the language of a part, without an effort to embody the character. But when she endeavored to assume the tone and mien befitting the joyous, caustic Beatrice, the attempt proved signally infelicitous. Miss Doran enacted Hero, and her presence exerted some stupefying influence.

In the stage versions of Shakspeare's plays a large portion of the original text is omitted. Numerous passages, which were tolerated in the lax days of the Virgin Queen, are suppressed, as a matter of course. Yet not a few objectionable phrases remain. These are delivered or expunged at the discretion of "stars;" but the regular members of the company are expected to follow the copy in the prompter's hands. Mr. Oakland had erased from Stella's volume of Much Ado About Nothing certain witty but offensive lines. Stella passed them over at rehearsal. Mr. Allsop, without reflecting upon their import, prompted her, in his usual business-like manner.

"I do not speak those sentences," was her mild reply.

Miss Doran thought this an admirable opportunity to hold up her rival to ridicule. She hid her face in her hands with an air of mock confusion, exclaiming, "O, dear! how modest we are! Mr. Allsop, I 'm shocked! How *could* you — how *could* you, you naughty man, prompt such dreadful lines! O, what a blessing it is that we 've got a saint among us! I 'll order ascension robes to be made in the wardrobe at once! We 're all safe to go to heaven, hanging on to her train!"

Everybody but Stella laughed. The angry sensations into which she had twice before been betrayed were kindled anew. The wrathful reply which sprang to her lips was stifled with difficulty.

Mr. Finch now called every one to order, and the play proceeded without further interruption, except an occasional sneer from Miss Doran whenever Stella threw a touch of lightness into her part.

Unequal to the task of representing Beatrice as Stella deemed herself in the morning, she was not prepared to be weighed in the scale and found so lamentably wanting as she was proved at night. The personation of a dashing comic part requires greater ease and more thorough stage knowledge than a sublime tragic embodiment. Stella made a vain effort to depict the sparkling, rollicking brilliancy, the half-spiteful mirth, the meaning glances, the ringing laughter, of the merry lady who misprized all she looked upon. The exuberant witticisms of Beatrice fell pointless upon the ears of her auditors. Stella tried to laugh, but the notes died hoarsely away in her throat. Her air of forced gayety might have been mistaken for affectation rather than mirth. Even her step, which should have been rapid and elastic, was slow, and almost heavy. Her countenance owed half its beauty to bright, rapidly-varying expressions; but this evening her visage was, at times, a perfect blank — it had never looked less lovely. A constrained, unnatural smile only touched, without wreathing, her lips, while her eyes were clouded by the most opposite expression. Her Beatrice was, indeed, "heavy lightness — serious vanity."

Miss Doran had *out*-dressed her. The rich brocade, with its scarlet flowers interwound with vines of gold embroidery, the coquettish Spanish hat, and long waving plumes, threw Stella's less costly blue satin and plumeless head-dress into the shade. She was painfully conscious of the inappropriateness of her quiet costume to her lively rôle. But, in the midst of her perplexities, her eyes more than once rested upon a talismanic bouquet which she carried, and then, for a moment, the wonted radiance returned to her face. Those flowers had been found in her dressing-room at the theatre. The few lines which accompanied them Stella had not tossed into the dressing-case, nor had she confided to her watchful dressing-maid from whence they came.

Every time the young actress was required to appear upon the stage, she notified Mattie whereabouts she would make her exit, and bade her be there with the book. The instant Stella passed out of sight of the audience, she seized the volume from her attendant's hand, and studied without pause.

In one scene alone did she, in some degree, redeem the sombreness and feebleness of her delineation. It was that in which Beatrice indignantly defends her friend, and urges Benedict to espouse the injured Hero's cause, and call Claudio to account. Through the whole of the play, which had seemed to her to drag its slow length unendingly along, it was the only time that a hand was raised in testimony of encouragement.

She learned that, if public favor may be quickly won by brilliant efforts, it is as rapidly lost, or at least jeoparded, by a single night's insufficiency.

"Will you permit me to escort you home?" asked a well-remembered voice, as Stella and Mattie emerged through the stage-door into the street. Stella mutely accepted the proffered arm. In vain

Mr. Percy ignored her failure in Beatrice; his praises did not remove her deep sense of mortification. She entertained too great a veneration for her art to be satisfied in the absence of self-approbation.

"Can I not make you think as little of to-night's performance as I do?" he asked, as they parted.

"No — I fear not."

"I might, if I could make you think more of — of *me*."

"Good-night," was Stella's unsatisfactory reply, as she entered her home.

That night she lay awake for hours, reäcting Beatrice in thought. Now she wondered how she could have delivered such a passage so stupidly, how she *could* have been guilty of such blundering readings; now she felt indignant with Miss Doran for outdressing her, for outshining her. Yes, *outshining* her; for the simple but lovable character of the wronged Hero had been invested with a prominence which left a dull Beatrice in the back-ground. Stella could not banish the play from her thoughts. It seemed as though some invisible being turned over the pages by her side, and read aloud in her ears. At last, thoroughly exhausted, she sank to sleep, but woke stifling with the successless attempt to execute a mirthful laugh. When she slept again, the dream was only repeated with increased vividness, and a hideous variation of torment. It was too dreadful; she would not — dared not sleep again. She rose, seated herself by the window, and looked out into the silent, gas-lighted street. Immediately beneath the lamp-post stood a theatrical placard bearing her own name and that of Beatrice in huge letters. How she loathed the very sight! She turned impatiently away, threw herself on the bed, and wept until morning.

When she joined her mother at breakfast, Mattie brought in the daily papers. Stella seized them with avidity. There was no cautious friend at hand to shut from her sight all indiscriminate, haphazard commendation or blame. Both are pernicious to the youthful artist, who is too apt to be wildly elated or unduly depressed. In the very first journal she opened Stella found her name linked with severest strictures. The critic was merciless, but she was forced to acknowledge that he was *just*. This gall tasted the more bitterly because the honey of unqualified praise still lingered on her lips.

As she walked to rehearsal, with her veil thickly folded over her face, and her eyes bent on the ground, she felt like some guilty creature, whose misdeeds were the theme of every tongue. She could not bear to encounter the members of the company. She was certain they would triumph over her threatened downfall.

A repetition of Evadne was selected for that night. The rehearsal was of Romeo and Juliet. That tragedy was to be enacted on the succeeding evening. Mr. Belton had called a rehearsal both on Tuesday and Wednesday, that Stella might be familiarized with the varying character of Juliet.

"What ails you, my dear child?" inquired Mrs. Fairfax, who was representing Juliet's garrulous nurse, — a master-piece of acting.

Stella drew her aside, before she replied,

"You did not see last night's shameful failure; you were not here!"

"No; but, of course, I heard of it: one hears everything in a theatre. A novice should not have undertaken Beatrice. But, as Mr. Tennent selects the plays, of course you had no choice."

"I never suffered so much in my life! I did not know that I *could* endure such frightful sensations. My head has felt as though it were bursting ever since, and I hardly know what I am doing."

"My dear Miss Rosenvelt," said the experienced actress, taking both of the young girl's hands in her own, "this is the ordeal through which all who attain eminence must inevitably pass. Do not let it conquer you. Rouse yourself, and you will be victorious over these trials."

Stella was not consoled. She exclaimed, in a tone of anguish, "O, I feel so humiliated! I cannot bear to lift my eyes to any face. What a presumptuous fool all these people must think me! How evidently they scorn me!"

"Not exactly; but, give actors a fair chance, and they are sure to ridicule one another. They particularly rejoice over the dimming of a star, because it proves that there is not such decided superiority of the greater luminaries over the lesser. Act greatly to-night! Personate Evadne as they tell me you did a few evenings ago, and your Beatrice will sink into oblivion; all memory of it will be lost in their admiration."

"See," said Stella, baring her lacerated and now inflamed arms. "We *fight* for favor here, and may glory in our scars, it seems. There were nails purposely thrust in the statue, to tear my arms when I clasped it, and to hinder my delivering Evadne's noble rebuke to the king. But the nails did not make me flinch; they could not have stopped me, had they pierced the very soles of my feet!"

"What a cruel act! Who could have done that? Was it not, perhaps, some carelessness of the property-man?"

Stella communicated her suspicions concerning the perpetrator of the deed.

Mrs. Fairfax sighed. "I know too well that the tendency of this profession is to generate the bitterest sensations of envy in narrow natures. I have even seen husbands and wives so envious of each other, that when their dramatic talents were unequally contrasted, the most rancorous hatred seemed to exist between them. But to liberal and well-regulated minds these passions find no admission, or they are only called forth to be conquered."

"And this — *this is the life*," exclaimed Stella, bitterly, "which so many young, light-hearted beings, who watch the brilliant actress through her brief hours of triumph, are panting to adopt! — which they believe to be so full of allurements, of bewildering delights! This life, which —"

"Nurse and Juli — et — et — *et!*" shouted Fisk; and Stella could not proceed.

Mrs. Fairfax had not given her falsely flattering hopes. Her shortcomings in Beatrice were not only forgotten by the actors, but by the audience, when they beheld her grand performance of Evadne; — forgotten by every one but herself. But the excited state of her mind only intensified her embodiment.

She was deaf to Miss Doran's sneers, unconscious of her impertinent surveillance. The spectators rewarded her with an unprecedented ovation. But did Stella's former exultant state return? No; while she stood before the audience, she lost all recollection of herself; but, the scene once over, the words of the pitiless critic haunted her again.

Her slumbers were not more soothing than were those of the preceding night. She was representing Evadne, in place of Beatrice; but, no longer acting in triumph, she imagined herself delivering the language in a ludicrous bombastic tone; now forgetting the words; now constrained, in spite of herself, to adopt Miss Doran's inflated style; now pierced to the very heart by bayonet-like nails; now frantically clinging to the statue, which gave way and fell, crushing her with its ponderous weight.

When Mrs. Fairfax met her young favorite at the second rehearsal of Juliet, she was struck by the strangeness of her manner, the incoherence of her replies, the wild gleaming of her eyes, her crimson cheeks and burning hands.

"My dear Miss Rosenvelt! — *Stella,* do try to calm yourself! These excitements are too much for you. I fear you are ill — quite ill!"

"Ill? No, no!" laughed Stella. "You see I can laugh at the very idea. Nobody must be ill here! nobody must suffer! Or, if they do, they must seem as if they did not. One must enjoy an immunity from all mortal ills, to be an actress. Such are the stage's tyrannous requirements. It's quite laughable! It makes me merry! If I could only have laughed so in Beatrice! Don't look at me with such an alarmed face. I 'm not ill; I 'm nothing but what Juliet was. Her head must have grown giddy after she quaffed the potion, and swam as mine does now. But *I* have only drank the draught which the kind, judicious, lenient public offered. It may poison — who knows? But I 'll not throw away the cup until I reach the dregs!"

There was an unsettled look in her glittering eyes, an abruptness in her speech, which became more and more apparent. Mrs. Fairfax took Mattie aside:

"I am distressed about Miss Rosenvelt; she has studied too much. I am afraid of the effect of this constant tension of her nerves. Will not her mother persuade her to take a few days' rest?"

"Ah! ma'am, how is Miss Stella to be *persuaded?* She *will* have her own way, — that's her one fault. When I talk to her, she tells me that she has bound herself to the hardest of task-masters, the public, and that the public will not allow her to rest without stripping her of the honors she has won."

"But her mother's urgent entreaty would have some weight?"

"Her mother could hardly be made to see her state; if she did, she would only grieve, but not argue with her. My mistress never could bear the exertion of doing that."

Mrs. Fairfax was not to be discouraged in her attempt to snatch this young girl from her perilous situation. She had met Ernest Rosenvelt in the profession, and resolved to write and warn him of his sister's danger.

Stella's state throughout the day gave Mattie deep

concern. Sudden bursts of hilarity were succeeded by fits of gloom; deep, abstracted silence, by voluble mirth. Her mother told her that she had grown *eccentric* since she became an actress. Mattie looked at her sorrowfully, and entreated her to rest. When it wanted but half an hour of the time at which she must leave for the theatre, she was persuaded to lie down. She fastened her watch to the pillow, in dread that the moments would slip away unnoted—that she would be late. She closed her eyes for a few seconds, then roused herself to look at the watch, then shut her eyes again, but in a minute turned to the watch again; and in this manner the half-hour passed.

Shortly before she appeared upon the stage, that night, she encountered Perdita, weeping bitterly. Floy was trying to console her, in a strange, affectionate fashion of his own, patting her wet cheeks, smoothing down her hair, laying his uncouth face on her shoulder, and whispering to her, tenderly, "Such a house! such a house!" as though that information were a panacea for all human ills. His language was limited to two or three phrases, and these were the only words he ever used in the theatre. His feelings were conveyed by variations of tone, as expressive as the most appropriate utterance.

And why was the usually tranquil Perdita weeping so violently? Stella paused to inquire, though her question was oddly framed.

"Tears, Perdita, off the stage! Tears! what sheer waste of dramatic material! We all 'weep for hire' here, and can't afford to spend our tears for naught. Paint them this passion before the footlights, or what is the good of tears?"

"Such a house! such a house!" reiterated Floy, rebukingly; his intonation conveyed that it was very ungrateful of Perdita to weep when she had that first of theatrical blessings, a crowded audience.

Stella pressed the sobbing girl for an explanation. Her father, whose duty it was to represent one of the guests at Capulet's festival, had entered the theatre in such a besotted condition that he could not even be persuaded to dress. He would be dismissed if he failed to appear. The ball-room was so scantily supplied with guests that his absence would undoubtedly be noticed. What was to become of him, if he lost this situation? Unworthy as he appeared, Perdita was devotedly attached to her degraded parent:

> "For, like the lowly reed, her love
> Could drink its nurture from the scantiest rill."

She would rather a misfortune befell herself, or even her witless brother, than be visited on him.

"Where *is* your father?" asked Stella.

"There he lies."

He was doubled up in a corner, not very distant from the prompter's seat, sleeping so profoundly that there was very little chance of rousing him.

"Juliet call — all — all — *alled!*" said Fisk, capering up to her; and then he added, "Look out for fun to-night; Pottle 's your maternal antecedent, and is n't she rigged off within an inch of her life! Only the fun 's gone out of her, a deal, since the night of the fire. Wan't that a fine conflagration of her own? But Pottle 's got the *blues!*"

Juliet appeared upon the stage for a few moments with her nurse and mother, and then was led by Paris into the ball-room of Capulet's stately mansion. Immediately after she entered, the dancing commenced. Stella sat watching Perdita's pliant form floating through the dance. The aëriality of her motions, and the pensive sweetness of her countenance, rendered her conspicuous among her less-refined companions.

O, light, glancing feet of the poor ballet-girl! who, in that admiring audience, dreams of the heavy heart thou art bearing through the mazes of the dance? Who imagines that the limbs thou art moving so gracefully to harmonious sounds are weighted down by aching weariness; that the glittering gauds which rise and fall with every breath are stirred by the beating of anguish-quickened pulses?

Juliet was the most faultless of all Stella's personations. She threw off the trammels of stage conventionalities, and struck out new beauties, undiscovered by the hackneyed actress who treads in the beaten steps of some great predecessor. Stella's embodiment was characterized by an impassioned self-abandonment that bore her spectators with her as upon an impetuous tide. Her audience became a finely-tuned instrument in her hands, and responded to the plaintive sweeping, the loud smiting of the strings, — shared in her dreamy musings; her ingenuous, impulsive confessions to Romeo; her sportive cajoling of her nurse; her bursts of pretty petulance; and, as the character of Juliet gradually expands, echoed her devotion, her intense agony, her heroism, her firmness of purpose, and the horrors through which her spirit is plunged when she quaffs the Friar's potion, and, calling upon the name of Romeo, sinks into death-like insensibility.

The fourth act of the play closes with the entranced Juliet lying on her couch, surrounded by her weeping parents, her nurse, her affianced husband, and the holy Friar. The scene was near its conclusion when suddenly there was heard a crashing fall behind the scenes, accompanied by a loud cry of horror. One side of the curtain rapidly descended, but without injuring any one upon the stage, for the performers were all gathered around Juliet's bed. A ponderous weight, by means of which the curtain was elevated, had given way. The opposite side of the curtain was now carefully lowered. Stella, though she was startled by the sound of the heavy fall, did not stir until the audience were excluded from view. As she rose up, she beheld a crowd of actors all running towards one corner, near the seat of the prompter. She was eagerly following them, when Mrs. Fairfax threw her arms about her, and forcibly attempted to impede her progress, ejaculating, "Come back! don't look! don't look! It is too horrible! O, poor fellow!"

Stella had already caught one glimpse of the prostrate figure; the head crushed in by the iron weight; the spouting crimson stream; the limbs still writhing in a death agony.

"Who is it? What is it?" gasped Perdita, pressing through the throng, followed by Floy. "Not my father! O, not my father! He would lie there!" Mr. Martin seized Perdita's arm, and held her back. Floy had thrown himself on the body, and, at the sound of his piteous lamentations, she broke from the actor's grasp.

Stella, completely stunned, was supported by Mrs. Fairfax and Mattie. Mr. Finch's voice reached their ears. He was addressing the prompter. "Bid the orchestra strike up quickly, that the audience may not hear that poor boy's cries. If they get wind of this accident, the theatre will be empty in a moment. The shock will hurt our business for a week. Make haste, Allsop! Don't stand there, man, as though you were petrified! Speak to them through the trumpet. Make them play loudly, at once."

Such was the stage-manager's cold-blooded order, in the very presence of death!

Stella, with a convulsive movement, slipped through the arms that supported her, and sank upon the ground. She had now lost all self-control, and broke forth into a succession of hysterical screams and sobs.

Mr. Finch lifted her in his strong arms, and bore her shrieking to her room. Poor Mattie was almost distracted. Mrs. Fairfax, with tender care, used her best efforts to restore the composure of the horror-stricken girl. Her labors proved quite fruitless. After a time, Mr. Belton knocked for admission. He entered, took a seat beside Stella, and addressed her somewhat austerely.

"Miss Rosenvelt, you really *must* compose yourself. It is absolutely necessary. You cannot be *indulged* any longer. The play has been interrupted for some time. Fortunately the audience is kept in ignorance of the sad accident, but the curtain has been down for such an interval that the people are now becoming impatient. I must insist upon your exerting more self-control, and preparing to finish your part."

The unexpected, the apparently inhuman request, amazed Stella into sudden quietude.

"My part! I can't—I can't act any more to-night! I can't, after witnessing that terrible sight,—that dying man, his wretched children!—the audience cannot expect it."

"The audience have nothing to do with the private distresses of those whose business it is to entertain them," replied Mr. Belton, in a severe tone. "The play cannot be interrupted. You have but one short scene more, in which you have only a few lines to utter; you *must* manage to get through them."

"Impossible!"

"Very possible, if you will make the effort. Probably you thought it impossible to stop screaming, a moment ago. We are losing time. Mrs. Fairfax, I depend upon your kindness to hasten Miss Rosenvelt's preparations. Bring her down at once."

There was an intonation of command in Mr. Belton's voice that compelled obedience. He left the room, and Mrs. Fairfax, without a remark, commenced unfastening Stella's dress, that it might be exchanged for the rich garments in which, according to the custom of her country, Juliet is decked for her interment. Mrs. Fairfax's manner seemed to imply that there was no appeal from Mr. Belton's decision. His voice was "all-potential." Stella was so much awed, bewildered, astonished, that she could not resist. During her rapid toilet the wild expression which had before attracted Mrs. Fairfax's attention returned to her eyes.

Fisk came to the door, but his voice was subdued to a husky whisper, as he announced that Mr. Belton had sent him, with his compliments, to say that the curtain had risen. Mattie noticed that the boy's face was blanched, and he shook from head to foot. He was standing so near the spot, when the accident occurred, that his shoes were stained with the spirting blood.

"Come, my dear, let us go down," said Mrs. Fairfax. "The scenes are not very long before Romeo bursts open the tomb, and I want to arrange you comfortably."

Assisted by Mattie, she almost carried the young girl down the stairs. They laid her upon the narrow sable-covered couch, in the supposed ancestral vault of the Capulets,—a square enclosure, formed of darkly-painted scenes. An antique lamp, which sent forth a lurid light, was suspended from the roof. Stella looked around with a shudder. Mrs. Fairfax, after arranging her dress in smooth folds, and whispering a few encouraging words, prepared to close the sepulchre-doors upon her. But Stella sprang up with a cry, and said, "Don't leave me! I can't stay here alone,—indeed, I can't; and I can*not* get through with the part!"

In a moment the scene would be changed, and the tomb disclosed to the audience; the doors could not then be opened until they were broken through by Romeo.

"Fasten the doors," said Mrs. Fairfax to the carpenters, who were waiting to complete their duty.

"I will stay with Miss Rosenvelt; I can hide myself here."

She pressed round to the side of the couch which was distant from the audience, and there crouched down in a painful position, but with her hand clasping Stella's.

The scene unclosed. They listened to the touching tribute of Paris to the memory of his lost Juliet, as he scattered flowers before her tomb:

> "Sweet flower, with flowers I strew thy bridal bed;
> Sweet tomb, that in thy circuit dost contain
> The perfect model of eternity;
> Fair Juliet, that with angels dost remain,
> Accept this latest favor at my hands,
> That, living, honored thee, and, being dead,
> With funeral praises do adorn thy tomb."

Then came the warning whistle of the boy, followed by Romeo's entrance, the combat between the lovers, the death of Paris.

"Now, courage, brave girl! In a moment more he will break open the doors. Do not stir; think how much depends upon your proving that you have not miscalculated your own powers — that you are fitted for the profession you have entered."

Mrs. Fairfax drew her hand away, and wholly concealed herself. The doors were forced apart. Juliet, in her bridal robes, lay motionless in sight of the audience. In defiance of good taste, the original scene was here supplanted by a stage version which is preferred by actors, but denounced by all critics. According to Shakspeare, Juliet does not wake until Romeo is dead. In the version sanctioned by stage custom, the "agonies are piled" Olympus-high, through the meeting of the lovers, after Romeo has swallowed poison. He bears the wakened Juliet from the tomb, and, after a scene made up of frantic demonstrations, expires. Juliet has but a few incoherent lines to deliver during Romeo's death-struggles. These Stella attempted to utter, but not one word was intelligible. After Romeo's death she paid no heed to the friar's entrance, made no answer to his queries, spoke not a single line set down; she seemed to remember but one act which she was to execute, and which would conclude the play. She silently seized Romeo's dagger, rose up, stabbed herself, and sank beside her lover's body. The woful, haggard expression of her face, her inarticulate utterance, her evident mental and physical exhaustion, gave effect even to this abrupt and original termination. The curtain fell amidst a tumult of applause.

Not till then was Mrs. Fairfax released from her painful captivity.

Mr. Belton requested Stella not to return to her room until she had acknowledged the summons of the audience. She answered him by a vacant stare, but allowed herself to be led across the stage in front of the curtain. Her look, as she made a mechanical obeisance, was almost ghastly. Her lips had not yet been taught to assume the forced *professional* smile with which the suffering actress veils her real emotions.

Stella was unable to walk home. Mattie went in search of a carriage. She encounted Mr. Percy, who awaited Stella at the stage-door, and related to him the terrible incident of the evening. He entreated her to return to Miss Rosenvelt, and allow him to find a conveyance.

Stella seemed scarcely cognizant of what passed around her; but, as some one lifted her, with tender solicitude, into the carriage, she recognized the voice which said, "You are suffering, and I cannot leave you yet; do not refuse me a seat."

Her silence was not construed into denial. She was totally unable to converse. Mr. Percy would not disturb her by a question, though he exchanged a few remarks with Mattie, which were chiefly designed for Stella's ear.

"Poor Perdita! Poor Perdita!" sighed Stella several times; but those were the only words she uttered.

CHAPTER IX.

The Watcher. — Orphan Mourners. — Perdita's Consolations. — The Ballet-Girl's Sorrows poured into the Bosom of the High-bred Maiden. — Rehearsal. — Mr. Tennent's Reprimand of the Novice. — Stella's Strangeness of Manner. — Performance of Hamlet. — Stella's Unusual Conduct behind the Scenes. — Her Interview with Mr. Martin in the Green-Room. — A Change in Fisk. — Stella's Personation of Ophelia Painfully Real. — Ophelia's Distribution of the Flowers. — Her La t Scene. — Last Impressive Words. — Unexpected Occurrences. — Edwin Percy among the Audience. — His Vain Appeals to the Door-Keeper. — Excited Imagination and Over-tasked Brain. — Consultation of the Manager with Mrs. Fairfax and Mattie. — Stella removed to her Home. — Maternal Anguish. — Devotion of Mrs. Fairfax. — Her Power over Stella. — Ravings. — Arrival of Ernest. — The Group beside the Bed of the Young Actress one Fortnight after the Night of her Débût. — Restored Consciousness. — Recognitions. — Farewells. — Conclusion. — An Open Book. — A Voice from the Invisible World.

Faithful Mattie, without communicating her alarm to Mrs. Rosenvelt, watched without Stella's door that livelong night. She could hear the young girl tossing restlessly upon her pillow, and now and then muttering unintelligible words. "Perdita! Poor Perdita!" were the only distinct sounds that reached Mattie's ear. Towards morning there was an interval of perfect stillness.

"She has fallen asleep at last, thank Heaven!" thought the distressed watcher; and then she stole, with light tread, to her own room, and lay down to rest. It seemed to her that she could not have slept more than a few moments, when she was awakened by a touch. Stella stood beside her.

"Is it too early to go yet, Mattie? No; it cannot be too early — they cannot have slept through this fearful night."

"To go where, Miss Stella, dear? How ill you look! You are as white as a sheet, and your eyes have grown twice their size in a night. Don't, don't look so! You frighten me sorely."

"Get up, then, quickly, and let us go."

"Go where?"

"To Perdita."

"At this hour, Miss Stella? Why —"

"Mattie, what is the use of arguing with me? You know I am headstrong — I don't heed remonstrances — I *can't* heed them; *I wish I could* — but I was never taught in the days when childhood's plastic mind may be shaped at will. It 's too late now. Affliction is the only tutor whose lessons I shall ever heed."

"Go back to bed, dear, for a while —"

"No; do you get up. I must see those wretched children. I shall never rest until I do. You know where they live, for you went for the last piece of lace."

"It 's a long walk for you — a couple of miles, at least. They live quite in the suburbs."

"The more reason that you should make haste. We need not return home; I can go from there to the theatre."

"But breakfast?"

"I can't eat; if you can, you may go back while I am at the theatre. Make haste!"

Mattie was ready in a few minutes. Stella left a hasty line to explain her absence to Mrs. Rosenvelt, then they set out. Stella took no notice of the distance they walked, and Mattie's occasional remarks were unheeded.

"This is the place," said the latter, stopping before a very humble tenement, the door of which stood open. "Perdita's family lodge up stairs."

They entered the close, untidy dwelling, and ascended to the second story. A low, continuous moaning told in which room some mourner lamented. Stella's repeated knocks were unanswered, though the plaintive sound still reached their ears. She lifted the latch softly, and they entered.

The body of the deceased lay on a mattress in the centre of the room. A sheet covered all but one arm. Floy was extended on the ground beside the corpse. The lifeless hand was clasped in his, and he lifted one cold finger after the other, and let them drop again, wailing piteously as every one fell. How fondly he touched that very hand which turned the fatal key, and locked the light of reason from his brain! He seemed to be struggling to comprehend that this hand was powerless now — powerless forever!

Perdita sat at the head of the corpse. The tears that rolled slowly down her wan face glittered upon the shroud she was making. She was as still, as collected, as ever; her spirit had long been nurtured by "Adversity's sweet milk," *patience.* With her

"Each grief, through meekness, settled into rest."

Inevitable affliction awakened no tumultuous sorrow.

There was one other occupant of the chamber. In the furthest corner, sleeping in her chair, Stella recognized the homely features of the kind-hearted but eccentric Mrs. Pottle.

It was not until Stella accosted Perdita that she looked up.

"I could not rest until I had seen you, Perdita!" Stella sat down by her side. "I could not rest until I knew how you bore this misfortune."

"It does not break my heart; that *cannot* break, or it would have broken long ago! But of all, all other trials, this is the most fearful! To die without one parting word — one blessing; to be hurried away so unprepared — and in his state — that is more dreadful than all!"

Stella knew not what to answer. Her silence seemed to imply that there was no consolation that could be offered.

"And yet he *could* not have died," continued Perdita, as if she divined her thoughts, "even by what people call an *accident*, if the fittest moment he could ever have known on earth had not arrived. The summons that comes unawares to man is known to God; there are no *accidents* but of his permission. He overrules them for good; he chooses the best hour for us all, though it may not always *seem* so. No, my father could not have died, had not death been better for him than life."

"Do you believe that?" asked Stella, doubtingly.

"I do; my mother taught it to me. It was the

consolation she gave her children when she was dying. Something within me bears witness to its truth."

Stella was silent again. Perdita fancied she was pondering upon ill reports she had heard of the departed.

"Do not judge him harshly," pleaded the devoted daughter. "God will not judge him so; for he knows the heart, and tempers all judgment with mercy. We are commanded 'judge not;' and do not — do not you, who knew nothing of his trials, his temptations, his sorrows, judge my poor father!"

"Heaven forbid! I only came to comfort you, Perdita."

"Your coming itself, your presence, comforts me. But my brother — Floy! Floy! will you not speak to Miss Rosenvelt?"

But Floy raised not his face. He continued caressing the frozen hand, and lifting one by one the stiffening fingers, and letting them drop again, moaning as before.

Mattie had taken the half-finished shroud out of Perdita's hands, and went on with the sad task. The high-bred maiden and the humble ballet-dancer sat side by side, conversing as sisters. Perdita's full heart unclosed; her sorrows were poured freely forth. She pictured her mother's struggles in the theatre,— her wasting away, yet laboring to the last; — her placid death,— the husband's anguish,— the envies and injustice through which he lost his position in the profession,— the revolution in his temper,—the mad infatuation which lured him to seek relief, oblivion, in the bowl.

"And have you no friends?" asked Stella; "none?"

"What time could we have to devote to friendships? We are always so busy! But that"—pointing to the slumberer in the corner—"that is one of the kindest friends we ever had, odd as she is."

"But how do you expect to live now?"

"We can only go on as before. That good Mrs. Pottle has promised to raise a subscription in the theatre for my father's"—she seemed choked by the words—"his funeral. Day after to-morrow it will be over. On Monday I will be forced to return to the theatre."

"So soon?"

"Yes; we are too poor, too miserably poor, to be able to give up even one week's salary. It was the same when my mother died. They gave me no time to recover from the shock. The public did not care; how could the manager? All goes on the same; my place in the ballet must be filled,—if not by me, some one else is engaged, and I may be left to starve."

Mattie had completed the shroud. This caused Stella to look at her watch. The hour for rehearsal had already arrived. She took a hurried leave, after kindly pressing Perdita's hand, and trying unsuccessfully to rouse the mourning boy.

Mr. Tennent, oblivious of his own example, remarked somewhat severely upon Miss Rosenvelt's want of punctuality. It was a bad sign, he said, in a novice; such carelessness did not augur well for her future success.

"Come, come! there has been delay enough! Allsop, be so good as to go on with rehearsal. Make your calls, Fisk," said Mr. Finch, in a displeased tone.

Stella made no apology.

The play was Hamlet. Mrs. Fairfax enacted the Queen-mother. She was the only person to whom the young actress that morning paid the slightest attention,—whom she even deigned to answer.

"There is something very singular about Miss Rosenvelt," whispered Mrs. Fairfax to Belton. "Do you see how her eyes glisten? For several days I have thought she was in a high fever; I am sure of it now."

"I dare say; she is so excitable, and has not been trained to govern her feelings. Will she be able to get through Ophelia to-night? That 's the question. We have no substitute,—Miss Doran can't sing a note."

"Stella will get through, I have no doubt; but I am troubled about her. She is such a lovely being,—so full of soul, of genuine love for her art! She is everything that the stage most needs. Do give her rest, as soon as you can. She is over-tasked; don't crowd her brain with fresh study."

"You are right; as soon as Tennent's engagement is over, I will advise her to recruit for a week. No doubt she will stand the wear and tear for three nights more."

The peculiarity of manner which she had remarked at rehearsal became even more apparent to Mrs.

Fairfax at night. Stella's unwonted, meaningless bursts of merriment, as she wandered about behind the scenes, even attracted the observation of the actors. During her brief professional career she had hardly exchanged a word with any of the company, save Mrs. Fairfax, Perdita, and Fisk; now she talked at random with every one whom she met, sometimes jokingly, sometimes in a vein of biting sarcasm. In her restlessness, she entered the green-room. Mr. Martin was extended on his customary bench. He was dressed as Ophelia's grave-digger. Stella abruptly accosted him with

"Are you a Catholic?"

"Yes—and no," replied Mr. Martin, surprised and gratified at her desire to converse with him. "A Catholic, but not a Roman Catholic. Why do you ask? Did you imagine that I was one?"

"Yes; because you are accepting your *purgatory* here. What a glorious life you lead, with your dark enemy, the rheumatism, dragging you one way, and your tyrant, the public, forcing you the other! Glorious! How many years have you sang over your mock grave-digging, to make the reflecting audience laugh?"

"I believe I first played Ophelia's grave-digger about twenty years ago."

"Twenty years digging, and you have n't buried Ophelia yet,—nor your own wits? Make an end of her to-night! Bury struggles, and hopes, and dreams; bury self-will and madness, altogether!"

Mr. Martin placed his crutches on the ground, and, supported by shaking hands, rose up in consternation.

16

"Miss Rosenvelt, I am afraid ——" He looked her steadily in the face, and could not finish the sentence.

She laughed until the old walls rang with the clear, piercing sound; it reached the very stage.

"That 's the Beatrice laugh! do you hear? I have learned it at last. What a misery it was not to be able to laugh before! But I shall do nothing but laugh now, in this merry, merry place! Last night a man was killed here, and did n't we all laugh as his spirit was taking its flight? An actor's laugh was an actor's fittest knell."

There was no acting in good Mr. Martin's emotion. He turned to Mattie, and whispered,

"Take her home, for pity's sake! She can't get through. Where is Mr. Belton? I will try to find him."

The old man regarded Stella once more with a look of mingled tenderness and pity, then hobbled in search of the manager.

"Ophelia called!" said Fisk. It was the first time he had ever approached her without a monkey-gambol. The impression left by the appalling accident had not yet worn away.

"Called! what for? What is it? Ophelia — yes, I remember. Mattie, where is the book? I have forgotten every line. Quickly, quickly,— the book!"

"I 'll fetch it, dear, from your dressing-room," replied Mattie.

"I have a copy," said Fisk. He ran off, and returned immediately with the play, found the right place, and gave the open volume into Stella's hands.

This was done with a grave, thoughtful kindness, very different from Fisk's usual manner.

Stella's thoughts were quickly concentrated on the part before her. As her cue was given, she smiled upon Fisk, returned the book, and walked calmly on the stage. Not a single syllable of the language was obliterated from her memory. She spoke and moved as Ophelia might have done before her mind became

> "Like sweet bells jangled out of tune, and harsh."

Mr. Martin had summoned Mr. Belton, and stood with him at the first entrance, regarding her.

"Really, Mr. Martin, you are growing fanciful yourself," said the latter. "There is nothing at all the matter with Miss Rosenvelt. She is delivering those lines beautifully, and she goes through the business of the scene with perfect propriety."

"If you had seen her in the green-room, you would have thought that, like poor Ophelia, she was

> 'Divided from herself and her fair judgment,'"

returned Mr. Martin, positively. "She almost frightened me out of my senses. I tell you this character has made a fatal impression on her mind. At all events, she is over-worked; nobody *can* deny that. It's downright cruelty, to my thinking. If she were a child of mine, I—"

"Why, Martin, this girl has bewitched you all! You are as bad as Mrs. Fairfax, who loves her as though she were her own. But make yourself easy; as soon as Tennent's engagement is over, I will give her a holiday. She will stand two nights more very well."

"Take care how you lay the last feather on your camel's back!" growled Martin, and he limped back to the green-room.

When Stella appeared upon the stage in the fourth act, — her hair unbound and dishevelled, her eyes dilated until they appeared of the jettiest black, and luminous with the peculiar light of insanity, her white drapery disordered, her movements rapid and uncertain, — her personation of the distraught Ophelia became painfully real.

As she sang,

"He is dead and gone, lady,
He is dead and gone;
At his head a grass-green turf,
At his heels a stone!

"White his shroud as the mountain snow,
Larded all with sweet flowers,
Which bewept to the grave did go
With true-love showers!"

the spell-bound spectators asked each other, "Was ever reason's overthrow so vividly counterfeited?" That her madness was but a thrillingly illustrated picture, seemed apparent from the correctness with which she delivered the text, and her exit made at the right moment.

Mattie awaited her at the wing, with Ophelia's crown of straw; Fisk stood near, his arms filled with loose flowers. With these Ophelia is decked before she returns to the stage for her last scene. Stella laughed as the fantastic coronal was placed on her head, and she snatched the bright flowers from Fisk, and laid them in the ample scarf which half enveloped her slender form.

"O, don't — don't!" pleaded Mattie. "When I hear you laugh so, it makes me feel as though it were all real; as though you *were*, for all the world, a poor, mad thing, like the one in the play!"

"Mad! Mad! Yes — that's it!" cried Stella, tossing the flowers in the air, and catching them again in her scarf. "Who is n't mad here? We are all mad! all mad! a jolly mad set!" And she laughed once more, as she fastened the reddest blossoms in her floating hair.

"*How now? What noise is that?*" exclaimed Laertes.

Stella recognized her cue, gathered up the scattered flowers, and glided upon the stage.

> "They bore him barefaced on the bier;
> Hey no, nonny, hey nonny:
> And in his grave rained many a tear!"

she sang. The audience once more listened entranced. Then came her touching distribution of her floral burden:

"There's rosemary, that's for remembrance; pray you, love, remember; and there are pansies, that's for thought.

Laertes. A document in madness; thoughts and remembrance fitted.

Ophelia. There's fennel for you, and columbines; there's rue for you; and here's some for me; we may call it herb of grace o' Sundays — you may wear your rue with a difference. There's a daisy! I would give you some *violets; but they withered all when my father died;* they say he made a good end:

> '*For bonny sweet Robin is all my joy.*' —

Laertes. Thought and affliction, passion, hell itself, she turns to favor and to prettiness."

Then she broke forth, more wildly and plaintively than before, singing,

"And will he not come again?
And will he not come again?
No, no, he is dead!
Go to thy death bed —
He never will come again!

"His beard was as white as snow,
All flaxen was his poll;
He is gone, he is gone,
And we may cast away moan;
Gramercy on his soul!"

Kneeling on the ground, she shaped a coffin with her long scarf, and strewed it with flowers, as she sang. She rose up repeating the words,

"Gramercy on his soul!
And of all Christian souls! I pray Heaven,
Heaven be with you!"

They are the last sentences Ophelia speaks. Every syllable fell from her lips slowly, solemnly; her arms were extended as though for a world-wide benediction. Ophelia should then make her final exit; but Stella stood immovable, her arms outstretched, her eyes fixed.

Mrs. Fairfax gently took her hand to rouse her; she uttered a cry that was the mingling of a laugh and shriek, and fell upon her friend's bosom.

"Gracious heaven!" whispered the actress, "she does not know what she is doing! Mr. Swain, carry her away; help me to take her off the stage."

Mr. Swain, who enacted Ophelia's brother, attempted to raise Stella in his arms; but she violently resisted — she would allow no one but Mrs. Fairfax to touch her. The latter, with some difficulty, bore her from the stage.

The tragedy proceeded without interval; the dethronement of a young girl's intellect was too trivial a circumstance, in theatrical estimation, to interfere with the regular movement of the play — to deprive the public of their purchased amusement. But there were those present who never, in after-life, forgot her eloquent, world-embracing attitude, her loving yet stony countenance, and the electrifying tone in which she said:

> "*Gramercy on his soul!*
> *And of all Christian souls! I pray Heaven,*
> *Heaven be with you!*"

Edwin Percy sat in that audience, his mind convulsed with distracting doubts. The instant Stella was no longer in sight, he hurried to the stage-door, and entreated admission of the theatrical Cerberus. It was against rules to enter. Percy pleaded, threatened, offered a large bribe, but the door-keeper was inexorable. Disregard of orders, in Mr. Belton's establishment, was forfeiture of situation.

Meantime Stella was conveyed to her dressing-room by Mrs. Fairfax and Mattie. The former was forced to return to the stage in a few moments, to recount the hapless Ophelia's watery end. The self-control acquired by years of discipline hardly sufficed the dismayed actress to go through her scene without betraying more emotion than befitted Hamlet's mother at the untimely death of the maiden whom she thought to welcome as her son's bride.

When Mrs. Fairfax returned to Stella, she found her talking in a wild strain ; the horrors of the night previous were reënacted in the young girl's imagination.

"Hark! Do you hear that heavy crash?" she muttered. "See! his brains are quite dashed out. Look, how the blood gushes! It has spouted up to Perdita's bosom, and Floy's hands are all dabbled. Must she play Juliet after that? Was it she, or I?"

Then she sang,

> "They bore him barefaced on the bier!"

but stopped suddenly. "No, they won't carry him barefaced; it would be too horrible a sight. Strew the flowers over him — hide him! Hide his mangled head from the staring crowd!" And she tore off the flowers that were fastened about her dress, and flung them about with frantic gesture.

It was not possible to change her attire; nor would she permit the crown of straw to be removed, nor her loosened tresses to be gathered and bound.

Mr. Belton consulted with Mrs. Fairfax and the almost broken-hearted Mattie. It was necessary that the young girl should be conveyed to her home without delay, and medical attendance summoned. Mr. Belton seized an opportunity when Stella sank back exhausted and powerless, and bore her down the stairs. Mrs. Fairfax longed to accompany her home, but she was compelled to appear on the stage in the fifth act.

"If Mrs. Rosenvelt will permit me, I will come to you as soon as the play is over," she said to Mattie; "Stella seems to recognize me, and I may be of assistance."

As Mr. Belton placed his unresisting burden in the carriage, Mr. Percy, who stood at the stage-door, grasped Mattie's arm. "Merciful powers! What has happened? She is not ill? She is not dying?"

"No, no," replied Mattie, soothingly, for his terrified manner touched her accessible heart; "but she no longer knows us — this horrible life has been too much for her."

"Let me go with you — she will know me. Stella! Stella!" he murmured, leaping into the carriage.

But Stella gave no sign of recognition, though she was now sitting quite erect beside Mr. Belton. When they reached her residence she seemed able to walk. Percy had alighted from the carriage first, and received her as she descended. She took his arm mechanically; preceded by Mattie, and followed by Mr. Belton, they entered the house.

Mrs. Rosenvelt rose in surprise, but not in alarm. Mr. Belton introduced himself. She saluted the gentlemen courteously, then turned to Stella:

"You have come home in your Ophelia dress to show it to me!" she exclaimed, with a gratified air. "How very picturesque! I am much obliged to you, gentlemen, for accompanying her!"

Mattie hid her face in her apron; Mr. Belton bent his eyes sorrowfully on the ground; Mr. Percy looked the very incarnation of mute despair. Stella stood vacantly gazing in the distance.

"Stella, dear, why do you stand there? How

strangely you look! Stella, my child, why don't you answer me? Mattie, what ails her? What have they done to her?"

"Hush! hush!" whispered the young girl, and the muscles, a moment before so rigid, now relaxed. "He 's dead, quite dead! His brain crushed in! Why am I lying alive in Juliet's tomb, while he is waiting for a grave? Here 's one ready made; lay him here!"

Mrs. Rosenvelt turned towards the perturbed manager. "Is it her part she is rehearsing? I have heard her rehearse often, but not in this manner. Why does she not notice any one? What ails her? She 's not — not — O God, not mad? Tell me, my child is not mad!"

"Give me the address of your medical attendant, madam, that I may go for him myself. Her brain has been overtasked. No doubt rest and a physician's care will restore her."

The mother, stupefied by the sudden shock, was incapable of giving the desired direction. Fortunately, it was remembered by Mattie. Mr. Belton wrote down the street and number, and departed.

Mrs. Rosenvelt lavished upon her daughter the most tender epithets; but words of endearment bore not their healing sweetness to her wandering mind. Mr. Percy had gently placed her in a chair; she had removed her straw garland, and was tearing it into bits. She offered him a fragment, repeating:

"There's *rue* for *you,* and here is some for *me!*"

He clasped the sad token to his breast, and gazed upon her as though his tortured soul would rush through his eyes; then turned to the afflicted mother, and asked, "Is there nothing, madam, I can do?"

"My son — send for my son — write to him by to-night's post!"

(These incidents occurred before the telegraph was in operation.)

Percy almost regretted his question. To comply with Mrs. Rosenvelt's wish, he would be forced to leave Stella. He bent over her, whispering her name, and imploring her to bestow upon him one look — one word.

Mrs. Rosenvelt noticed that he lingered, and said, "You want his address? 'Ernest Rosenvelt, New York,' will reach him. Tell him — prepare him for this blow. Do not lose time; write at once."

Mr. Percy was forced to take his leave.

Mrs. Rosenvelt and Mattie were kneeling on either side of Stella's chair, when Mrs. Fairfax entered. At the sound of her voice, the young girl looked up and stretched out her hand.

"*You* are staying with me; you are so good! You will not leave me in this dark tomb alone! Hold fast my hand — don't draw it away. I know the cue, and will loosen it at the right moment. The combat is not over yet — Paris is not dead. Romeo will not burst open the doors until then."

She clung eagerly to Mrs. Fairfax, who, after many attempts, succeeded in luring her to her mother's chamber before the physician arrived.

"Brain fever, produced by injudicious mental stimulus," pronounced the man of science, after examining his patient attentively. "The most absolute quiet is necessary for her recovery."

But neither quiet nor medicine seemed likely to effect that promised restoration. For three days she lay wildly raving, and recognized no one. Now she imagined herself triumphing on the stage, floral showers falling around her, and the plaudits of a delighted multitude ringing in her ears; now failing in some grand, laborious part, overwhelmed with shame and confusion; now subjected to Miss Doran's merciless persecutions; now witnessing again the appalling death of the captain of the supernumeraries.

Mrs. Fairfax was constantly by her couch. It was marvellous how the actress could discharge her morning and evening duties at the theatre, and yet watch beside Stella, night after night, with undiminished strength. Mrs. Fairfax had never experienced the pangs and joys of maternity, but her heart adopted this young girl almost from the moment when, at rehearsal, her arm enfolded that trembling form.

Mr. Percy had, every day, many brief interviews with Mattie. The shattering of Stella's intellect had razed from its dream-laid foundation, and dashed to atoms, his mansion built of many hopes.

Ernest, apprised of his sister's perilous illness, obtained leave of absence for a few days, and arrived in Boston on Sunday morning. His presence wakened no harmonious chord in Stella's unstrung mind. As he sat by her couch, in tearless anguish, he could not help saying to Mrs. Fairfax:

"I foresaw this; I dreaded the effect of this turbulent existence upon her; but she would not heed my counsel. God grant that she may listen to it better when she recovers."

"*When* she recovers!" Mrs. Fairfax sadly repeated to herself; "*when?* Alas! alas!"

The next evening, towards sunset,—about the hour that, one fortnight before, the novice had been robed in her Virginia attire, prepared to be ushered upon her perilous stage life,—the watchers noticed a decided change in their beloved invalid. She slept calmly, for the first time during her illness. The mother and son were seated near the head of the bed; Mrs. Fairfax, a short distance from them; Mattie stood at the foot, but not alone. She had hearkened to Perdita's earnest pleadings, and allowed the sorrowing girl to gaze once more upon the lovely features of her almost worshipped friend.

Only a few whispered words were spoken, but those breathed of hope. Stella lay as white and still as sculptured marble. The arms, that had been incessantly tossed about, were folded on her breast; the features, so constantly distorted, had settled into a holy calm; the burning glow on her cheek had faded out, and the labored breath was now lightly drawn. She moved feebly; then, with a deep sigh, opened her eyes. The glittering light, the vacant expression, the wild stare, had gone from them.

"My mother!"

"Thank God! thank God!" murmured Mrs. Rosenvelt, sinking upon her knees. "She knows me! She will recover!"

"Ernest, is that you? How came you here? I was rash; I did not heed you. If I can but prove to you how much I—but it's too late! Who is that by you? My friend, my kind friend! Kind to every one, but kindest of all to the headstrong novice! All that could be done to help her — to smooth the rough path — you did!"

Mattie pressed forward, but Perdita shrank behind the curtains.

"My own faithful, uncomplaining Mattie, how I have made you suffer! God bless you! Don't forget that I loved you always; you were so patient, so devoted! Brother, take care of my good Mattie!"

A low sound of weeping now issued from one at the foot of the bed, and the curtains shook.

"Who is that? Who moves the curtains? *Is it — can it be ——?*" and her face became suddenly effulgent with a hope which her tongue refused to betray.

At those words Perdita issued from her concealment, and bathed the outstretched hand of her friend with dewy messengers of love and gratitude, sent from her heart.

"What, Perdita! you? It was not you of whom I was thinking; and yet I am so glad you are here! Brother, this orphan and her poor brother — I hoped, but cannot now — I thought to help them — *you will?* And, Mattie, you will never forsake them? My memory on the stage — let it be embalmed by one, this one good deed. There is something else I want to say, but I cannot speak it — *some one else.* Lift me up; I am stifling!"

The terrified Ernest raised and supported her. She looked imploringly in his face, and struggled to speak; but her lips moved without producing a sound. Her eyes rested, with a look of love unutterable, upon every countenance in turn; fainter and fainter grew her breathing; more and more glassy became her distended orbs; and now the heavy lids drooped slowly over them. Never more would those eyes be dazzled by the glare of stage-lights; never more would that stilled heart swell or sink at the world's applause or blame. The meteor, which flashed its resplendent lustre for a moment athwart the dramatic horizon, moved in a heavenlier sphere!

Ernest led his mother from the bed of death to Stella's unoccupied chamber. A volume of Shak speare lay open on the table. The hand now lifeless had marked those passages which the young girl loved best. Ernest pointed out the book to his mother. In the violence of her grief she would have pushed it aside, as though it had some conscious instrumentality in her sorrow. But her son gently prevented the action, and pointed out the unclosed page, which bore the trace of Stella's pencil. A voice from the unseen world seemed whispering in the ears of the mourners, as, through their blinding tears, they perused the inspired lines:

"Heaven and yourself
Had part in this fair maid; now Heaven hath all,
And all the better is it for the maid.
Your part in her you could not keep from death;
But Heaven keeps his part in eternal life!
The most you sought was her promotion,
And 't was your heaven she should be advanced:
And weep ye now, seeing she is advanced
Above the clouds, as high as heaven itself?
O, in this love you love your child so ill,
That you run mad, seeing that she is well!" *

* Romeo and Juliet.

THE

PROMPTER'S DAUGHTER.

The sweetest thing that ever grew
Beside a human door. — WORDSWORTH.

THE PROMPTER'S DAUGHTER.

> The sweetest thing that ever grew
> Beside a human door. — WORDSWORTH.

CHAPTER I.

Property-Room of a Theatre. — Its Contents. — The Property Cradle and its Occupant. — Robin and Susan. — A Prompter's Trials. — History of the "General Utility." — The Prompter's Courtship. — "Asking in Church." — Wedding of the Hunchbacked Prompter and the "General Utility." — The Bride at Rehearsal. — Tina. — The Cricket on the Hearth. — Dot's Baby. — Tina's Débût. — A Touch of Nature. — The Infantile "Hit." — Susan's Prayer in the old Property-Room.

READER, have you ever stood in the "*property-room*" of a theatre? That mysterious receptacle of gilded sceptres and tinsel crowns, of stage wealth, stage honors, and stage appliances, for the use of representative heroes and heroines? It is in the property-room of a London theatre that our story commences. The room is about nine feet square. It is windowless, and might, by the *un*theatrical visitor, be called a closet; but the designation rudely painted over the door forbids. The words "property-room" stand out in glaring red letters and beneath "No admission." A gas-branch sheds its bluish light on a heterogeneous mass of objects, ranged and heaped together in disorderly-seeming order. Around three sides of the room run a set of shelves, nearly reaching to the ceiling. On the shelf nearest to the door stands a small chest, with drawers; within are portraits of absent lovers and lost children; lockets to be exhibited at some critical moment in the play; a golden-linked chain, with a heart attached,—such as Rosalind gives to Orlando, with the sweet words,

> "Gentleman, wear this for me,
> One out of suits with fortune,—that could give more,
> But that her hand lacks means."

A rude cross, "carved by no craftsman's hand," such as St. Pierre recognizes on the neck of Mariana, and thus discovers his sister; the snuff-box which that drawer of a long bow, Claude Melnotte, declares Louis the Fourteenth gave to his great-great-grandmother; and the diamond ring with which the same veracious individual asserts the Doge of Venice married the Adriatic. Watches of various sizes, and, apparently, varying value; the countryman's turnip-shaped silver time-teller, the large gold watch for the robber's booty, the glittering bauble of the dashing beau. A set of purses, of different textures, —the velvet purse of the benevolent lady, filled with golden coin, and opening easily to dispense charities; the dingy leathern purse of the miser, only unclosing to be filled; the honest-looking, well-stuffed purse of the farmer; the empty silken purse of the spendthrift. Pocket-books, swelling with bank-notes, for nabobs and rich uncles. Tossing among these sentiment-suggesting objects are huge pieces of tobacco for hoosiers, Yankees, sailors; fire-crackers for "little Pickle;" handcuffs for detected villains, &c. &c.

Upon a rack, at one side, hang a set of horse-pistols for mounted desperadoes; several sets of duelling-pistols for insulted individuals, called upon to protect their honor; tomahawks and calumets; bowie-knives for the lawless; swords of all ages and countries; daggers,—some too sharp for stage use, others that spring back harmlessly into their handles; bunches of keys — large, ominous-looking ones — for prison-doors; small clusters to dangle at the waists of notable housekeepers. One gigantic key hangs by itself; it is the one with which the Duke locks up the fiery Juliana, informing the audience that there is "much virtue in a lock and key," but forgetting to tell them that the true "padlock" is "on her mind." A little further on is suspended an antique lamp of grim aspect and classic shape, which does service in Juliet's tomb, dungeons, and all subterranean and sepulchral places.

On the shelves lie truncheons; golden sceptres; a velvet cushion, with a crown; the three coffers from which Portia's lover must make his choice to win a wife; the rustic basket, filled with berries (made of red flannel), which Parthenia bewitches the rude Ingomar into carrying; the golden goblet which she wreathes with flowers while humanizing the barbarian with her innocent prattle (weaving an invisible chain as she twines the flowery band); baskets of painted fruits and mimic haunches of venison, such as adorn the table of the Banished Duke, when Orlando rushes in with drawn sword, commanding them to "forbear and eat no more" until his famished companion has feasted; tempting plum-cakes (concocted of *papier maché*); canvas-backed ducks (manufactured out of canvas); bottles of different sizes, labelled "champagne," "brandy," "soda," "poison," but, when used, harmlessly filled with treacle and water; glasses containing ice-cream (that is, raw cotton); a huge punch-bowl, innocent of anything stronger than sweetened water or lemonade; by its side stands the nut-shell mug which Juliana, in her angry mood, offers to her husband's guest. In seemingly dangerous proximity you may see a red-hot poker that never cools, and sets of icicles that never melt; the bell that rings a deafening peal when Romeo kills Tybalt, and all Verona is roused by the jarring of the rival houses; golden inkstands, that will not hold ink; a couple of quills (obviously *uncut*), which write the parting words of despairing lovers, sign fatal contracts, add disinheriting codicils to rich uncles' wills. Just beyond is Virginia's "last task," with Icilius' likeness so faithfully delineated in water-colors that the portrait is very evident to her father's eyes, though the audience usually fail to detect the resemblance.

In one corner stand brooms for "singing chambermaids;" crooks for shepherds and shepherdesses; spears and staffs; walking-sticks and canes of all descriptions,—from the gold-headed cane of the opulent old father, the rough stick of the uncouth farmer, whose duty it is in all plays to protect injured innocence, the whalebone whip of the dandy, to the well-worn walking-crutch of Juliet's nurse.

But in that opposite corner — that less cumbered, well-shaded nook — how strangely unsuited to the place seem the objects there! A cradle, carefully curtained, stands alone,— a "*property-cradle*," it is true; but the tiny form within, the little white arm thrown over the baby head, those slightly-parted lips, those closed eyes, with their deep fringes lying on the soft cheek,— are those also the crafty handiwork of the theatrical property-man?

A noiseless foot passes the threshold of the door; a young girl, attired for the stage as an English peasant, approaches the cradle. She stoops down gently, and gazes upon the little sleeping face. She almost hushes her breath to stifle back an involuntary sigh; she crouches close to the cradle, with her hands clasped on her knees, and watches the infant with a look full of tender sadness. For some time she sits silent and motionless; then is heard the tinkling of a bell, the sound of some heavy object unrolling, and a fall as it touches the ground; it is the descending curtain at the close of an act. There is a great bustle without, and the running to and fro of rapid feet; they are "setting the stage" for another act.

"Does the *birdie* sleep?" asks a low voice at the door.

"Hush! hush! Robin," is the whispered answer.

"Better wake her up gently, Sue; the scene is nearly set."

The speaker was Robin Truehart, the hunchbacked prompter of the theatre. Like all hunchbacks, he was stunted in his growth, and looked older than his years. Everybody designated him as the "old prompter," yet he had hardly passed his prime. His fine, expansive brow was completely bald, and the few remaining locks that fringed his head were touched with silver. There was the unmistakable stamp of intellectuality on his pallid countenance; yet its most marked expression was of patience — patience the result of long discipline — patience which nothing could weary out, nothing disturb.

And well may the lesson of patience be learned in a theatre by its prompter! His is, perhaps, the most harassing, temper-trying, of all situations within those walls. He bears the whole burden of the play on his shoulders, but receives none of the applause. In thought he acts every part while seated in his own quiet nook; he follows every line, groans over every error, gives notice for every "call," and has a host of responsible duties to discharge, of which the audience are in ignorance. It is chiefly upon the prompter that the irritability of the actors is visited. One falls into a rage because he has been prompted when he did not need "the word;" another gets into a passion because he was not audibly prompted when he did need it; a third charges his own forgetfulness to the prompter, who, by watching him too closely, caused his obliviousness. Do what he may, the prompter is always accused of being in the wrong. In this severe school he either becomes highly irascible, or he is rendered patient in the extreme, bearing hard words and undeserved rebukes without self-defence; accepting them as unavoidable evils of his lot, which he is bound to endure.

And who is the fragile-looking girl of eighteen seated upon the ground so close to that cradle, with her eyes riveted upon that baby face, and almost keeping time, in her own breathing, with the infant's lightly-drawn breath? She is the wife of that hunchbacked prompter; the mother of that sleeping child.

Susan's parents and grandparents had been actors for as many generations as they could trace back. The stage had descended to her as an inheritance; she knew no other vocation, never thought of adopting any other. Her parents had held responsible, but not high, positions in the theatre. She had just entered her fourteenth year, when an epidemic, then raging in London, made her an orphan. There were none near of kin to protect or counsel her; none upon whom she had a claim, save that of charity. She was retained in the theatre in the capacity designated as "general utility." It is the duty of the "utility" to speak a few unimportant lines, to deliver notes and messages on the stage, to sing in choruses, take part in ball-room scenes and dances where numbers are required, and assist in filling up groups for tableaux.

Susan was tall; her figure had that willow-like slenderness which betokens a rapid shooting up of the form, outstripping the strength. Her drooping shoulders and slight stoop seemed to indicate the bending humility of her character. Her features were too delicately fine to strike those who gazed upon her through the barrier of foot-lights as beautiful. They only noted the profusion of auburn hair, which some might have termed *red* (the color which the old masters loved to paint), the soft brown eyes, and exquisite fairness of complexion; and many wondered whether she were indebted to art for the latter, until the flush that came with a gesture or a word gave evidence that the hues were by

"Nature's own sweet and cunning hand laid on."

The melodious tones of her voice would sometimes attract, but no opportunity was ever afforded her for the exhibition of talent. There are a thousand agencies at work in every theatre, of which the uninitiated know nothing, to prevent those in humble positions from rising. The might of great genius will force its way upward; but lesser talent, unaided by *influence,* is a fountain pent within a stony barrier, raised by jealous hands. The fountain may bubble and sparkle, but, unless it have strength to burst its bounds, the waters remain unacknowledged. So was it with Susan.

There were those in the theatre who felt sure that she had fine dramatic powers; but their desire to keep her back, to drive her into the shade, and preclude her taking a higher rank in her profession, became all the greater. Her natural timidity amounted to diffidence, and prevented the lonely, friendless girl from associating freely with those around her. From the manager, Mr. Higgins, a money-loving, bold, dissolute man, she shrank with instinctive repugnance. He was struck with her ideal style of beauty; his quick eye soon discovered she had hidden abilities; he would have placed her in a position to display them; but she shunned his presence, and met his insulting manifestations of admiration with that species of womanly dignity which awes even a libertine.

She was but sixteen at the period alluded to, but she had had no childhood to *put away;* she knew none of childhood's buoyant joys,—its careless lightness of heart, its elastic gambols over meadows and lawns. Her memory looked back upon no time unfilled by the daily routine of duties at the theatre. Yet she could scarcely be termed unhappy. She accepted her portion humbly, never rebelling at her lot, never questioning why a lot so lowly should be hers. She knew no unhallowed desires; gave entertainment to no evil thoughts. Through temperament and through culture her mind was a quick recipient of all holy influences. From the lips of a virtuous mother she had learned the great lesson of submission to the will of Providence; learned to do the work which her hand might find to do, and to do it with all her heart. He who learns this lesson, does this work, can never be classed among the unhappy.

After the death of her parents, the hunchbacked prompter was her chief friend in the theatre, her tacit protector. It was he who conducted her each night to the humble lodgings which her parents had occupied at their death; he who, when he could snatch a moment's time, instructed her in her duties; he who whispered a few comforting words when she was terrified by the harsh rebukes of the stage-manager.

One day Susan had been deeply wounded by some coarse expressions uttered by Mr. Higgins, and alarmed at his threat of dismissal if she maintained her habitual reserve. That night, as Robin was conducting her home, he could feel the arm that was locked in his tremble violently. He kindly inquired the cause of her agitation; the poor girl burst into tears. In a voice broken with sobs she confided to her sole friend the insults to which she had lately been subjected. Poor Robin! this was a critical moment in his life. Day by day he had watched that human flower expanding in unsullied purity; he had unconsciously appropriated it, in thought, because it seemed as if no other had been sent for its guardianship. His deep and tender affection had strengthened in secret. He had never spoken to the young girl of love. It seemed so preposterous for him, a cripple, the "old hunchback," as the actors called him, to offer his heart to a being so young and so beautiful! But his protection would be invaluable, she needed it so much; she seemed to cling to him, to come to him as her sole refuge,—he must speak!

"Sue," he said, in a husky tone. "Sue, I wish I were your father, or your brother! I would take such tender care of you; no one should insult you, or make you weep as you do to-night. Sue, I can't be your father or your brother, and I am a poor cripple, though not dwarfed or crippled in heart; and there is something I might be. Don't weep so, dear! don't be offended! It 's only for your good that I offer it; not that I don't love you,—I do, Sue; I love you as well as any father or brother could, as well as one who was blessed with that other name could. Sue, you understand me?"

Susan's sobs had suddenly abated, but she did not answer.

"I have not grieved you? I have not vexed you?" asked Robin, in an alarmed tone.

"O, no," murmured the young girl; "you are always so good to me; you are the only friend I have!"

"Then, Sue, perhaps, for your own sake,—for I should never venture to ask it for mine,—perhaps you would give me the right to that dearer name, which I hardly dare to speak?"

There was no reply.

"Will you, Sue? May I hope for it?" urged Robin, encouraged by her silence, and the entire cessation of her sobs. It seemed to him that she held her breath, she had grown so still; perhaps the new thought half stunned her. She could not speak; but, at his repeated questions, she clung more closely to the arm he held. He felt that answer was enough, and, returning the pressure, thanked and blessed her, and told her that he would be the truest husband that ever woman had, though he was but a poor man and a cripple. And then the exquisite words of Miranda, which Susan had so often heard delivered on the stage, flashed through her mind:

——"My affections
Are, then, most humble; I have no ambition
To see a goodlier man."

They said no more that night, but parted at the street door of Susan's lodgings. She lay down with a strange sensation at her heart; wonder and pleasure mingled with a sense of pain which she could not comprehend. Her first thought in the morning was, "Have I dreamt all this?" Then she remembered Robin's tone and manner, and began to say to herself how much better she loved him than she imagined, the night previous, would be possible. The sense of pain had almost passed away; she had some one to lean upon, some one to look up to, some one to render happy, some one to fill up all the voids of her dreary life!

There was a rehearsal at ten o'clock, and, strange to say, she was there before the hour,—a rare occurrence for any one connected with the profession, except the prompter. His arduous duties commence in advance of rehearsal. Robin was sitting at his table, arranging the "calls" in the book before him. He could not have heard her light step when she entered the half-dark stage; but he felt her presence, and rose to meet her, and conducted her to his seat with a tenderness of manner which he had never before dared to use. There was no one in the theatre at that hour, except the carpenters, at work at the back of the stage. They could not hear Robin's petition that Susan would not postpone the time when he might call her his.

"It is Saturday; the bans must be published on three Sundays,—why not to-morrow?" said Robin, hurriedly. "Why will you not be asked in church to-morrow, and, after service on the day of the third asking, let me call you wholly mine? The sooner that I can feel I am your protector, the better."

Susan started and colored, but recovered herself

instantly, and said, "To-morrow, then, Robin." At the same moment she rose hastily from the prompter's chair, for the actors began to make their appearance at the wings. She retired to a quiet seat, behind the scenes, to think over all that had passed; and remained there, unnoticed, until she was summoned to rehearse her few lines. She did not see Robin again, that day, except in his prompter's seat, apparently engrossed by his duties. At night he took her home as usual, but they were both too meditative to converse much.

Robin had been in the habit of accompanying Susan to church every Sabbath; the church her parents had attended ever since they came to that neighborhood. They had chosen it, at first, because it was the nearest to their residence. Of differences of creeds and doctrines, and disputations concerning the exposition of Scripture, they thought not. Susan's mother was a being made up of sweetness and humility. Like the Syrophenician woman, in Holy Writ, she would have been content to feed from the crumbs that fell from the Lord's table, not asking for the children's meat. But at that church this lowly-minded woman and her husband had received spiritual food in such rich abundance, that their souls were constantly strengthened and refreshed. The love of *good* gifted them with an instinctive perception of *truth;* they never cavilled or questioned; God gave, and they received. They belonged to the class of the *simply good,* who *accept* heavenly truths with delight, but cannot *argue* about them.

Robin and Susan sat side by side in church that next Sabbath; and, when, with the usual formality, the names of Robin Truehart and Susan Fairlie were announced by the minister as desirous of being united in wedlock, few were aware to whom these names belonged. Had any scanned the countenances of those who sat just in front of the altar, in the free seats, the seats for the poor, two countenances would have betrayed the secret. The one kindled up with a flush of grateful joy, and there was a proud swelling of the breast upon which the chin was resting, as though the heart beneath were growing too large for its fleshly bonds. The other face was turned in maidenly modesty towards the ground, the dropped lids hiding the eyes, and a mantle of crimson blushes veiling the cheek.

That week they saw little of each other, except during the usual walk home at night, and neither was sufficiently self-possessed to allude to the event which filled the thoughts of both. The church was not so distant from the theatre that what transpired in the former was not quickly known in the latter. Susan was bantered upon her singular choice. Some sneeringly wished her joy of her *young* and *handsome* intended. Some openly chided her for throwing herself away. She had but one answer for all — "I am content."

The next Sabbath, when Robin Truehart and Susan Fairlie were again "asked in church," both manifested a decorous composure. For an instant Susan's eyes were raised to Robin's face, as if already she were beginning to turn confidingly to him ; and his lips moved as though murmuring words of endearment that he had not before had courage to utter. The next moment, the attention of both was fixed upon the minister.

Another week passed almost as the former had done, except that Robin made arrangements with Mr. Gildersleaf, the property-man, for a room at his house. Mrs. Gildersleaf had formerly been an actress, but the care of a large family became incompatible with her professional duties, and she now received a few lodgers, principally theatrical. Her husband remained attached to the theatre.

On Saturday afternoon, Robert was passing through Covent Garden Market, to make, out of his scanty means, a few purchases for the morrow. Among the profusion of delicious fruits and exquisite flowers, he noticed a bunch of newly-gathered daisies. Their fresh, bright, yet humble beauty, seemed to him so like that of Susan, that he purchased them. That night, as he parted from her at the door of her lodgings, he placed the flowers in her hand, and said, "Will you wear them to-morrow, Susan? They are so like yourself!"

When Robin came for her on the bright Sunday morning of that morrow, —came for his bride, —he found her attired in a simple dress of virgin white, and the bunch of daisies blooming on her bosom. The "eyes of day," they are poetically called; and they seemed to look at him from their pure resting-place, a cluster of eyes full of promise and love. Mr. and Mrs. Gildersleaf accompanied Robin and Susan to church. The bans were published for the third time; service was over; the congregation dispersed; the minister came forward; Robin and Susan rose and approached the altar. There was an expression of surprise on the face of the holy man, as the hunchback of half a century (for such he seemed to the casual observer, though he was, in reality, much younger) presented himself as the bridegroom of the girl of sixteen. Yet, illy-matched as these twain, at the first glance, appeared, the bearing of both was so indicative of serene composure and high purpose, that, as the clergyman proceeded with the ceremony, he thought he had never performed it before more intent and devout listeners, —never himself delivered the words more impressively. The blessing was given, and, for the first time, Robin pressed his young bride to his breast, and imprinted upon her chaste lips his first kiss.

They spent that afternoon sitting beneath the majestic trees, or wandering through the delightful walks of Kensington Garden, conversing with each other as they had never conversed before, communing as neither had ever communed with any human being. Susan often looked back on that day as the first in which the morning star of happiness had dawned through the severing clouds that enveloped her life.

On the morrow it was with her arm in her husband's that the youthful bride walked to rehearsal. As they entered upon the stage, Robin led her to Mr. Higgins, who stood talking to one of the carpenters, and said, "Allow me to present to you Mrs. Truehart, my wife."

"Your wife?" exclaimed the discomfited manager.

"Yes, sir; we were married yesterday morning."

Robin spoke these words in a tone so full of manly

pride, and his attitude was marked by such simple dignity, that the contemptuous sneer died away upon the manager's lips, and he exchanged it for a less scornful "I wish ye joy!"

Mr. Tuttle, the stage-manager, echoed the words of his superior. It was his wont to follow in the wake of the latter, and to take from him the cue which governed all his actions.

Some of the company tittered, and some congratulated Susan, who stood by, pale and trembling. It was a trying day for her; a long, painful rehearsal, and no chance of a word spoken to Robin. She concealed herself, as often as she could escape notice, behind the scenes; and when rehearsal was over, and Robin gathered up his books, and sought her out to conduct her again to her new home, she could no longer restrain her tears; — tears of joy, which fell upon the bosom of the poor prompter, as he wound his long, misshapen arms around the fragile form which he had henceforth the privilege of guarding.

They had been married two years at the period of which we now write, and Susan had known a mother's "*aching joys,*" and experienced the truth of the poet's prophecy,

> "——— a child's kiss,
> Set on thy sighing lips, shall make thee glad."

And Robin's toilsome existence within the walls of that gloomy theatre had suddenly been flooded with sunshine, — sunshine that ever played around the forms of his wife and child.

Robin still stood at the door of the property-room,

and Sue still knelt beside the slumbering child, forgetful of the time and place.

"We want the cradle, Mrs. Truehart," said Gildersleaf, entering hastily. "Scene just set—little one must be taken up."

"Then I *must* wake you, darling!" sighed Susan; and, with the timid carefulness which very young mothers use in touching the first living treasure intrusted to their keeping, she lifted the baby out of the cradle. The little features were drawn together as though the child were about to utter a cry; but the blue eyes opened on the mother's countenance, and the tiny puckered mouth relaxed into one of those shooting smiles which Wordsworth calls

> "Feelers of love, put forth as to explore
> The untried world."

The child was twelve months old, but remarkably diminutive, and its complexion had a whitely waxen hue. A blossom nurtured in the dark, that scarcely knew the sunlight and the fresh breezes of heaven, no wonder that it was colorless and feeble! The parents were too poor to pay an attendant. In their necessary absence, the infant was left in charge of the kind-hearted Mrs. Gildersleaf, but at her busy hands could receive but little attention. Often, of a bright morning, the young mother would awaken from her slumbers at dawn, and, hastily dressing herself and her baby, she carried the child to St. James' Park, and walked beneath the trees, singing in a low voice to her little one, and pondering upon her new blessings. But, though she rose with the sun, the walk was necessarily short. She had to return to prepare breakfast, then other duties must be hurriedly performed, and ten o'clock must find her at the theatre, ready for rehearsal.

Robin could seldom accompany her in her morning ramble, for he had undertaken the duties of assistant copyist, as well as prompter. The copying out of "parts" occupied almost all his leisure moments; but he received an extra remuneration — he could add to the comforts of his wife and child. He plodded through the additional labor cheerfully. His salary was but thirty shillings per week. Susan received one pound, out of which she had the larger portion of her theatrical costumes to furnish; thus her salary was diminished to a mere pittance. To-night the infant of twelve months was to make its first appearance on the stage — was to commence earning its livelihood!

The play was a dramatized version of Dickens' "Cricket on the Hearth;" an infant was needed for Dot's baby. The charge of supplying children for the stage falls to the property-man. The children, of course, receive a trifling compensation. Mr. Gildersleaf proposed to Sue and her husband to allow their child to commence a career which was inevitable. Both parents hesitated at first; but necessity, stronger than inclination, forced them to consent. *Tina* was carried to the theatre to make her débût.

The stage represented Dot's apartment, the kettle singing on the fire, and Dot seated near the cradle where slumbered her infant. A cold shiver ran through poor Susan's frame as she walked upon the stage and laid her smiling nursling in the cradle. It seemed the commencement of life's hard struggles for the child.

At Mr. Tuttle's authoritative "Clear the stage, ladies and gentlemen!" Robin took Susan's hand, and with some difficulty led her away. She stationed herself in the little nook behind his prompter-seat. He rang the bell which gave warning to the carpenters above, and slowly the curtain rose. Sue could see her child lying in the cradle which Dot was rocking. Its large eyes were wide open. It had no cradle at home; the rocking was something new and pleasant, and the infant's face beamed with delight. Presently Dot took up the child; she did not handle it dexterously or carefully, for the young girl who played the part was not a mother. Susan started forward, and, had not Robin stayed her in time, the probability is she would have rushed upon the stage.

The child, attracted by the bright foot-lights, stretched out its little arms towards them, and laughed. A touch of perfect nature, however simple, will electrify a whole audience. The infantile action drew down a round of applause, as though the child had well performed something which it had been taught. Tina saw the clapping hands, and sportively imitated the action. Then the applause, mingled with laughter, grew louder and louder, and round followed round. The unconscious child had made a "hit." How Susan's heart beat! She crept close to Robin, and whispered, "Look at her! look at her, Robin, dear!"

"God bless her!" said the hunchback, fervently; "I was thinking that perhaps she will smile just so on all the hardships that come to those who must labor under this roof, and that they will all be light to her! But don't talk to me, Sue, dear; it 's hard for me to keep my mind on the book. Somebody will be wanting the word, for they are all loose enough in their parts to-night."

No further conversation passed between Robin and Susan. He seemed absorbed in his book; and she stood by his side, with her eyes fixed on the child in Dot's arms. Various characters in the play took Tina. Still she chuckled and laughed, and turned to the bright foot-lights with outstretched hands, as though she would seize them.

At last the scene ended, and with one bound Sue was on the stage, and caught up the infant and covered it with kisses, as though it had passed through some great peril. She carried it to the old, crowded property-room, and then, when no mortal eyes were gazing upon her, she sank down upon her knees, with the baby clasped close to her breast, and prayed God to guard this little one from all harm — to let her be a lamb in the Lord's fold, to "crown her with tender mercies and with loving kindness." Involuntarily she repeated the baptismal blessing which the minister had uttered over the infant on the last Sabbath: "The Lord bless thee, and keep thee; the Lord make his face to shine upon thee, and be gracious to thee! the Lord lift up his countenance upon thee, and give thee peace!"

So ended Tina's first night on the stage.

CHAPTER II.

Time and his Wonderful Works. — The Seasons Dramatically Represented. — Time and his Symbols. — Rough Treatment of the Infant. — Maternal Fears. — Melting of a Stern Heart. — Tina in Fairy Pageants. — Evenings at Home. — Rehearsal of Pizarro. — Tina as Cora's Child. — Mr. Upton. — Incident at Rehearsal. — Comparative Value of a Child's Arm and a Tragedian's Point, in the Estimation of Mr. Upton. — Interference of Mr. Higgins. — Subserviency of Mr. Tuttle, the Stage-Manager. — Virtue of a Leathern Girdle. — Tina and a Stray Sunbeam. — The Sphere of Childhood. — Its Effect in the Theatre. — Tina and her Father. — Gold and Silver Rain. — The Temptation. — Performance of Pizarro.

THE "Cricket on the Hearth" was repeated a number of nights, and Tina always appeared as Dot's baby, always arrested the attention of the audience. A grand *spectacle* was in preparation, entitled "Time and his Wonderful Works." The wonders which Time effects by gradual steps were exhibited as taking place instantaneously, through a succession of marvellous transformations — well-executed stage delusions. The sower strewed seed upon the bare earth; Time passed over the furrows with his iron-shod feet, and, lo! the ground was decked with verdure and bloom, and cities suddenly sprang up where fields of corn waved a moment before. The young lover wooing his coy nymph in a bower of roses was breathed upon by Time — the bower vanished ; in its place appeared an old-fashioned fireside, and the enamored pair were metamorphosed into the antiquated Darby and Joan shivering in the chimney-corner. The seasons were also represented gliding, with rapid transitions, one into the other. Through very elaborate scenic effects, Spring was so minutely depicted, that the spectators almost fancied they inhaled the breath of flowers, and hearkened to a chorus of birds. In reality, a fine imitation of their tuneful throats, through the medium of musical whistles.

A golden-haired child, just dawning into maidenhood, crowned with swelling buds, bedecked with young leaves and fruit-tree blossoms, presided over the year's first holiday. Time flitted across the scene ; the flowers expanded into perfect bloom, the trees were covered with foliage, birds twittered on the boughs, butterflies flew about in the air, the roseate light took a warmer, more gairish hue ; the maiden in her spring time disappeared, — a woman of oriental beauty, in the full lustre of her charms, reposed upon a bank luxurious with flowers. Garlands floated from her shoulders ; roses were scattered amidst her unbound locks, and dropped their leaves to cushion her feet. Time glided by ; the trees were hung with fruit ; the leaves exchanged their emerald green for crimson and yellow tints ; the gathered harvest shone in the distance, and beyond appeared a vineyard laden with amber and purple grapes. The recumbent Summer goddess was gone, and a majestic-looking being, of mellower, statelier beauty, stood in her place. The masses of her chestnut hair glittered with bright-hued fruit interwoven with the long pen-

19

dent tendrils of the vine, shooting downward like a veil. Her waist was girdled with autumnal leaves; in her hand she carried a basket filled with the most delicious produce of the vines and trees. Time passes once more — the leaves fall; the bare trees sparkle with icicles; the ground is suddenly sheeted over with snow; mountains gleaming in the perspective are coroneted with snowy wreaths; the regal-looking queen of Autumn is displaced by one of even more imperial beauty. Her severely classic features are colorless, passionless; a diadem of icicles surmounts her black, braided hair; her vesture shines as with sleet; the evergreens she holds in her hands are covered with ice; the red berries of the holly and the pearly mistletoe peep through the frosty covering. Those who look upon her can hardly repress a transient shiver.

Time carried a scythe in his right hand; an hour-glass hung at his girdle; his wings were large, and shaped like those of a bat; his white beard flowed to his waist; his blanched locks fell on his shoulders. His left arm enfolded an infant. A waxen doll had generally been used on similar occasions, but Tina's appearance as Dot's baby, and the attraction which the audience manifested towards her, induced Mr. Tuttle to request that the child would supplant the usual waxen representative. Robin and Susan had no alternative. It was a bitter winter for them — a winter full of struggles, and hard upon all the poor; the pittance that the child earned helped to supply its absolute wants — fuel, clothing, medicine, nutritious food.

Susan's maternal heart ached as she removed little

Tina's woollen wrappings, that a picturesque but very airy garment might take their place. The actor who personated Time was an uncouth, untender bachelor. He received the child from the arms of its mother as though it had been some inanimate piece of theatrical "property," and held it in the requisite position with a rough grasp. When he stalked upon the stage, he waved his scythe carelessly, and, as it glittered in the bright light, Susan trembled as though she feared that it would fall and crop her opening flower. The apparent danger made her forget that the scythe was only a harmless bit of pasteboard, and the "flash of steel" merely proceeded from the innocent covering of silver paper.

Little Tina seemed instinctively to become accustomed to the kind of life which she was destined to lead. She lay contentedly in the arms of Old Time, and even swept back from her cheek his white beard, and wound her fingers in his floating locks.

Susan met Time at his first exit, exclaiming,

"O, Mr. Crowfoot! I am so fearful you hold the child too tightly! She is very delicate; pray do —"

"Get out of the way, my good woman! The child is doing well enough; it 's not crying. Don't bother me, or I shall forget the cues, and then we shall have Tuttle forfeiting us both. Tuttle is great on forfeits — they help old Higgins' treasury. Stand back, will you? and leave the child alone!"

She dared not address him again, but while Mr. Crowfoot was looking over his part she stealthily clasped Tina's hand. The cue was spoken more suddenly than the actor expected; he thrust his book in his bosom, and, not having noticed Susan's fond action, rushed on the stage so abruptly that Tina was almost jerked out of his arms. The young mother was more cautious after this; but she took her post at every wing where Time was forced to make his exit. She had asked Robin to tell her all the cues, and she now ventured to throw a warm shawl over the child's light drapery, taking care to remove the needful protection the instant the cue was given.

The last marvellous transformation was over. Time made his final exit, dropped his scythe, half-tossed the child into its mother's longing arms, and unbuckled his heavy wings, seemingly as glad to get rid of his animate as his inanimate emblematic accessories.

The *spectacle* found favor with the public, and was repeated some thirty nights. Every night Tina lay nestling in the rude bosom of Time. Perhaps she melted the stern heart beneath by the soft pressure of her innocent form; for gradually the actor grew more tender towards her, touched her more gently, and became more respectful to the mother. One night, when Susan placed her as usual in his arms, the infant looked up so confidingly in his face that he involuntarily kissed the smiling mouth; but, ashamed of the action, he laughed, with a half-scowl, saying that he hated the "little imps." He even made some insolent speech to Susan about kissing the pretty mother through the child. But Susan well knew that the child's angelic look had won the kiss; she comprehended in what manner the hard-hearted actor was softened better than he understood himself, and paid no heed to his audacious words.

Shortly after the spectacle of Time was withdrawn, a succession of fairy pageants was produced, and Tina was constantly in requisition. She could now walk, and had commenced to prattle intelligibly. Sometimes the audience beheld her curled up in a mammoth rose. At the sound of music the flower unfolded, and the child sprang out, with butterfly wings and a silver wand, the fairy of the flower! Sometimes she represented the infant that Titania stole from its earthly mother; sometimes she was a Cupid, speeding shafts in all directions; sometimes a hobgoblin.

Towards the close of the season, burlesques and fairy pieces gave place to legitimate dramas, tragedies, melodramas, comedies. Then Tina had rest, and even her rejoicing mother was now and then exempt from theatrical toil, and could spend the evening at home, alone with the child. Sometimes she was lured into Mrs. Gildersleaf's cosey sitting-room. With Tina on her knee, and her work in her hands, she alternately chatted with her kind landlady, instructed the child, or sang snatches of opera melodies, in which Tina instinctively joined; but never did the busy fingers cease their employment. These were evenings of calm happiness, which had but one auxiliary wanting for their completeness — Robin's presence. He, of course, was in the theatre, at his nightly post, long before the curtain rose, and forced to remain until it descended for the last time.

One night he brought Susan the information that Mr. Upton, who was then starring in a number of tragically terrible parts, would enact Rolla on the ensuing evening, and that Tina was cast as Cora's child. This was the first regular drama in which Tina had appeared. Susan herself was to personate one of the priestesses.

Susan had never seen the play. At rehearsal, instead of remaining in the green-room until summoned by the call-boy, according to the usual custom of actors, she carried a small bench to one of the wings, and sat down to watch the action of the scene.

When Tina first appears, — or rather Cora's child, — Cora is seated on a mossy bank, playing with the child at her knee; Alonzo (the father) is leaning over them with delight. The following dialogue is delivered:

"*Cora.* Now, confess, does he resemble thee, or not?

Alonzo. Indeed, he is liker thee — thy rosy softness, thy smiling gentleness.

Cora. But his auburn hair, the color of his eyes, Alonzo — O, my lord's image and my heart's adored! (*Pressing the child to her bosom.*)

Al. The little darling urchin robs me, I doubt, of some portion of thy love, my Cora. At least, he shares caresses which till his birth were only mine.

Cora. O no, Alonzo! A mother's love for her sweet babe is not a stealth from the dear father's store; it is a new delight, which turns with quickened gratitude to him, the author of her augmented bliss.

Al. Could Cora think me serious?

Cora. I am sure he will speak soon; then will be the last of the three holidays allowed by Nature's sanction to the fond mother's heart.

Al. What are those three?

Cora. The ecstasy of his birth I pass; that, in part, is selfish.

But when first the white blossoms of his teeth appear, breaking the crimson buds that did encase them, that is a day of joy ; next, when from his father's arms he runs without support, and clings laughing and delighted to his mother's knee, that is the mother's heart's next holiday ; and sweeter still the third, whene'er his little, stammering tongue shall utter the grateful sound of Father ! Mother ! O, that is the dearest joy of all !"

Susan drank in every word, and involuntarily murmured, "O, *I* could play Cora with my whole soul! I have felt all that; I have had those holidays with my Tina. But they would never give *me* such a part to act; they would not trust me with it; though I *could* play it—I feel I could!"

Alonzo and Rolla go forth to fight the Spaniards. Alonzo is taken prisoner by Pizarro. Rolla breaks to Cora the fatal intelligence that her husband is either slain or captive to the Spaniards.

She determines to seek him, even in the Spanish camp; and, deaf to Rolla's prayers and remonstrances, snatches up the child, distractedly exclaiming: "My child, everywhere we shall be safe! A wretched mother, bearing a poor orphan in her arms, has Nature's passport through the world!" and rushes forth.

Cora is next seen in a thick forest, her child asleep on a bed of leaves; the elements are supposed to be at war. The order is given (theatrically) for abundance of thunder and lightning and rain at night. Manufactured tempests are omitted at rehearsal. Cora covers the child with her mantle and veil, and, faint and weary, watches beside the leafy couch.

Meantime Rolla has sought Alonzo; has found means to enter his dungeon, and, by a stratagem, to set him at liberty, remaining a prisoner in his place. Alonzo is passing through the very forest which Cora has just reached, on her way to the Spanish camp. Cora recognizes his voice in the distance, and, starting up, joyfully flies to seek him.

Two Spanish soldiers enter, see the slumbering child, and bear it away. The child is taken by the soldiers to Pizarro, and brought before him during his interview with Rolla. Rolla incautiously speaks of the boy as Alonzo's child. Pizarro, on hearing this, determines to keep the infant; for, through him, Alonzo is again his prisoner. Rolla argues — pleads with him; forgets the warrior, and sinks upon his knees, imploring that the child may be given back to the agonized mother. Pizarro remains obdurate.

Then Rolla indignantly starts up, draws his sword, and cries, "Then was this sword Heaven's gift!" He darts forward, seizes the child by the arm, and, whirling him round with a wild, melodramatic action, holds him at arm's length above his head.

Tina uttered a shrill cry of pain, as she was tightly grasped by the tragedian and whirled aloft. That cry pierced the mother's heart, and she sprang up from her concealed seat, and ran on the stage.

"O, sir, you have hurt her! Give her to me! Put her down, — pray, put her down! You have dislocated her arm!"

A stifled moan from the child showed that she was acutely suffering, and the actor dropped his arm, saying, "What is the brat whimpering about? If she is going to do that at night, she 'll play the deuce with my best point!"

Susan was examining Tina's arm, and questioning the gentle child, who, even at that early age, exhibited wonderful self-control and power of endurance. Robin, too, had left his prompter-seat, and was stooping anxiously over the little one. Fortunately the arm was not dislocated, only slightly sprained. The probabilities were that, in a second experiment of the kind, especially if made during more impassioned acting at night, the child's fragile arm would be dislocated or broken.

"What is the meaning of this interruption?" demanded Mr. Tuttle, in a dignified tone of rebuke. Mrs. Truehart, leave the stage! Proceed, sir, with your part," addressing the actor; "try that point over again."

But Susan's maternal nature conquered her habitual timidity. She stood up erect and determined before the cold-blooded stage-manager, holding Tina's hand.

"Not with my child, sir," she answered, in a voice such as no one had ever heard her use, it was so firm, and clear, and almost defiant. "Would you have her arm dislocated or broken? Do you think she would shriek unless the pain had been terrible,—she who hardly knows what it is to cry? She never cried, as other children do. He must have almost broken her arm. *He shall not* lift her in that manner again!"

"I'd not miss making that point for the arms of a dozen children!" said Upton, excitedly.

"Then, Mrs. Truehart, we must find another child; and, if the new child fill *one* part, she must fill all during the season. We do not want two children regularly engaged in the theatre," answered Tuttle, unconcernedly.

Susan turned deadly pale, and was seized with an inward trembling. The loss of the situation to the child, and her own discharge, which would probably follow, were calamities that would bring starvation to her door. Still she stood resolute, and replied,

"Discharge us both, sir, if you please; better that we should starve, without employment, than that I should see my child crippled."

"It would only be the fashion of the family," sneered Mr. Upton, in an under tone; but the unfeeling taunt reached the ears of both Robin and Susan.

"Susan, take *our daughter* home!" said Robin Truehart.

Our daughter! It was the first time she had heard him designate the child as "our daughter," and there was a strange solemnity mingled with pride in his tone. His countenance had grown more ashy than hers through suppressed emotion. High hopes had he builded upon that child's successes in the theatre; in an instant they were dashed to the ground.

Mr. Higgins, who had been writing at the stage-manager's table, now stepped forward. He was a shrewd, calculating, selfish man. The dislocation of a child's arm would to him have been a matter of very little importance; but he knew how valuable Tina was in the theatre. He remembered that he paid both father and mother a much smaller sum than would procure equally good substitutes for their situations; he had noted the effect produced by that child upon the audience whenever she appeared; and, though his own heart had now and then warmed towards her, it was *interest* rather then any nobler feeling which prompted him to interfere.

"Is there no safer manner of lifting the child?" he inquired of the enraged actor.

"No, sir; my point depends upon my holding a drawn sword in one hand, and Cora's child in the other, with my arm extended, while I stand in this attitude" (exemplifying); "and I would n't spoil that point for all the crying children in Christendom! If this puny thing won't do, let me have a child that *will* play the part."

Mr. Upton was drawing large houses; that fact entitled him to the manager's respect; his wishes must not be thwarted. The piece was a favorite one; it could not be withdrawn. Mr. Higgins was puzzled. Not so Mr. Tuttle. As soon as he suspected his superior's desires, he changed his tone.

"Not, for the world, have the little darling injured!" patting Tina's head, and speaking in a tone that he meant to be meltingly tender. "The point is easily managed. Mr. Gildersleaf, bring me a leathern girdle."

The girdle was soon selected out of some of the heterogeneous heaps in the memorable property-room. Mr. Tuttle fastened it securely around the child's waist.

"Now, Mr. Upton, elevate the child by means of this belt; hold it firmly here, just at the back; you will find your point equally effective. I have seen it done a hundred times."

"No; let me try it first," said the still alarmed

mother, as she made an awkward attempt to imitate the melodramatic movement of the Peruvian hero.

"Mother, me not afraid!" said Tina. "Please do it!" looking up winningly in the actor's face.

The tragedian petulantly caught up the child, throwing himself in a fine heroic attitude. Tina smiled down upon her mother, to show her that she felt safe and was unhurt.

Rolla continued:

"*Rolla.* Then was this sword Heaven's gift, not mine! Who moves one step to follow me, dies upon the spot."

He rushes out, pursued by the Spaniards, and is next seen crossing a high bridge, bearing the child. These stage-bridges are often hurriedly and carelessly erected, and cause frequent accidents. Susan could hardly choke down an exclamation of horror. The soldiers fire on Rolla, but the firing is not rehearsed. At night this would be another dreadful moment. How could she endure to see the guns pointed at her child? Some of them might accidentally be loaded!

A ball is supposed to strike Rolla. When the audience next behold him, he staggers into Ataliba's tent, reels towards Cora, places the child in her bosom, and, at her frightened exclamation of "O Heaven! there 's blood upon him!" gasps out, "'T is *my* blood, Cora!" and, an instant afterwards, dies.

Susan had been deeply interested in the plot of the drama; but the rehearsal, towards its close, had caused her a succession of agonies. That bridge, those guns, they haunted her the rest of the day.

Again and again she charged Robin to try the bridge himself, and to inspect every gun carefully. He promised to do so, and there was little fear of his breaking his word.

Night came, and Susan half forgot her fears as she dressed Tina, and found how lovely she looked in her snowy tunic and golden girdle, beneath which the important leathern band was safely fastened. A white fillet circled her curling locks, which had taken the hue of amber when it reflects back a ray of the sun. The child had been gifted with uncommon beauty; beauty of an ethereal, highly spiritual character. Her limbs were exquisitely symmetrical, though so diminutive. The brilliant whiteness of her complexion had almost an unearthly aspect, and Susan would never allow a touch of stage *rouge* to profane the child's colorless cheek. Her singularly dilated eyes, but for their soft expression, would have seemed too large for her delicate face.

> "—— The moist,
> Unfathomable blue of those large eyes
> Gave out its light as twilight shows a star,
> And drew the heart of the beholder in." *

Her brow was high, and, when the clustering curls were gathered back, the most careless eye would note that its development strikingly resembled that of her father. She inherited, too, her father's imperturbable patience; but her patience had not, like his, a touch of sadness. It had not been the offspring of trial. It was a natural gift, which early training daily perfected. Her mother's softness seemed to

* N. P. Willis.

have been infused into her own more vivacious spirit, and evinced itself even in the midst of the exuberant joyousness, the sportive glee, that neither father nor mother had ever known. All her motions were light, rapid, full of untutored freedom.

The wonderful elasticity of her limbs supplied the want of strength. The life of exertion which commenced from her cradle had inured her to bear great fatigue without injury. How few, save those who have had their faculties called into constant action, know what wonders habit will accomplish!

There was something about the child, an indescribable hallowing presence, which produced a marked effect throughout the theatre. I once saw a sunbeam stealing through a crevice in the roof, and glancing upon the darkened stage, at a rehearsal. That single streak of golden light, falling upon the dust, and paint, and faded scenery, and glaring imitations of nature, spoke to me, with a thrilling tone, of green murmuring foliage; of air voiceful with rural sounds; of the flower-studded earth; of nature's rich storehouse of vernal treasures; of all that sunbeam shone upon, far away from this mockery and drudgery, this mimicry and misery. As I watched the beam illuminating the surrounding gloom, my mind was filled with fresh and strengthening aspirations, that belonged not to this life of representation, that had no affinity with the place and the hour. It is years ago, yet I have never forgotten that one ray of light, and the sensations and reflections which it called into existence.

Tina is closely associated with that sun-ray in my thoughts; she was the living sunbeam shining through the darkness of selfishness and strife in the theatre to which she belonged. She lured all things on to love her; she discovered and unconsciously threaded her way, through some vulnerable avenue, into almost every heart. Voices softened when they spoke to her; unsmiling lips grew blander at her caress; unloving eyes shone with something like affection when they looked into hers. The purifying sphere of innocence — the sphere of the angels about childhood, which, though invisible, is so often *perceived* — gradually penetrated, with its holy influence, the spirits of all those with whom she communicated.

Susan, too, was treated with more consideration and respect, because the child was hers. Robin, whose quiet, upright consistency of conduct won him spontaneous esteem, since Tina's advent in the theatre had become a person of decided importance. Those who, a few years before, had either spurned or pitied the "old hunchback," regarded him with a feeling akin to envy, when that lovely child would spring upon his knees, and wind her arms about his neck, and cover his furrowed cheeks with kisses, and tenderly pat the protruding hunch, as though it were an especial object for caresses.

And what was the child to Robin, the poor prompter, whose days were passed within the sunless walls, whose evenings in the gas-lighted glare of the theatre? — upon whose very soul "stage-dust" had fallen in such thick clouds that they shut out all nature's pastoral loveliness; who breathed but gaseous air; who only knew beauteous sounds and sights, and noble deeds, and heroic sacrifices, through the inspirations of the poets which he heard declaimed, and saw represented, until his brain whirled with imaginings which the eye and the heart longed to pronounce realities! All that his life had lacked before, all that it had foregone, Tina was now to him.

> "He pineth not for fields and brooks,
> Wild flowers and singing birds;
> For Summer smileth in her looks,
> And singeth in her words."

The child and its mother had transformed his life of care and anxiety into a paradisiacal existence.

But, to return to Pizarro. The drama was enacted with more than usual éclat. Tina's appearance called forth a warm welcome. Pieces of silver and gold were showered upon the stage. Tina already knew something of the value of money — already comprehended the privations and necessities of her parents. She looked at the glittering coin with wishful eyes, that would not be withdrawn. She had been taught that she must not stoop and gather these showered donations. True, they were intended for *her*; but stage etiquette, of long-established standing, had decreed that money thrown upon the stage should become the perquisite of the carpenters and property-men. Once Tina put her foot upon a half-sovereign; she thought that no one saw her; her lithe limb quivered with the strong temptation; she might so easily pick it up; it would buy coal for her mother! Then came a sensation of having committed some indefinite wrong; a fear, an oppression; she pushed the shining golden coin away, and averted her eyes. Thus early was she tempted; thus early did she learn resistance!

So great were Susan's heart-flutterings when Rolla drew his sword and seized Cora's child, that the anxious mother hid her face. The leathern girdle might not be securely fastened — might break! She could not look! She heard the well-known words, heard the thunders of applause which the tragedian's favorite point always elicited, and then Robin's whisper greeted her ears, "All right, Sue; the *birdie's* quite safe! See how lovely she looks, and how she smiles at you!"

Then Susan dared to look up.

Rolla rushed from the stage with the child still held aloft, ran rapidly past Susan, and ascended the steps which led to the bridge without lowering his burden. Of course, the instant he appeared upon the bridge, the guns of the Spaniards were levelled towards him. They were fired so suddenly that Susan saw the danger was over before she had time for a new alarm. She hurried round behind the "flats," to the left-hand wing, where Rolla, after crossing the bridge, had made his exit. She found him dabbling her child's dress and his own with red paint — a darkish imitation of not very healthful blood. Susan did not venture to address him. The work was accomplished rapidly and silently. Again Rolla appeared before the audience; Cora received her child, the hero died; soon after, the curtain fell, and Tina, in her blood-stained dress, bounded joyfully into her mother's arms.

That same season, she enacted the Count's child, in the Stranger; the petted child, in Grandfather

Whitehead; one of the Babes in the Wood, and a number of similar parts. Now and then, Susan experienced the delight of appearing upon the stage with her child. On these rare occasions, what artist would not have thought the face of the hunchbacked prompter, as he watched them both, a study?

CHAPTER III.

Precocious Mental Development. — Religious Training. — The Young Sunday-school Teacher. — Miss Amory's Proposition. — Building the Mansion in which we shall dwell in the Great Hereafter. — The Child-Actress at Sunday-School. — Miss Amory's Horror of a Theatre. — Miss Haughtonville's Recognition of Tina. — The Discovery. — A Scene in Sunday-School. — Robin's Disclosure to his Child. — Life's First Bitter Lesson.— Change in Tina. — Juvenile Persecutions.

As the atmosphere of the hot-house forces the flower into rapid development, so Tina's premature training produced a precocious mental expansion. With unwearied devotion, her parents seized every leisure moment to instruct the child. Neither reflected that they were cultivating her brain at the expense of her *physique;* making large drafts upon the former which must inevitably impoverish the latter; undermining her finely-moulded organization for the transient display of its marvellous construction.

To sow the seeds of religious knowledge as early as her infantile mind could receive them, was not to commit a similar error. As soon as she could lisp, she had been taught to fold her hands and bow her knees, and lift up her soft voice in prayer. The Word of God had grown familiar to her ears before she could read, and her puzzling questions often tested the theological knowledge of her parents. As the mother wondered over the child's quick perception in all scriptural matters, she would say to herself, "Children are so much nearer heaven than we! It must be so; for does not Holy Writ tell us that *their* angels — the angels who watch over them — do always see the face of our heavenly Father?"

She had no thought of ever sending Tina to school; that is, to any but the Sabbath-school of the neighboring church. There she became a pupil at five years old. One of those saintly young girls, whose life fashion could not fill up and satisfy, who yearned to bestow on others the good gifts she had received, whose heart longed to perform uses and dispense blessings,—finding that her position in aristocratic society closed many avenues to this exercise of good, offered herself as a teacher in that Sunday-school. She was very zealous in seeking out little lambs to bring into the fold of Sabbath-day instruction. She had noticed Tina in church, and one Sunday accosted Susan, and asked her to allow the child to join a class just forming. Susan gladly consented.

When she and Robin talked over Miss Amory's proposition, he said, "Perhaps they may teach her more than we know! Let 's give the *birdie* all the knowledge of the other world we can, that it may be a help to her in this. Truth will be a staff for her to lean upon, to keep her feet from stumbling on the rough road. Did you mark, Susan, what the good old clergyman said in his sermon, this morning? — that every day, every hour, every minute, we spend here, has its effect upon our lives in eternity. That we are every day building the mansion in which we are to dwell hereafter; that we may lay broad and deep, and erect a noble edifice, or so cramp our souls that they will only be fit to inhabit a narrow and sunless home in the eternal future. How something stirred within my spirit, and responded to his words when he said that if we loved the Lord in our inmost hearts there would be *no difficulty about the ways and means of serving Him*; that He would surely give us the desired opportunity. He would afford us facilities for developing all that is good and true within us. He would meet us in our business, our social intercourse, our very recreations. That we would no longer look upon life as so much drudgery, so much to be done for the mere sake of a subsistence, but that all things would be seen in the light of *uses*, of things to be done in order to exercise the heavenly quality of benefiting and blessing those around us; that this quality would thus daily grow and expand our souls; that the blessings of life would be continually multiplied, and trials and temptations, and troubles and misfortunes, would all turn to blessings! Were not those his words, Sue? Do you remember them?"

"Yes, every syllable, and who can feel their truth better than you and I, Robin?"

The next Sabbath found Tina at Sunday-school, seated with a group of little girls in Miss Amory's class. When the bells began to toll, and the school was dismissed, Tina's young mother and hunchbacked father were standing at the door awaiting her. They could not bear to be separated from their child in church. Their holy enjoyment of the service was not complete unless she sat between them; for those three were all this world to each other — all of human existence they asked to make heaven of the other world.

Thus Sabbath after Sabbath passed. Tina and her parents loved this day of rest and worship better than all others. The child became a great favorite with Miss Amory; but the latter knew nothing of Tina's history. A theatre the young Sunday-school teacher had never entered. She had adopted the social *fiction* — had become the dupe of that ignorant prejudice which caused her to look upon the temple of dramatic art with a half species of horror. She entertained a mysterious sort of belief that a theatre was some "dreadful place," replete with baneful influences; that none but worthless people found employment there. A theatre, and the angelic-looking child over whose spirituality, gentleness, and intellectual brilliancy, she had so often wondered, were never associated in her mind. But it was not possible for this state of things to last.

Tina had become so great an attraction at the theatre that plays were constantly selected for the very purpose of displaying her histrionic talents. She now began to personate important parts. Her naturalness of manner, richly-cadenced voice, her correct enunciation, and fine elocution (the result of her father's careful training), and the impulsiveness with which she threw herself into her rôle, produced startling effects. It chanced that one of Tina's Sunday-school companions, belonging to a proud but *parvenu* family, saw Tina at the theatre, recognized her, looked for the name on the play-bill, found it "Tina Truehart," the same as that of her youthful associate. The ill-bred girl grew indignant at the recollection of the familiar manner in which she had conversed with the little actress; she remembered that she had made room for the pretty child to sit by her side; had begged her not to occupy any other place; had coaxed Tina to use her books; had encircled her waist with her arm when they were reading from the same Bible. The wrath of Miss Haughtonville rose in proportion to the measure of kindness bestowed on the juvenile but unrecognized actress.

The next Sunday Tina entered the school at a later hour than usual; she had been much fatigued during the week, and Susan could not bear to wake her from the deep, refreshing sleep which sealed her eyelids long after daylight. She entered radiant with smiles, her fair hair dropping in a shower of natural curls around her hueless face, which even her rapid walking had failed to tinge. She was breathing so quickly, from the hurried exercise, that she could hardly wish her teacher good-morning. She took her seat, as usual, beside Miss Haughtonville; but the young girl, who was by four years her senior, cast upon her a look of serio-comic disdain, rose, and changed her place.

"Don't go away, Miss Clara! There is room enough; why are you going?" said Tina, affectionately, though still panting for breath.

"I did not know that I had been associating with an *actress*, Miss Tina Truehart, and I would not demean myself by sitting beside an actress' daughter."

"An actress!" exclaimed the young teacher.

"An actress!" echoed several of the elder scholars.

"Yes, an *actress!*" replied Miss Haughtonville. "I saw her on the stage, myself, last Friday night, all dressed out in gauze and spangles; and I saw her mother too! They're both actresses! It's perfectly shocking to think of her being here associating with *us!*"

Tina's very pulses seemed suspended, so great was her amazement. She sat staring at Miss Haughtonville as though some waking nightmare possessed her. No one spoke. When her power of utterance returned, she bent towards her teacher, and gasped out, "Shocking! What does she mean?"

Miss Amory was so startled at the sudden revelation that she quite forgot the child's possible sensations, and could only say, in a deprecatory tone, "It's not true! You don't belong to such a shocking place as a theatre?"

"*Shocking* place!" and Tina started up. "We don't belong to any shocking place! My dear mother and my father, they are as good — as good — as good as you want me to be when you tell me I must be one of God's children!" Tina's slight frame shook violently, and her voice was so tearfully tremulous that she could hardly articulate.

"Is your mother an actress? — are you an actress?" asked Miss Amory.

"Yes, father is prompter and assistant copyist, and mother acts 'utility parts,' and I act the children," replied Tina, becoming more composed through the conviction that no just reproach could attach itself to them; "and what has that to do with anything *shocking*, with anything wrong?"

The child's innocent face, the guileless tone of her

voice as she uttered these words, and the earnest, indignant manner in which she defended her parents, recalled Miss Amory to herself. The thought flashed through her mind, "I have unintentionally wounded and injured this poor child! What do I know about theatres? The theatre *may be* the terrible place they say it is, but I have found nothing but godliness in this little child."

Tina stood looking in her teacher's face, her eyes glittering with unshed tears, and her usually pallid countenance crimsoned by a sense of shame which she could not herself comprehend.

"Sit down, Tina, and we will say no more about it," said Miss Amory; "you are here to learn your catechism and lesson from the Word, and I have always found you a good little girl, and very obedient and studious. I have no fault to find with your conduct here."

The child remained standing. "But my mother! my dear mother! you do not think — you will not let these young ladies think she could do anything shocking! O, Miss Lucy, you don't know my mother, and how good she is!"

"You are right to love her, Tina; no doubt she is very good; there, sit down."

Tina obeyed, and took her seat as far as possible from any of the other children. She did not comprehend the charge brought against her or her beloved parents, but she was instinctively conscious of a barrier raised between herself and her former companions. In vain she attempted to fix her mind upon her book; she kept involuntarily repeating the words, "*Shocking* — shocking — how is it shocking? How is it bad? What *could* they mean?"

When Sunday-school was over, and she joined her parents, they noticed her sweet eyes impearled with tears, her flushed cheeks, and agitated manner. The hearts of both were troubled with a vague fear that half divined the truth. The service seemed very, very long, that day. When it ended, and they were in the street again, Tina, in a hurried, excited manner, related all that had passed.

"Ah, my *birdie*, has the knowledge of the world's prejudice, the world's injustice to us poor slaves of an ungrateful public, come to you so soon?" said the father. "You must e'en learn to bear all their hard sayings, hoping never to deserve them."

"But, father, what did they mean by *shocking?* What did they mean by calling the theatre a *shocking* place?"

"I don't know how I can make you understand it clearly, precious *birdie;* but to theatres there have sometimes belonged bad persons, bad men and women, who were actors and actresses, and their sinfulness was made known to the world. Generally it was exaggerated, and believed to be far greater than it was; and so it came about that some people are prone to think that every one belonging to a theatre is degraded. But it is not so, my child; we have among us — as the annals of crime show that other professions (even the highest, the ministry of God itself) have — unprincipled and wicked people; but we have true, honest, God-fearing people, also. When you hear any one say otherwise, think of your dear mother," — and he pressed Susan's arm as on that day when he promised to be all to her,— "and remember that what the world thinks cannot harm you. It is *what the Lord thinks*,— the Lord, who sees your heart, your actions and intentions, — what *He* thinks alone has true importance."

"But must I go to the Sunday-school again, father, when I know they think ill of me and of my mother, and that I belong to a *shocking* place?" That word *shocking* grated so harshly upon Tina's young ears! She could not forget it.

"Yes, my daughter, you must go, and you must bear whatever slights you may meet with. You may have to encounter them in life, and they cannot harm you. When we reach home I will read to you about some great and good men, the benefactors of their country, who have been reviled and misjudged all their lives; but those who were holy-minded performed their duties courageously, all the same, and their spirits were not broken because they were ill-used and misunderstood."

As the week glided on, Tina, for the first time, dreaded the approach of the Sabbath, though she never thought of shrinking from the trial through which her father wished her to pass. Sunday came, — a lovely, calm, bright day; the bells chimed so musically, everything animate and inanimate seemed to know that it was the Sabbath of their Lord. With a slow step and drooping head Tina entered the Sunday-school. Her eyes were cast down, as if she dreaded to meet the many curious looks turned upon her; for the news that she belonged to that mysterious place, a theatre, had rapidly spread throughout the school, and the children leaned their heads together and whispered as she passed them. She joined her own class. Miss Amory accosted her kindly. Without lifting her eyes, she seated herself meekly apart from the other scholars. No words were spoken except on the subject of the lesson; no allusion was made to the occurrences of the Sunday previous.

From that day her whole demeanor underwent a change. The frolicksome child was no more; all her buoyancy disappeared; her features wore a subdued and chastened expression; her ease of manner was displaced by a fawn-like fearfulness, that shrank from contact with strangers. She had learned her first sad lesson in life! There was a chill about her young heart which could not be warmed away. Her deep, dreamy eyes still smiled constantly, smiled on all they looked upon,—and the smile of the eye says more than that upon the lips,—but the dimpling laughter that was wont to irradiate her face was hushed forevermore.

Many Sabbaths passed in the same manner as this. Tina was wholly separated from her former friends; that is, she withdrew herself from them, dreading that they might shun her. But there were many who longed to speak to the little girl; many who were touched by her sweet submissive ways. Some had lately seen her on the stage, and were curious to approach the public favorite nearer.

One Sunday she reached the school unusually early. The superintendent and teachers were not present. Only a few scholars had assembled. These mustered courage to gather around Tina, and ask her questions. She answered shyly, but politely.

"Won't you walk on your toes for us?" said one saucy little miss.

"Do," said another, "and make us a pirouette, won't you? I do so want to see what they call a pirouette!"

"You might *act* a little for us before the teachers come," said another; "now, don't be ill-tempered, but *show off!*"

"Yes, show off! show off!" cried all the children.

Tina was so surrounded that she did not know which way to turn; her juvenile persecutors met her on all sides. None heeded her embarrassment, her prayers to be left to herself; the children only urged her more pertinaciously to "show off." They even seized her, and tried to drag her to the platform where stood the superintendent's desk and chair, — children are such cruel tyrants at times! In vain Tina remonstrated and struggled; they were forcing her upon the platform, when the entrance of one of the teachers occasioned her release.

It was not easy to resmooth the ruffled plumage of Robin's poor *birdie,* and her little heart fluttered like that of any bird when pursued by vultures; but Tina remembered her father's words, and she sank down in her quiet corner without uttering a complaint.

CHAPTER IV.

Genius. — Sensations of the Youthful Actress. — Tina's Personation of the Young Duke of York. — Jealousy of Richard's Representative.—Tina's First Call before the Foot-Lights.—Sudden Deafness of Mr. Tuttle.— Mr. Higgins' Command and Motives.—The Hunchbacked Prompter's Delight.— Duke of York metamorphosed. — Merriment of the Audience. — Rumors heard by Mr. Higgins.— Robin bound by a Contract. — Discovery that he has been Over-reached. — Tina as Prince Arthur.— Falling from the Wall.— Mr. Upton softened. — William Tell. —Tina as Albert. — A Tragedian's Generosity. —The Hunchback's Gratitude.

Tina had just entered her sixth year when she was intrusted with the rôle of the young Duke of York, in Shakspeare's tragedy of Richard the Third. The pulse of true genius stirring within her soul, always exultant when her high gifts were brought into use, caused her to experience an inexplicable, indescribable fascination for her profession, — a fascination that counterbalanced the weariness, the anxieties, the trials, that crowd the actor's smoothest pathway. Even at that early age she was a close student of her art. She had an intense love for the poet's conception and for its lifelike embodiment, rather than any undue fondness for applause. The latter was only valued as a token that she had fitly interpreted her author, that she had done her duty. The power of mental concentration, of total self-forgetfulness, is the first great element of dramatic success; and this she possessed in an eminent degree. The character of the young Duke of York she studied with an all-absorbing enthusiasm.

In act fourth, the Duke of York enters with the Archbishop of York, Queen Elizabeth, and the Duchess of York. The following is the dialogue:

"*Duchess.* I long with all my heart to see the prince;
I hope he is much grown since last I saw him.
Q. Eliz. But I hear no; they say my son of York
Hath almost overta'en him in his growth.
York. Ay, mother, but I would not have it so.
Duchess. Why, my good cousin, it is good to grow.
York. Grandam, one night, as we did sit at supper,
My uncle Rivers talked how I did grow
More than my brother. Ay, quoth my uncle Gloster,
Small herbs have grace, great weeds do grow apace:
And since, methinks, I would not grow so fast,
Because sweet flowers are slow, and weeds make haste.
Duchess. Good faith, good faith, the saying did not hold
In him that did object the same to thee.
He was the wretched'st thing when he was young,
So long a growing, and so leisurely,
That, if his rule were true, he should be gracious.
Arch. And so, no doubt, he is, my gracious madam.
Duchess. I hope he is, but yet let mothers doubt.
York. Now, by my troth, if I had been remembered,
I could have given my uncle's grace a flout,
To touch his growth nearer than he touched mine.
Duchess. How, my young York? I prithee let me hear it.
York. Marry, they say my uncle grew so fast
That he could gnaw a crust at two hours old:
'T was full two years ere I could get a tooth.
Grandam, this would have been a *biting* jest.
Duchess. I prithee, pretty York, who told you this?
York. Grandam, his nurse.
Duchess. His nurse? Why, she was dead ere thou wert born.
York. If 't were not she, I cannot tell who told me.
Q. Eliz. A parlous boy! Go to, — you are too shrewd."

These salient points were given with an earnest archness that evinced how thoroughly the child comprehended the character she assumed.

In act third the young Duke enters again, accompanied by Hastings and the Cardinal. His elder brother, the Prince of Wales, thus greets the youthful Duke:

"*Prince.* Richard of York, how fares our loving brother?"

A touch of childlike deference mingled with the tone of affection in which the young Duke replied:

"*York.* Well, my *dread* lord, so must I call you now.
Prince. Ay, brother; to our grief, as it is yours.
Too late he died that might have kept that title,
Which by his death hath lost much majesty!
Gloster. How fares our cousin, noble lord of York?
York. I thank you, gentle uncle. O, my lord,
You said that idle weeds are fast in growth;
The prince, my brother, hath outgrown me far.
Gloster. He hath, my lord.
York. And therefore is he idle?
Gloster. O, my fair cousin, I must not say so.
York. Then is he more beholden to you than I.
Gloster. He may command me, as my sovereign;
But you have power in me, as in a kinsman.
York. I pray you, uncle, then give me this dagger.
Gloster. My dagger, little cousin? With all my heart.
Prince. A beggar, brother?
York. Of my kind uncle, that I know will give;
And being but a toy, which is no grief to give.
Gloster. A greater gift than that I'll give my cousin.
York. A greater gift? O, that 's the sword to it!
Gloster. Ay, gentle cousin, were it light enough.
York. O then, I see, you 'll part with but *light* gifts;
In weightier things you 'll say, a beggar: nay.
Gloster. It is too weighty for your grace to wear.

York. I weigh it lightly were it heavier.
Gloster. What! would you have my weapon, little lord?
York. I would that I might thank you as you call me.
Gloster. How?
York. *Little.*
Prince. My lord of York will still be cross in talk;
Uncle, your grace knows how to bear with him.
York. You mean, to bear me, not to bear with me.
Uncle, my brother mocks both you and me;
Because that I am little, like an ape,
He thinks that you should bear me on your shoulders.
Buckingham. With what a sharp provided wit he reasons!
To mitigate the scorn he gives his uncle,
He prettily and aptly taunts himself.
So cunning and so young is wonderful!
Gloster. My gracious lord, wilt please you pass along?
Myself, and my good cousin Buckingham,
Will to your mother, to entreat of her
To meet you at the Tower, and welcome you.
York. What! will you go unto the Tower, my lord?
Prince. My lord protector needs will have it so.
York. I shall not sleep in quiet at the Tower.
Gloster. Why, sir, what should you fear?
York. Marry, my uncle Clarence's angry ghost;
My grandam told me he was murdered there.
Prince. I fear no uncles dead.
Gloster. Nor none that live, I hope?
Prince. An' if they live, I hope I need not fear.
But come, my lord, and with a heavy heart,
Thinking on them, go I unto the Tower."

The prince twines his arms around the reluctant York, who looks back to Gloster with a doubtful glance, shaking his head mournfully while he goes out, as if some dark foreshadowing of his fate were flitting across his mind.

Will it be credited that the hearty applause called forth by Tina's acting excited the displeasure of the distinguished tragedian who represented Richard? He felt as though the child's delineation of her part rendered her too prominent in a picture where he had the right to stand in solitary conspicuousness. He desired alone to engross the public eye. His surroundings must all be subordinate accessories, satellites that would not interfere with his more luminous shining. That he could exhibit envy towards a child may seem an absurdity to many; it will be recognized as an incident of constant occurrence by those who move within the narrow circle of the profession.

At the close of the play, there was, of course, a call for Upton, who had personated Richard. But he had scarcely made his bow before the foot-lights, when a second cry arose for the young Duke of York. The child had never before been honored by a similar summons, one which actors highly value. After the exertions and fatigues of the evening, the call before the curtain is to them a refreshing mark of approval, which "stars" are very unwilling to forego.

Robin, from his prompter-seat, heard the name of his child rising in peals. His breast glowed with tumultuous transport, yet stage etiquette forbade him to apprise Tina, or in any manner to notice the wishes of the audience, until the stage-manager sent forth his orders. Mr. Tuttle adhered to the principle of never putting an actor forward, for fear that he might rise above his control, or demand an increase of salary. He listened to the call, comprehended it perfectly, secretly admitted its justice, but to all appearance remained singularly deaf. He issued no commands ; he hoped the audience would grow weary, and the applause die away. But the impression made was too deep ; the acclamations only grew louder when the audience found their demand was unnoticed.

Mr. Higgins, who, from his post in the box-keeper's office, could overhear all that took place, now hastened behind the scenes, and demanded why Tuttle had not "sent on" the child. It was the manager's policy to encourage this favoritism of his patrons, for it rendered Tina doubly valuable to him. As for spoiling the Trueharts, he had no fear of that; he had too great a hold upon them. Who but *he*, he asked himself, would have engaged a hunchbacked prompter? Did he answer himself that when Robin Truehart applied for a situation that hunch had given the wily manager a pretext for cutting off one third of the prompter's usual salary? O, no, he forgot that small item, and actually persuaded himself that he had employed Robin out of *charity*.

"Send on Miss Truehart at once, Tuttle," said Mr. Higgins, majestically.

Mr. Tuttle bowed, and declared he was just on the point of doing so; then ordered the prompter to notify Miss Truehart to appear before the curtain without delay, also to summon the Richmond of the evening to conduct her.

Robin's heart beat with a stroke that was almost audible. Up the long, narrow flight of stairs he scrambled, taking two steps at a time.

Susan had not anticipated this tribute to her child's talents ; she had disrobed Tina of her black-velvet tunic, glittering with bugle embroidery. The child was now attired in a coarse red calico dress, and a white bib. She was sitting on her mother's knee, half asleep, when Robin knocked at the door; for the dressing-room was appropriated to half a dozen ladies besides Susan. In an agitated tone, he told Susan to bring out Tina.

"What is it, Robin, dear?" asked Susan, opening the door.

"Bring the *birdie*, quickly! She is called — called before the curtain! Do you hear those shouts, wife? They are calling for her — for our little one! She played magnificently! Come, come quickly."

Susan had never heard her grave, tranquil husband speak so rapidly, so incoherently; she was lost in amazement, and so was the suddenly-awakened child; but Robin took the latter in his arms, and ran down the steps. Such an interval had elapsed, he feared the call would cease. The gentleman who personated Richmond was standing by the curtain, waiting for it to be drawn back.

Susan only recovered her presence of mind in time to say, "You are to curtsey, darling, as you cross the stage, — curtsey several times, — as often as they seem to want."

When the audience beheld, instead of the noble Duke of York, in his rich ducal garb, the little girl, evidently startled out of sleep, in her calico dress, and white bib, and rough shoes, there was a general laugh. But Tina curtseyed gracefully, and half laughed herself, comprehending their cause of merriment. She had established a species of magnetic communication between herself and her audiences, and this response to their mirth drew her more closely to them. They saw, too, how lovely was this child in her mean attire; how little costlier raiment had contributed to display her infantile grace and beauty.

Susan could hardly sleep for joy that night, and Robin lay in a waking dream; but Tina's slumbers were undisturbed by the weight of her fresh laurels.

Richard the Third was repeated several nights in succession. Tina's performance was an acknowledged feature, which added to the popularity of the tragedy. She was always called before the curtain; but Susan was too hopeful of the repetition of that honor again to substitute the red calico dress for the ducal vestments.

Even Mr. Upton's heart was not proof against the child's witchery of manner; she continued so docile, was so unelated by adulation.

Rumor whispered in Mr. Higgins' ear that other theatres were about to make Robin advantageous offers. The hit made by his daughter had been noised about London. The manager was quite aware that father and mother, as well as their little one, could command much better salaries than he allowed them, — salaries that would place them in comparatively easy circumstances. Before these whispers of preferment could reach Robin, the prompter was summoned to the box-office. Mr. Higgins praised Tina in a highly sententious and condescending manner, and then inquired whether Robin would not like to sign a contract for the engagement of himself, his wife, and his child, for three years. The wily manager took great care to impress upon the poor prompter's mind that he meant to confer on him and his needy family an especial favor. As a mark of his generosity he proposed to raise Tina's salary from ten shillings per week to fifteen. Robin's upright nature harbored no suspicions; he thankfully signed the contract, which, already drawn up, lay upon the table.

On his return home, he was rejoicing with Susan over this increase in their funds, and describing to her Mr. Higgins' unusual suavity of manner, when a letter was placed in his hands. It contained an offer for his services and those of Susan and Tina, at the Princess' Theatre, with a salary of ten pounds per week! And he had engaged with Higgins to receive three pounds and a quarter weekly, for three years!

Robin crushed the letter in his hands, after he had perused it. "Higgins must have known this!" he exclaimed. "He has bound me by that wicked contract, and prevented my rendering you and the *birdie* comfortable, besides laying up something for a rainy day. He has outwitted me, and what is to be done?"

Nothing *could* be done. Truehart was forced to abide by the contract, from which Higgins, when he was told of this more lucrative offer, showed not the slightest intention of releasing him.

King John was the next Shakspearian revival, and it was selected principally to give Tina an opportunity of appearing as Prince Arthur. Her gift of personation now revealed itself in a striking manner. There was a strong contrast between her piquant, shrewd, *parlous* Duke of York, and the tender, melancholy, loving Prince Arthur. The scene in which Arthur pleads with Hubert, when he is commissioned to put out the prince's eyes, moved the audience to tears. A look of premature sorrow pervaded the whole mien, the weight of early care betrayed itself in the child's very step, when Arthur enters, and greets Hubert with a subdued "Good-morrow, Hubert."

"*Hubert.* Good-morrow, little prince.
Arthur. As little prince (having so great a title
To be more prince) as may be. You are sad.
Hubert. Indeed, I have been merrier.
Arthur. Mercy on me!
Methinks nobody should be sad but I:
Yet I remember, when I was in France,
Young gentlemen would be sad at night
Only for wantonness. By my Christendom,
So I were out of prison and kept sheep,
I should be merry as the day is long;
And so I would be here, but that I doubt
My uncle practises more harm to me;
He is afraid of me, and I of him.
Is it my fault that I am Geoffrey's son?
No, indeed, is 't not; and I would to Heaven
I were your son, so you would love me, Hubert!
Hubert. If I talk to him, with his innocent prate
He will awake my mercy, which is dead;
Therefore I will be sudden and desperate. (*Aside.*)
Arthur. Are you sick, Hubert? You look pale to-day.
In sooth, I would you were a little sick,
That I might sit all night and watch with you:
I warrant I love you more than you do me.
Hubert. His words do take possession of my bosom!
Read here, young Arthur. (*Showing a paper.*) How now, foolish rheum (*aside*),

Turning dispiteous torture out of door!
I must be brief, lest resolution drop
Out at mine eyes, in tender, womanish tears.
Can you not read it? Is it not fair writ?
Arthur. Too fairly, Hubert, for so foul effect:
Must you with hot irons burn out both mine eyes?
Hubert. Young boy, I must.
Arthur. And will you?
Hubert. And I will.
Arthur. Have you the heart? When your head did but ache,
I knit my handkerchief about your brows
(The best I had — a princess wrought it me),
And I did never ask it you again.
And with my hand at midnight held your head,
And, like the watchful minutes of the hour,
Still and anon cheered up the heavy time,
Saying, what lack you? and where lies your grief?
Or, what good love may I perform you?
Many a poor man's son would have lain still,
And ne'er have spoke a loving word to you;
But you at your sick service had a prince.
Nay, you may think my love was crafty love,
And call it cunning; do, and if you will.
If Heaven be pleased that you must use me ill,
Why, then you must. Will you put out mine eyes?
These eyes, that never did nor never shall
So much as frown on you?
Hubert. I have sworn to do it,
And with hot irons must I burn them out.
Arthur. Ah, none but in this iron age would do it!
The iron, of itself, though heat red hot,
Approaching near these eyes, would drink my tears,
And quench his fiery indignation,
Even in the matter of mine innocence;
Nay, after that, consume away in rust,
But for containing fire to harm mine eye.
Are you more stubborn hard than hammered iron?
An' if an angel should have come to me,

And told me Hubert should put out mine eyes,
I would not have believed no tongue but Hubert's.

Hubert. Come forth! (*Stamps. Enter attendants, with cord, iron, &c.*) Do as I bid you do!

Arthur. O, save me! Hubert, save me! My eyes are out,
Even with the fierce looks of these bloody men.

Hubert. Give me the iron, I say, and bind him here.

Arthur. Alas! why need you be so boist'rous rough?
I will not struggle, I will stand stone still.
For Heaven's sake, Hubert, let me not be bound!
Nay, hear me, Hubert! drive these men away,
And I will sit as quiet as a lamb;
I will not stir, nor wince, nor speak a word,
Nor look upon the iron angrily.
Thrust but these men away, and I 'll forgive you,
Whatever torment you do put me to.

Hubert. Go, stand within; let me alone with him.

1 *Atten.* I am best pleased to be from such a deed.

(*Exeunt attendants.*)

Arthur. Alas! I then have chid away my friend!
He hath a stern look, but a gentle heart;
Let him come back, that his compassion may
Give life to yours.

Hubert. Come, boy, prepare yourself.

Arthur. Is there no remedy?

Hubert. None, but to lose your eyes.

Arthur. O Heaven! that there were but a mote in yours,
A grain, a dust, a gnat, a wandering hair,
Any annoyance in that precious sense!
Then, feeling what small things are boist'rous there,
Your vile intent must needs seem horrible!

Hubert. Is this your promise? Go to, — hold your tongue.

Arthur. Hubert, the utterance of a brace of tongues
Must needs want pleading for a pair of eyes.
Let me not hold my tongue; let me not, Hubert!
Or, Hubert, if you will, cut out my tongue,
So I may keep mine eyes! O, spare mine eyes,
Though to no use but still to look on you!

Lo, by my troth! the instrument is cold,
And would not harm me!
Hubert. I can heat it, boy.
Arthur. No, in good sooth; the fire is dead with grief,
Being create for comfort, to be used
In undeserved extremes. See else yourself;
There is no malice in this burning coal;
The breath of Heaven hath blown his spirit out,
And strewed repentant ashes on his head.
Hubert. But with my breath I can revive it, boy.
Arthur. And if you do, you will but make it blush
And glow with shame of your proceedings, Hubert.
Nay, it perchance will sparkle in your eyes;
And, like a dog that is compelled to fight,
Snatch at his master that doth tarre him on.
All things that you should use to do me wrong
Deny their office; only you do lack
That mercy which fierce fire and iron extend —
Creatures of note for mercy-lacking uses.
Hubert. Well, see to live! I will not touch thine eyes
For all the treasures that thine uncle owes.
Yet am I sworn, and I did purpose, boy,
With this same very iron to burn them out.
Arthur. O, now you look like Hubert! All this while
You were disguised.
Hubert. Peace! No more; adieu.
Your uncle must not know but you are dead;
I 'll fill these dogged spies with false reports.
And, pretty child, sleep doubtless and secure
That Hubert, for the wealth of all the world,
Will not offend thee.
Arthur. O Heaven! I thank you, Hubert."

The escaped prince next appears in act fourth, scene third, upon a wall before the castle, and speaks thus:

"*Arthur.* The wall is high, and yet will I leap down.
Good ground, be pitiful, and hurt me not!

There 's few or none do know me ; if they did,
This ship-boy's semblance hath disguised me quite.
I am afraid, and yet I 'll venture it.
If I get down and do not break my limbs,
I 'll find a thousand shifts to get away :
As good to die and go as die and stay ! "

He leaps down, and, after the fall, feebly groans out the words :

" O me ! my uncle's spirit is in these stones :
Heaven take my soul, and England keep my bones !
(*Dies.*)"

The wall was sufficiently high to cause a shudder when the prince leaped down. Dread that the child was in reality injured was increased by the pathetic tone in which the last lines were delivered.

Pembroke, Salisbury, and Bigot, enter ; the body of Arthur is not at first perceived ; then Pembroke, bending over the corse, gives utterance to that exquisite line,

" O, Death, made proud with pure and princely beauty ! "

Hubert brings the glad tidings that Arthur is safe, and is shown the boy, stark and dead upon the ground. When accused of his murder, he replies,

' 'T is but an hour since I left him well :
I honored him, I loved him ; and will weep
My date of life out for his sweet life's loss."

The child is borne out in Hubert's arms, and it was not until the close of this protracted scene that the anxiety of Tina's parents was relieved, and they found that she had escaped injury. She was so light and supple that, by relaxing her limbs when she fell, and making no resistance, she might have dropped from a much more alarming height without receiving a bruise.

Her performance of Prince Arthur had made so deep an impression that the papers now began to trumpet her praises.

Mr. Upton, whose admiration for the child's dramatic gifts, and attraction to her lovable character, had overcome his former sense of professional envy, proposed the production of William Tell, and Tina's appearance as Albert. There was a long discussion at the manager's table. Tina could, doubtless, enact Albert, and make what the low comedian humorously styled a "hard hit," a "striking hit;" but her exceedingly delicate features, her fairy-like proportions, were particularly unsuited to the bold, sturdy mountain boy.

"We expect to see a tall man when Othello is personated," suggested Mr. Upton; "but I believe no one remembered Mr. Kean's diminutive stature when he represented the Moor. His genius lifted him up until he looked grander than the men of six feet who surrounded him."

This argument was conclusive; the play was cast, and Tina commenced studying Albert. The character inspired her with fresh delight. When the appointed night came, Mr. Upton's judgment proved correct. Her vigorous step, the width and decision of her movements, the power of her voice, the rustic boldness of her bearing, caused the unsuitableness of her stature to be overlooked. In the opening scene, the boy springs down the rocks at the call of Emma, his mother. The replies to her two first queries, though so simple, were spoken in a tone of deep reverence, which the child could not have simulated, had not her heart been full of unaffected devoutness.

> "*Emma.* Knelt you when you got up to-day?
> *Albert.* I did, and do so every day.
> *Emma.* I know you do; and think you, when you kneel,
> To whom you kneel?
> *Albert.* I do.
> *Emma.* You have been early up, when I, that played
> The sluggard in comparison, am up
> Full early; for the highest peaks alone,
> As yet, behold the sun. Now tell me what
> You ought to think on, when you see the sun
> So shining on the peak.
> *Albert.* That as the peak
> Feels not the pleasant sun, or feels it least,
> So they who highest stand in fortune's smile
> Are gladdened by it least, or not at all!
> *Emma.* And what 's the profit you should turn this to?
> *Albert.* Rather to place my good in what I have,
> Than think it worthless, wishing to have more:
> For more is not more happiness so oft
> As less.
> *Emma.* I 'm glad you husband what you 're taught.
> That is the lesson of content, my son;
> He who finds which, has all — who misses, nothing."

Albert's shooting, his desire to emulate the heroic mountaineer his father, his attention to Tell's instructions concerning the use of the bow, all these interested the audience; but it was not until the second act, when Albert encounters Gesler fainting upon a rock, gives him to drink, and offers to show him the way to Altorf, that the dramatic abilities of the child were tested.

"*Albert.* You 've lost your way upon the hill?
Gesler. I have.
Albert. And whither would you go?
Gesler. To Altorf.
Albert. I 'll guide you thither.
Gesler. You 're a child.
Albert. I know
The way: the track I 've come is harder far
To find.
Gesler. The track you 've come! What mean you? Sure
You have not been still further in the mountains?
Albert. I 've travelled from Mount Faigel.
Gesler. No one with thee?
Albert. No one but God.
Gesler. Do you not fear these storms?
Albert. God 's in the storm.
Gesler. And there are torrents, too,
That must be crossed.
Albert. God 's by the torrent, too.
Gesler. You 're but a child.
Albert. God will be with a child.
Gesler. You 're sure you know the way?
Albert. 'T is but to keep
The side of yonder stream.
Gesler. But guide me safe,
I 'll give thee gold.
Albert. I 'll guide thee safe without.
Gesler. Here 's earnest for thee. (*Offers gold.*) Here—
I 'll double that,
Yea, treble it, but let me see the gate
Of Altorf. Why do you refuse the gold?
Take 't.
Albert. No.
Gesler. You shall.
Albert. I will not.
Gesler. Why?
Albert. Because
I do not covet it; and, though I did,

It would be wrong to take it as the price
Of doing one a kindness.

Gesler. Ha ! who taught
Thee that ?

Albert. My father.

Gesler. Does he live in Altorf?

Albert. No ; in the mountains.

Gesler. How ! a mountaineer ?
He should become a tenant of the city ;
He 'd gain by it.

Albert. Not so much as he might lose by it.

Gesler. What might he lose by it ?

Albert. Liberty.

Gesler. Indeed !
He also taught thee that ?

Albert. He did.

Gesler. His name ?

Albert. This is the way to Altorf, sir.

Gesler. I 'd know thy father's name.

Albert. The day is wasting — we
Have far to go.

Gesler. Thy father's name, I say ?

Albert. I will not tell it thee.

Gesler. Not tell it me !
Why ?

Albert. You may be an enemy of his.

Gesler. May be a friend.

Albert. May be ; but should you be
An enemy — although I would not tell you
My father's name, I 'd guide you safe to Altorf.
Will you follow me ?

Gesler. Ne'er mind thy father's name ;
What would it profit me to know ? Thy hand, —
We are not enemies.

Albert. I never had
An enemy.

Gesler. Lead on.

Albert. Advance your staff
As you descend, and fix it well. Come on.

Gesler. What, must we take that steep?
Albert. 'T is nothing. Come,
I 'll go before — ne'er fear. Come on — come on!
[*Exeunt.*]"

Gesler and Albert are next seen at the gate of Altorf.

"*Albert.* You 're at the gate of Altorf.
Gesler. Tarry, boy.
Albert. I would be gone; I 'm waited for.
Gesler. Come back:
Who waits for thee? Come, tell me; I am rich,
And powerful, and can reward.
Albert. 'T is close
On evening; I have far to go. I 'm late.
Gesler. Stay; I can punish, too.
Albert. I might have left you,
When on the hill I found you fainting, and
The mist around you; but I stopped and cheered you,
Till to yourself you came again. I offered
To guide you, when you could not find the way
And I have brought you to the gate of Altorf.
Gesler. Boy, do you know me?
Albert. No.
Gesler. Why fear you, then,
To trust me with your father's name? Speak.
Albert. Why
Do you desire to know it?
Gesler. You have served me,
And I would thank him, if I chanced to pass
His dwelling.
Albert. 'T would not please him that a service
So trifling should be made so much of.
Gesler. Trifling?
You saved my life.
Albert. Then do not question me,
But let me go.
Gesler. When I have learned from thee
Thy father's name. What, hoa!

Sentinel. (*Within.*) Who 's there?
Gesler. Gesler!
Albert. Ha! Gesler. (*The gate is opened.*)
Gesler. (*To soldiers.*) Seize him! Wilt thou tell me
Thy father's name?
Albert. No!
Gesler. I can bid them cast thee
Into a dungeon. — Wilt thou tell it now?
Albert. No!
Gesler. I can bid them strangle thee. — Wilt tell it?
Albert. Never!
Gesler. Away with him!
(*Soldiers take off Albert through gate.*)"

In act third, William Tell has been taken prisoner, and brought before Gesler. Albert refuses to recognize his father, whose life he fears he may endanger. Tell, also, sentenced by the tyrant to die, will not acknowledge the boy, and bids him farewell as though he were the child of another, sending by him a message to his mother. But when Albert is sentenced to death by the inhuman Gesler, the father is overpowered; he yields to conquering nature, embraces his child, confessing that he is a parent. Then Gesler offers him freedom if he will shoot an apple from his child's head; risking that child's life, or an eye, or the mangling of his cheek, his lips, — the lips his mother has so often covered with kisses. After a fierce mental struggle, the father consents. The moment for the trial arrives; the arrow is aimed — faithfully sped — the boy is safe — father and son are free!

Albert has not many words to utter during this last thrilling scene; but the variations of the child's eloquent countenance, the spontaneous gesticulations, the "by-play" (as it is styled in stage parlance), spoke more emphatically than language, filled out the part even more fully and beautifully than it had been conceived by the poet.

Tina's graphic delineation of Albert had assisted Mr. Upton in his personation of Tell, — he was generous enough to admit the fact. The instant the green curtain had fallen between the actors and the audience, he turned to Susan, and said, "Ah, you may well be proud of her! She will make the first actress of the day. I never saw anything so true to nature."

The "call" was now deafening all ears.

Mr. Tuttle advanced: "They are calling you, Mr. Upton; be so good as not to keep the audience waiting. Miss Truehart, don't go to your room; they are calling you also; you will go out afterwards."

"No," said Upton, warmly, "she richly deserves the call! She shall go on with me."

A star, who is supposed to receive all first honors and never to share them, to propose conducting before the foot-lights, in answer to his own summons, a child, one of the stock company, the prompter's daughter, — this was indeed an unprecedented condescension!

The tragedian led Tina out, and the unusually hearty welcome of the audience implied a recognition of the courteous act. This would have repaid him, had he not been more amply compensated by that internal sense of delight which emanates from the consciousness of having performed a generous deed. He found an additional reward in the expression of Robin's countenance, as he held back the curtain for them to make their exeunt, and said, in a low, feeling tone,

"I thank you, sir! Very few *stars* would have done what you have just done!"

CHAPTER V.

Tina's Musical Gift. — Mr. Higgins' Ideas of a Theatrical Establishment. — The Tempest. — Spurious Edition. — Tina "cast" as Ariel. — Discussion between the Manager and Stage-Manager. — Exultation of Susan and Robin on reading the Cast. — Excitement in the Theatre. — Miss Mellen's Sarcasm. — Night of Performance. — The Prompter's Nook. — Ariel's Appearance. — Tina's Delineation. — Fifth Act. — Ariel Flying. — Entangled Wires. — A Mother's Terror. — General Confusion. — Frightful Catastrophe. — Robin's Presence of Mind. — The Rescue. — Night Watchers in the Green-Room. — Bearing Tina Home. — Incidents by the Way. — The Child's Answer to her Father.

Operatic melodies were as familiar to Tina's infant ears as the cradle lullaby to those of ordinary children. Susan had always taken part in choruses. She possessed a sweet though not powerful voice, and a very accurate ear. Before her child's lisping tongue could prattle fluently, the mother commenced instructing her in one of the most important branches of her profession.

Tina was in her seventh year before her musical faculties were discovered in the theatre. She was then required to sing in a burlesque. The music apportioned to her was a parody upon several popular airs. The gush of birdlike melody that broke from her lips at rehearsal, the clear, warbled notes, took all ears captive, and hushed every other sound. Those within hearing could not choose but mutely listen. Then her face sang; her eyes "shot out vocal light;" her whole frame was penetrated and thrilled through and through with the spirit of melody. The leader of the orchestra was in ecstasies. Need the effect upon the audience, at night, be related? From that time the new songster carolled nightly to enchanted ears.

Mr. Higgins announced to his stage-manager that Shakspeare's Tempest would be the next attraction presented to the public. Let it not be imagined that this refined selection was an evidence of Mr. Higgins' cultivation and taste. He was merely a judicious caterer for the public amusement; he had the skill of feeling the pulse of his audiences, and discovering their requirements. Of *high art*, of the true purposes and ennobling objects of the stage, he knew nothing. The theatre was simply his means of gaining a livelihood,—his *workshop*, where dramas to suit his customers were provided and manufactured, and where artisans were paid as charily as possible for their labor. As for the elevated or debasing tone, the morality or immorality, of the plays presented, these were not subjects upon which he wasted a thought.

It so chanced that the class of audience who supported his theatre were attracted by unobjectionable plays; such, therefore, were placed before them, dished up by Mr. Higgins as a hotel purveyor serves his viands, consulting merely the appetite, not the health, of his guests. Had the patrons of his establishment preferred plays of an opposite character, Mr. Higgins, as far as the licenser permitted, would have surfeited them with the most highly-seasoned immorality that could be concocted.

The Tempest was to be produced from the original text. The reader may not be aware of the existence of a stage version, in which hapless Will Shakspeare is unmercifully mutilated. The noble Prospero has a spurious scion grafted on his stock; and the peerless Miranda is furnished with a sister, — an excrescence as unresembling herself as Goneril was unlike Cordelia.

The character of the "dainty Ariel," the "delicate sprite," belongs, according to stage conventionalities, to the singer of the theatre. That its delineation should be intrusted to a child was a novel idea; yet such was Mr. Higgins' proposal to his stage-manager. Tina's great popularity, and the spell of her flute-like music, induced Mr. Higgins to make this bold experiment — a decided innovation on theatrical usages.

Mr. Tuttle, accustomed as he was to bow and say "Ay" to every suggestion of his superior, now ventured to demur. He urged that the singer of the theatre, Miss Mellen, would probably "throw up" her engagement. The part belonged to her by right, — that could be proved by all precedents; then the music was difficult. Could Miss Truehart master it in time? Could she execute it at all?

Mr. Tuttle vehemently heaped his objections one upon the other; and Mr. Higgins coolly swept them away, as though they had been a child's edifice of cards. He was one of those persons whom opposition always renders inflexible.

"Cast the piece, sir, with Miss Truehart as Ariel.

I will arrange matters with Miss Mellen; if she choose to throw up her engagement, so much the better. Miss Truehart will more than fill her place, one of these days. That child is invaluable to the establishment, and I can foresee what she is destined to become."

And Tina was cast for Ariel.

The cast of plays is hung in a glass frame, in a conspicuous part of the green-room. It is the duty of every actor to inspect this cast daily. Concerning its preparation the members of the company are not consulted by the stage-manager. In all well-regulated theatres, however, every actor is entitled to a certain line of business, and cannot be called upon to undertake any character which does not belong to the class for which he is engaged.

Great was Susan's wonder and delight, when, glancing over the cast of the Tempest, she read Tina's name as Ariel! A rehearsal was called, to take place the next day. Away she ran to the stage, in hope that the business of the morning had not yet commenced, and she could communicate the good news to her husband; but the first act had that moment begun. It is an infringement of rules for any person not engaged in rehearsing to cross the stage, or address the prompter, or in any way interfere with his duty. Susan and Robin had been accustomed to adhere strictly to all regulations, not merely from a dread of seeing their names inscribed in the awful forfeit-book, which, in its glaring red cover, lay threateningly on the stage-manager's table, but because obedience was a duty. A strict adherence to duty in trifles rendered easier the fulfilment of duty in matters of importance.

Tina was not needed at the theatre that morning, and there was no one near with whom Susan could share her delight. The happy mother could not speed her way home, and gladden the child with the good intelligence, and bid her commence studying forthwith; for Susan had a small part to rehearse, and could not absent herself. Soon she was summoned to the stage. She delivered her few lines, and had only to play the listener for some time. Then the temptation became so great that she could not forbear drawing nearer to the prompt-table than was customary, and, catching Robin's eye, she whispered, "O, Robin! such good news!"

Robin looked at her inquiringly, and smiled because she smiled; but he was too strict a disciplinarian to induce her to say any more.

At last rehearsal was over, and Susan could give vent to her pent-up feelings of joy. She caught Robin's arm as he was gathering up his books and papers.

"Robin, have you seen the cast of the Tempest? Tina, our Tina, is cast as *Ariel!*"

"Is it possible?—Ariel? Wife, you are dreaming. It is Miss Mellen's part."

"It is our Tina's; they have cast it to her! Come, come, and see!" and she drew him to the green-room, where several of the company were examining the cast. One of them read aloud,

"*Prospero*, Mr. Olderman.

"*Miranda*, Miss Lovelace.

"*Ariel*, Miss Truehart."

Robin and Susan waited not to hear the possible comments. It was true; and, if Tina was successful in this character, as they felt sure she would be, they might look forward to a glorious future for her. Already they began to build castles in the clouds; they pictured her at the topmost pinnacle of her profession, a *star*, released from half the trammels that render the stage an existence of perpetual weariness, trial, mortification, to underlings! More; they painted her, in fancy, independent, rich, bidding adieu to the stage while she was still in the bloom of womanhood; giving her heart to one who was worthy of a woman's boundless devotion, at whose feet she would gladly cast her laurels down, rejoicing, more than she ever rejoiced in wearing them, to feel herself

"—— fit
Beside an unambitious hearth to sit
Domestic queen!"

Upon this vision of the future their minds revelled in a species of mental intoxication. Never had their quiet natures been so stirred, so elated. When they reached home, they could scarcely restrain themselves from confiding to the child all their hopes. But Tina's thoughts were quickly absorbed by the difficulties of the character. With the perception of an artist, she felt the weight of the true artist's responsibility. A few shelves, suspended from the wall, held her little library. Five minutes after her parents entered the room, she was hunting among her books for the Tempest. The rest of that day beheld her seated on a low stool near the window, her head buried in her hands, and the open book upon her knees. She was reading and re-reading, and pondering over Shakspeare's fine poetic creation, and gradually moulding a conception in her own mind. As to the language of Ariel, that was memorized almost unconsciously. High cultivation will impart to the memory of an actor a rapidity in receiving impressions which becomes a kind of mental daguerreotyping.

Tina had no part to enact that evening, and could remain at home. Before Susan left for the theatre, the child begged her to sing the airs which Ariel executes. Fortunately Susan was familiar with all of those peculiarly bewitching and fantastic melodies.

The next morning, before the play was rehearsed, the leader of the orchestra proposed to instruct Miss Truehart in the music. His report to the manager was that she sang with such wonderful fidelity and expression it was a delight to teach her. "And what will it be to hear her at night?" he added, enthusiastically.

"You see, Mr. Tuttle," said Higgins, with a self-congratulating air, "my judgment has proved *somewhat* better than yours, sir."

Mr. Tuttle very humbly admitted the fact, asserting that it was no wonder, for Mr. Higgins' judgment always *was* better than that of anybody else, and nobody was more willing to admit this superiority than Mr. Tuttle himself.

All the theatre was in a state of excitement at the expected performance; for, in spite of the jealousies which seem inseparable from the profession, true genius, once recognized, wins an involuntary reverence. Envy gives place to a species of characteristic generosity, and actors are magnetically attracted towards an individual whose talent surpasses their own.

Even Miss Mellen came to the wing to hear Tina sing at rehearsal, and found no fault except that which was contained in the remark:

"Shakspeare's Ariel was not a child; that 's what makes it ridiculous."

"Ariel was a sprite, a spirit," retorted one of Tina's warm admirers; "and, I suppose, as none of us ever saw a sprite or a spirit either, it would be difficult to give any authority for its not being personated by a wonderfully-gifted child."

A week elapsed, during which the Tempest was rehearsed daily. Then came the appointed night for its performance. The fair, fragile child, in her gossamer robe, looped here and there with sprays of bright sea-weed; with her shining, filmy wings: her floating hair interwound with branches of white and scarlet coral: her girdle and bracelets of shells: looked the island sprite indeed,—a being scarce earthly!

Robin had not seen her Ariel attire, for the piece was one that required the closest attention, and tasked all his powers.

The prompter's seat was a sort of nook on the right of the stage, close to the audience. It is worth describing. A high desk with a tall stool. On one side, five leathern pockets, marked "letters for Act 1st;" "for Act 2d;" "for Act 3d;" "for Act 4th;" "for Act 5th." A sixth pocket, with marriage contracts, parchment wills, and various legal documents. Near the desk are fixtures for turning off gas to darken the stage, or turning it on to increase the light. A speaking-trumpet, through which the prompter directs the musicians. A little bell, the wire of which runs upward into the "flies," and gives notice to elevate or lower the curtain. A second bell, for the descent of golden cars from which mythological personages alight upon the stage, or for the lowering of rose-tinted clouds, where Cupids and other visionary beings make their appearance. Then there is a peep-hole through which the prompter has a view of the stage, and can watch the actors. A second peep-hole (not legitimate), by means of which he can get a bird's-eye view of the audience. Here sat Robin, in the midst of these stage appliances, anxiously waiting until the moment came when Tina half bounded, half glided on the stage, exclaiming to Prospero:

> "All hail, great master! grave sir, hail! I come
> To answer thy best pleasure; be 't to fly,
> To swim, to dive into the fire, to ride
> On the curled clouds; to thy strong bidding task
> Ariel, and all his quality."

Her appearance evoked a tremendous burst from the audience, which reverberated loudly and long. It would be useless to attempt to describe the quaint, original, inimitable acting.

After the scene with Prospero, Ariel next appears luring in Ferdinand, to whose eyes the spirit is supposed to be invisible. Ariel is playing on a lyre-like instrument, and sings:

"Come unto the yellow sands,
And then take hands;
Curtseyed when you have and kissed
(The wild waves whist),
Foot it featly here and there;
And, sweet sprites, the burden bear.
Bur. Hark, hark!
Bough, wough.
The watch-dogs bark:
Hark, hark! I hear
The strain of strutting Chanticleer
Cry cock-a-doodle-doo!"

The very first notes, ringing with silvery clearness from her lips, brought the actors from the green-room to cluster around the wings. At the close of the air, not a few of their hands spontaneously joined in the rapturous applause of the audience. As the melody ceases, Ferdinand says, in a tone of wonder:

"Where should this music be? — I' the air, i' the earth?
It sounds no more, and sure it waits upon
Some god of the island. Sitting on a bank,
Weeping again the king my father's wreck,
This music crept by me on the waters,
Allaying both their fury and my passion,
With its sweet air; thence I have followed it,
Or it hath drawn me, rather — but 't is gone.
No, it begins again!

Ariel sings.

Full fathom five thy father lies;
Of his bones are coral made.
Those are pearls that were his eyes;
Nothing of him that doth fade
But doth suffer a sea change
Into something rich and strange.
Sea-nymphs hourly ring his knell —
Hark! now I hear them — ding, dong, dell!
(*Burden.* Ding, dong, dell!)"

We cannot follow the performance step by step, but hasten to the more important close.

It is usual for Ariel to appear flying across the stage. This flying process is generally performed by *a double,* costumed closely to resemble the true Ariel. It would have been difficult to have found a child that so nearly resembled Tina as to deceive the audience; and to destroy an illusion is to rob any play, especially one highly poetical, of a powerful charm. It was therefore arranged that she should execute the feat herself, but not until the close of the fifth act, when Prospero gives Ariel his liberty.

To produce the appearance of flying, wires, invisible to the spectators, are attached by means of hooks and a strong band to the shoulders and waist of Ariel. The child first mounts a high platform on the right of the stage, behind the scenes; by the aid of pulleys, she is then drawn along the wires, but apparently floated through the air. In this manner she traverses the whole length of the stage. As she passes out of sight of the audience on the left hand, the wires are gently lowered until her feet touch the ground. The sensation experienced is singular, and rather terrifying; but the child of genius was too much absorbed in her part to be susceptible of fear.

The fifth act commenced. Tina had thrown around the audience her most potent spells, singing,

"Where the bee sucks, there suck I;
In a cowslip's bell I lie;
There I couch when owls do cry.
On the bat's back I do fly,
After summer, merrily;

Merrily, merrily, shall I live now,
Under the blossom that hangs on the bough."

Twice more Ariel appears for a few moments; once with the Master and Boatswain amazingly following, and then driving in Caliban, Stephano, and Trinculo. The faithful sprite then receives the promised boon of liberty from Prospero. There is a slight transposition of the original passages to give the performer a few moments to prepare for her aërial travelling. The time allowed is very short. After her exit, Tina bounded up the ladder, closely followed by her watchful mother. Susan had never felt prouder, more exulting, more hopeful, in her life. Alas for such moments in the human heart! Mr. Gildersleaf was standing on the platform. He carefully adjusted the wires to Tina's waist and shoulders, and tested their strength; then gave a signal to the carpenters above. The pulleys were drawn — Ariel appeared before the audience in mid air! The waving of those graceful arms moved the light wings, while the ransomed spirit smiled farewell to the group upon the stage. How the people cheered! Many rose from their seats and leaned forward; the delusion was so perfect it seemed as though she must be winging her flight through the atmosphere without support. The floating form was almost out of sight, when suddenly it stopped. The arms were still waved, and the light wings responded, but the figure remained immovable. The wires in some inexplicable manner had become entangled, the pulleys refused to work; the child — Heaven guard her! she was suspended immediately over one of the side-lights used to illumine the back portion of the stage!

A heart-rending shriek, that pierced every ear, burst from Susan's lips, and gave the first announcement of the impending danger. Regardless of the audience, she dashed frantically across the stage, crying, "Cut the wires! my child, my child! she will be burned to death!"

Beneath the spot where hung the child she fell upon her knees, flinging up her despairing arms, and uttering cry after cry, which broke out from the very depths of her tortured soul.

All was confusion. Numbers of the audience leaped upon the stage, which was now thronged with actors; the carpenters, apparently paralyzed with fear, vainly strove to make the pulleys do their duty.

Mr. Higgins ran from the box-keeper's office, exclaiming, "Save her! that child is the most valuable person in my establishment! A reward for the man that saves her! Save her for my sake—save her!"

Not for the poor child's sake, not for the sake of her agonized parents, but because she was of *value* to *him*, the sordid man offered a reward that her life might be saved. As if humanity contained a monster that would save her for a reward who could have saved her and did not *without!*

Thus far Tina, with wonderful heroism, had remained in a state of stony quietude, though perfectly conscious of her danger. But now the intense pain of her scorching feet, every moment increasing, drew from her the most piteous wails.

And where was Robin? The only person present who retained anything like presence of mind, he had rushed to the property-room, snatched a hatchet, seized the ladder on the right of the stage, dashed down the platform which it supported, and, with a strength imparted by terror, the usually feeble cripple was seen bearing the heavy ladder across the stage as powerfully as though it were held in a Titanic grasp. He placed it beside his child, mounted as lightning flashes, severed the wires with strong blows of the hatchet, and caught the child in his arms just as her gauzy raiment became one sheet of flame. Fortunately, he had not loosed from his neck the cloak which he always wore at night, to protect him against the draughts that whistled around his exposed seat. The child was quickly enveloped in its ample folds, and the flames extinguished.*

There was a physician among the crowd of people who, in the hope of rendering assistance, had gathered upon the stage. Accompanied by him, Tina was borne to the green-room — but, O! what a spectacle for her mother's eyes! Her tiny silver slippers were literally burned from her feet, and a large portion of the silk stockinet which encased her limbs was also consumed, and showed how the flames had fed on her delicate flesh.

Excruciating were the little girl's sufferings while the stockinet was gradually removed, yet less terrible than those of her parents. Susan would not yield up her child to other hands, though her own

* The idea naturally suggests itself that this accident might have been prevented by the immediate turning off of the gas; but the incident took place as related, and not one person in a crowded theatre remembered that the child could be saved by this simple process.

shook violently as they performed the trying offices. Tina, ever thoughtful of her mother, in spite of the torturing pain uttered not a single cry, and only now and then an irrepressible moan escaped her lips. The oil with which the burns were immediately bathed produced a soothing effect, and her mangled limbs were now covered with raw cotton, and tenderly bound up. She lay upon a small sofa, from which it was found impossible to remove her without danger. Dr. Welldon ordered her to remain undisturbed that night.

With what altered feelings Susan and Robin sat down to watch beside her! Their exulting pride had suddenly been changed almost to despair. Yet were their hearts full of thankfulness that the child's life had been spared. But the shock to her constitution must be so great, those burns were so terrible, might she not yet die? Neither dared ask that question, but it shone in the eyes of both when they looked into each other's faces for comfort.

After pity, curiosity, and interest, had all been satisfied, the green-room was gradually deserted, save by Susan and Robin. They sat together, hand clasped in hand, the whole of that long, fearful night, watching their child. An opiate had caused a half-sleep, but pain did not seem wholly lulled. She lay with her eyes partly open, for their shining blue glittered through the long lashes; her breath was labored, and now and then she flung her arms from side to side, and feebly groaned.

The kind physician returned soon after daylight, and ordered the little sufferer to be carried upon the sofa to her home. Mr. Gildersleaf and one of the carpenters, who had remained in the theatre all night, would have borne her; but the poor hunchback insisted that he himself must aid. Tina was covered with shawls; — the father took the head of the couch, and the sympathizing "property-man" the foot, and they set out. Susan walked by the side of her child. The carpenter followed, for he well knew that Robin's strength would give way. It was too early in the morning to meet any but a few stragglers, and these paused in surprise and pity, and some asked questions of the carpenter. One woman said to another, as they passed, "That 's the poor little lamb who was nearly burned to death last night. She looks as white as if she were dying now."

What words for the mother's ears!

Robin heard them also; they curdled his blood, and took from his limbs their little remaining strength.

"Set her down, Gildersleaf! I can't — I can't take another step!"

They set down the sofa. Tina was now quite conscious; the fresh morning air had revived her. She opened her eyes, and said, in a faint tone, "I am better, father; I 'm so glad you 're taking me home!"

The carpenter now occupied Robin's place, and Robin walked beside Susan, who sorely needed his support. As she clung to his arm, she whispered, "That woman said she was so *white*, that — that — but she 's always *white*, Robin, dear; you know she 's so fair! She 's not *whiter* than usual, is she?"

In a few moments they were at the door of their humble lodgings. The sofa was carried up that narrow stair with some difficulty, and at last the prompter's family were once more in their own neat but poverty-betokening room. Tina uttered no groan as her father lifted her up and laid her tenderly on the bed, though every movement rendered her sufferings more acute.

"Ah, my *birdie!* my *birdie!* this is a terrible blow to fall on you!" said the anguished parent.

"Father," she whispered, "did you not tell me good comes out of every affliction which we bear *patiently?* I mean to be patient; O, so *patient,* if you and mother will help me!"

"We *will* help you, my own *birdie!* We will all be *patient,* and the Lord will not take thee, our only treasure, away from us! No, he will not!"

"Not — not unless it be for your best good and for mine, father!" replied the child.

The poor prompter bowed his head. They were his own teachings, — could he rebel?

CHAPTER VI.

A Mother's Vigils. — Mr. Higgins' Rule concerning Invalids. — Sympathy of the Charitable. — Visit of the Sunday-school Teacher. — The Mother's Pang of Jealousy. — Reticence. — Convalescence. — Susan's Return to the Theatre. — First Glance at the Place of Peril. — Tina at Kew Gardens. — The Child's First Recognition of Nature. — A Relapse. — The Hunchback's Fears for his Wife. — Two Minds in One. — The Seasons of Love.

When Dr. Welldon visited Robin Truehart's humble lodgings that day, he found Tina in a heavy sleep; but her sharp, quick breathing, the crimson spot on either cheek, betokened the presence of high fever. The doctor's whispered inquiries and his light touch upon her throbbing pulse aroused her. She opened wide her large eyes, now shining with unusual lustre, but they looked vacantly around. Her mother bent tenderly over her, but no answer came to her anxious questions. Then suddenly the child raised herself on her pillows, and broke out in song. The liquid notes rang through the chamber, as she warbled,

> "Where the bee sucks there suck I;
> In a cowslip's bell I lie!"

Susan no longer wept or trembled. Her bending, reed-like nature rose up strong and firm under the heavy pressure of this trial. Her tears were petrified by the greatness of her affliction. With an unfaltering step she followed the physician from the chamber.

"Doctor, will she *live?* will my child *live?*" was all she said, and the words were uttered in a calm tone.

"I trust so," was his evasive answer. The mother's fear-quickened perception construed the reply aright.

At that moment the child's voice again struck on her ear,

> "Under the blossom that hangs on the bough,
> That hangs on the bough, that hangs on the bough!"

sang Tina. The day before Susan would have thought it impossible that she could shudder at the sound of that delicious melody. She returned to the bed-side of the child, who now sank back oppressed with sleep, now started up, murmuring snatches of Ariel's song —

> "Ding, dong, dell! — ding, dong, dell!"

She repeated that burden, the knell sang by the sea-nymphs, over and over, until Susan at last felt as though the whole universe were filled with that one haunting sound, that melodious knell. She heard it when the child's lips were mute; night and day it echoed in her ears, and drowned all other tones.

The accident occurred on Monday, and through that long week Robin had to fulfil his duties at the theatre as usual. Susan kept her sleepless vigils beside the couch of the child. Her engagement was, of course, relinquished; with it her salary and Tina's. It was Mr. Higgins' rule not to pay salaries to actors who were indisposed or disabled. If he were to do that, he argued, his company would always be *dangerously ill*—he would keep a hospital, not a theatre. It is true that Tina had so won her way into some accessible corner of his cold heart that he experienced a strong desire to make her a solitary exception to this stern law. It was not without a secret pang that he decided against the act of liberality, as injurious to his theatrical discipline. But he quieted his conscience by sending the mother a message of condolence, accompanied by a guinea.

With this diminution of their weekly salary, and the great increase of expenses consequent on Tina's illness, the situation of the Trueharts would have been one of fearful privation, but for the beneficence of strangers who were interested in the child's public career. Not a few noble ladies despatched their maids or footmen to Robin Truehart's dwelling with messages of sympathy, money, dainties for the sick, fine linen for the dressing of the little girl's burns, &c. &c. One thoughtful lady furnished Tina with a small elastic bed,—an especial comfort to the suffering child. Tina had been accustomed to share the couch of her parents; and so great was their fear of disturbing her, that until this welcome gift arrived neither father nor mother, since the night of that fatal accident, had lain down. A few benevolent ladies, not content with intrusting the mission of charity to their domestics, called themselves; but these visits were a tax upon Susan's patience, rather than a consolation to her. It distressed her to answer the numerous queries of curiosity or kindness. She needed all her thoughts, all her time, for her child. The members of the company were not behindhand in their warmly-tendered sympathy, their proffers of assistance in ministering to the youthful patient; but Susan would not allow any one to share her maternal duties; she could not bear her child to receive a cup of water from the hand of another.

In a few days the fever abated, and Tina's consciousness returned. Though she was too feeble to speak, the grateful smile which repaid every office of love brought sunshine back to her mother's heart.

Meantime Miss Amory learned from the public journals that her favorite pupil's life had been in danger. At first she hesitated about visiting the lodgings of a poor actress, one of that class she had been taught to contemn; but true charity conquered the scruples of an unworthy prejudice. As she opened the door of the little apartment, Tina uttered an exclamation of delight, and stretched out her arms towards her young preceptress.

"O! I knew you would come!" she feebly murmured. "Miss Lucy, that is my dear mother; and," she added, in a whisper, her eyes filling with tears as she recalled the scene at Sunday-school, "she 's not '*shocking,*' but good—heavenly good!"

Miss Amory greeted Susan cordially, and told her that she had come to assist in tending the beloved little invalid.

Susan could not decline her services, for she knew

that they would be welcome to the child; but a jealous pang shot through her heart.

"You look very much worn out, Mrs. Truehart," remarked the young girl, in a tone of sympathy.

"Do not think of me," answered Susan; "now that I dare to hope my child will recover, I shall have all the strength I need."

From that time Miss Amory came daily, and spent many hours with her former pupil. The kind-hearted girl read to her, conversed with her, amused her. Susan sat silently by. It was not easy for her to talk to strangers at any time; but now she shrank more than ever within herself. She remembered Miss Amory's prejudices against the stage, but had not sufficient strength of character to enable her to combat them. In the most distant corner of the room, half concealed by a friendly window-curtain, sat the mother, hiding her emotions when she found her place occupied by another. Through those long daily visits she chid her own heart for its discontent, and repeated internally, over and over again, "My child is happier when Miss Lucy comes; what matter for *me?*"

At the end of a month Tina was pronounced out of danger; but it was obvious that some time must elapse before she could resume her profession. The liberal donations now ceased; those formerly received had been expended. Robin's family had only his small salary to depend upon. This could not meet the weekly outlay. Susan found herself unable to purchase the expensive medicines ordered by the physician. From that moment she said mentally, "I must to work again. O, what a heavy heart I shall carry to the theatre! But I must work that my little one may not want!"

Mrs. Gildersleaf offered to watch beside Tina during her mother's absence. The good landlady's presence was seldom needed, for Miss Amory came regularly at the hour for rehearsal, and remained until Susan's return. In the evening, before the latter left for the theatre, Miss Lucy was again at her post.

The first morning that Susan reëntered the theatre, when she stood upon the stage, and cast her eyes up to the spot where Tina had been suspended almost in the embrace of death, her blood suddenly congealed, her pulses ceased to beat, the place swam and then grew dark; she tried to take a step towards Robin, but fell senseless on the ground. She had fainted, for the first time in her life.

When consciousness returned, she found herself lying on the green-room sofa (the same sofa on which Tina had been conveyed to her lodgings). Robin supported her head, and a crowd of actors and actresses were kindly ministering to her.

"Ah! Sue, I felt just the same when I looked up to that fatal place. But cheer up, wife, for our *birdie* is spared to us," whispered her husband.

And Susan was comforted, and in a short time declared herself able to return to the stage. Robin seated her on a chair by one of the wings, and returned to his station at the prompter's table. Inadvertently he had chosen the very spot where she sat watching the rehearsal of Pizarro when Tina first enacted Cora's child. How well she remembered that day, and her own terror at the comparatively slight peril in which her child was then placed! She thanked Heaven that the veil of the future had not been lifted, and that no presage of a more terrible evil had entered her soul. The call-boy's summons aroused her from her revery, and, with a slow, staggering step, she "walked through" her trifling part.

Another month passed, and still another; and, at the end of the third month, Tina once more breathed the fresh air, and beheld the blue sky. At her young teacher's invitation, she was conveyed in an easy carriage to Kew Gardens. Little knew the poor child-actress of the wondrous beauties of nature. She had never dreamed of such a paradise as these gardens revealed to her. The memorable mammoth grape-vine, the extensive conservatories, the picturesque shrubberies, the magnificent old trees, the profusion of gorgeous flowers,—all these were a marvel. The flowers to which her young eyes had been too well accustomed were fabricated of bright tissue-paper or colored cambric; the "cut woods" were manufactured of canvas bedaubed with *impossible* trees; the stage groves and gardens she had nightly moved among were things of paint, and glare, and gaudiness. She saluted nature with a burst of joyous greeting, a loving recognition, though nature had heretofore been known only through a rudely-painted image. The child almost flew about, drinking in the balmy air, basking in the sunshine, kissing the flowers which she was not permitted to pluck, now lifting up her arms and her sweet face in mute wonder, her ecstasy now gushing forth in song. Her long-lost buoyancy of spirit, for the moment restored, vented itself in music. It was only a short period since she had been able to walk again, and generally the effort of taking a few steps caused her pain. But she was conscious of neither weakness nor suffering as she darted about over the lawn, until the buttercups had showered her feet with yellow dust, and she bade Miss Amory look at the golden slippers the flowers had given her.

At last she grew weary from the unwonted exercise, and lay down, with her head resting on Miss Lucy's lap, beneath the shade of a branching oak, catching glimpses of the sky through the wind-shaken foliage, and singing without pause,— singing as the birds sing, from that gleefulness within which turns to melody.

After they had passed several hours in this manner, the young Sunday-school teacher warned her companion that it was time to return; but Tina could not tear herself away from this newly-found elysium. She pleaded for a few moments more, and still a few moments more, until the trees began to cast long shadows, and the roseate light grew gray, and the perfumed air became slightly chilly. Then she was reluctantly conducted back to the carriage.

Her exuberant spirits sustained her while the excitement lasted, but a reäction succeeded its removal. That night the fever returned with increased violence. No words of blame were uttered by Tina's parents; but Miss Amory could not forgive her own unconscious imprudence. Her attention, her devotions, were redoubled. She was now seldom absent from the child's couch; she literally spent her days at Robin Truehart's lodgings.

In a few weeks the young sufferer rallied. Those beautiful gardens were forever a haunting memory stored up in her mind, but she did not ask to see them again. She seemed to be aware that her joy had not been temperate; she had been intoxicated by the exhilarating air, the pastoral sights and sounds; she had revelled in them until the golden rule of moderation was forgotten.

"I must not run any more risks, or ask for any more indulgences; I must get well and go to work again," she would often say. "How ill my poor mother looks! If I could only work, and let her rest!"

The anxieties of the last few months had wrought an alarming change in Susan. Her cheeks were daily growing more hollow; her weary eyes were deeply sunken, and circled with dark rings; her form, always slight, was becoming emaciated. Robin's watchful eyes saw the sad transition, and there was a mysterious admonition in his heart, — a foreboding of ill, which he could not stifle. He marked how wearily she went through her allotted duties; to what a faint key her voice had sunk; how uncertain her steps became. She never complained, and to his tender inquiries always answered that she was well, she did not suffer, she was very happy — was not her child recovering? She was so blessed in all things that she asked of her heavenly Father no added blessings; she only prayed to become worthier of receiving those she enjoyed.

Robin gazed upon her earnestly. Her cheek was so very pale, her eyes so dim, her whole mien pervaded by such an air of languor, that he could not help saying, "Then you are *not* suffering or grieving, Sue? You would not *hide* it from me, if you were?"

"Hide it? No, Robin, I have never concealed anything from you in my life!"

And it was true. Within her guileless heart there were no secret chambers, no curtained depths, which veiled the inmost sanctuary from her husband's eyes. Unlike as were these twain in all external appearances, there was a similitude of soul which daily joined them more and more closely together. The silver links of perfect sympathy had never been broken, or even jarred; the eyes of both were fixed on the same goal; the feet of both walked in the same path; all their thoughts were in unison; their faith was planted on the same rock; their knees bowed to the same God; theirs was the union of two minds whose strong affinity drew them into one. Not that their love was a dull, unvarying stream, gliding in smooth *monotony*. It passed through soft gradations into Love's different seasons, every one more perfect than the other, — seasons that are exquisitely described by one of our country's minstrels, in these lines:

"The *Spring-time* of love
Is both happy and gay,
For joy sprinkles blossoms
And balm in our way;
The sky, earth, and ocean,
In beauty repose,
And all the bright future
Is *couleur de rose!*

"The *Summer* of love
  Is the bloom of the heart,
When hill, grove, and valley,
  Their music impart;
And the pure glow of heaven
  Is seen in fond eyes,
And lakes show the rainbow
  That 's hung in the skies.

"The *Autumn* of love
  Is the season of cheer, —
Life's mild Indian summer,
  The smile of the year,
Which comes when the golden
  Ripe harvest is stored,
And yields its own blessing, —
  Repose and reward.

"The *Winter* of love
  Is the beam that we win,
While the storm scowls without,
  From the sunshine within.
Love's reign is eternal,
  The heart is his throne,
And he has all seasons
  Of life for his own!" *

* G. P. Morris.

CHAPTER VII.

Ill Effects of Mental Precocity. — Preparation for Christmas Pantomime. — Mr. Higgins' Visit and Proposition. —Tina resuming her Profession. —"Boxing Night." —The Fairy Queen. —The Pantomime. — The Child's Power of Will. — Last Night of the Pantomime.— The Last Painful Effort. — The Old Property-Room. — The Adieus. — Mr. Higgins and the Young Actress. —Stage Clothes laid aside for the Last Time. — King John. — The Prompter's Agony. — Blistered Pages of the Prompt-Book. — Susan forced to enact Patience in Henry the Eighth. — Toilet made by the Bedside of her Child.—The Young Sunday-school Teacher helping to robe the Actress.— Hymn sung by Patience to Queen Katharine, as she dies.—The Mother's Return Home.— Singing the same Hymn to her Child.—Robin's Entrance.— The Last Hymn. —Tina's Release.—The Mother's Last Offices. —Unnatural Strength giving way. — Robin's Parting Declaration.— Reunion of Mother and Child.— Self-Renunciation. — The Prompter's Victory.

Five months had elapsed since the night of the appalling catastrophe. Tina had not regained her former elastic vigor, but she persuaded herself and her parents that she was restored to health. Had her constitution been strengthened during these first seven years of her life by a close obedience to physical laws, the recuperative powers inherent in childhood might have effected a thorough restoration. It now became evident that the high cultivation of her precocious mind had sapped the springs of vitality. Her so-called recovery was simply toe healing of the burns, the returned facility of locomotion; not the ruddy glow, the bounding pulse, the functional activity, of positive health.

Christmas was approaching. The usual pantomime which celebrates the Christmas festivities was in preparation. One character Mr. Tuttle found difficult to "cast," — that of a Fairy Queen, whose duty it was to transform the young lovers, for certain disobedient conduct, into the customary Columbine and Harlequin, and metamorphose the crabbed fathers into Clown and Pantaloon. The fairy was only required to exhibit herself at intervals during the pantomime, and pronounce a few doggerel lines, as she dispensed her favors or dealt out retributive justice. The rôle was one technically called a "light part," but demanding "judicious" representation. Mr. Higgins became particularly anxious that this Fairy Queen might be personated by Tina. His audiences had fallen off, of late; her return to the stage would give a new impetus to his flagging business; she would be an especial attraction to the merry juveniles who thronged his boxes during the holiday season.

Mr. Higgins himself called at the lodgings of the Trueharts, and made the proposition to the child. She at once declared herself quite able to resume her duties. The manager left the house exulting.

The Fairy Queen first appears surrounded by her attendants, Coral-branch, Dewdrop, Roselips, Cowslip, Twinkle-star, Rainbow. Susan was cast as Coral-branch; she would have the felicity of standing on the stage beside her child, — a privilege rendered doubly dear by long privation.

Tina had not entered the theatre since the night of the accident, yet she betrayed no emotion at the first rehearsal of the pantomime. Perhaps she was too feeble to be subject to excitement, or it might be the love of her art returned with a strong tide that swept away painful recollections. She always experienced a deep internal satisfaction when the gifts with which she was endowed were brought into use.

She was welcomed joyfully by the whole company. Coldness, indifference, professional jealousy, all had melted away in the general sympathy awakened by her sufferings. Her presence seemed to spread gladness wherever she passed; scenic artists, carpenters, scene-shifters, door-keepers, dressers, basket-carriers, all left their employments, to throng around her and rejoice over her return.

"Boxing night," as it is termed, arrived. It is the night succeeding Christmas, — the first on which the theatre is opened after its regular close for a fortnight or three weeks, during the preparation of the pantomime. On Christmas eve and on Christmas night there is no performance in any theatre in England, — a rule not observed in America.

According to old-established usage, some gloomy, terror-inspiring tragedy always precedes the pantomime. George Barnwell, Jane Shore, Bertram, Douglass, Venice Preserved, are greatly in vogue on these occasions. But, although the tragedy is expected, nay, *required*, by the audience, and faithfully represented by the actors, to not one single sentence do the occupants of pit, gallery, or boxes, ever listen. The two former keep up a continual uproar, which would not be tolerated on any other night. Sometimes humorous conversations are shouted out between the individuals aloft and their acquaintances below. No attempt is ever made to prevent this violation of decorum. It is one of the traditional licenses of "boxing night." The tumult continues until the pantomime commences; and then, strange to say, a dead silence, only broken by occasional peals of laughter, reigns through the theatre. Silence while the performance on the stage is principally in dumb show; a deafening clamor while the tragic actors are straining their lungs to render audible their wrongs, miseries, and heroic resolves.

Once more Susan arrayed her child in the glittering apparel of the stage. Many and many a time did she kiss those poor little feet, now covered with purple scars, before she drew on the silken stockinet and tied the silver slippers. But when she tried to fasten the transparent wings on her child's shoulders, an icy bolt shot through her heart; she thought of those Ariel wings that had turned to wings of flame; her trembling hands wholly refused to perform their office. She turned away her blanched face, and silently motioned to the dresser to secure the fairy appendages.

When she was equipped, Tina stole to her father's side, and attracted his attention by gently touching him with her silver wand. As he dropped his book to take her for a moment in his arms, a deep shadow passed over his face, and he looked upwards as though internally praying for strength to bear some impending affliction.

The theatre was densely crowded; the tragedy

was over. The pantomime commenced. In the second scene the Fairy Queen is discovered in a crystal bower, surrounded by her nymphs. Tina's appearance was the signal for a perfect hurricane of acclamations. While she curtseyed in acknowledgment, Susan, who was standing beside her as Coralbranch, could not help glancing at the round, rosy, laughing faces that clustered in the boxes, and contrasting them with the pallid, wasted child, who received the juvenile greeting with a languid inclination and a faint smile. This prolonged clapping of little dimpled hands, this rapturous welcome, was all in honor of Susan's precious one; and yet it struck upon the mother's ears with a sound of mockery—her heart sank as it never sank before.

When the boisterous greeting was over, the pantomime continued. Tina's rôle was not one that displayed her dramatic abilities, yet the audience was predetermined to be delighted with her most trifling efforts. Her step had lost its springiness, her movements were undulating but nerveless, her voice was low and tremulous, its clear, ringing tone had quite gone; yet all these losses seemed to have no effect upon her popularity.

There was a deal of laughter elicited by Matthews' humorous clown. "Hot Codlins," as usual, excited the riotous mirth of the pit. Pantaloon was duly buffeted and bullied; the stereotyped traditional jokes played off upon him created as much amusement as though they had not been repeated every Christmas since the grandfathers and grandmothers present were chubby urchins themselves. Columbine and Harlequin and Sprite danced through the scenes at unanticipated moments, and there was a liberal expenditure of blue and red fire at the grand *finale,* when the Fairy Queen ascended in a gilded car.

Accidents had been carefully guarded against; everything passed off smoothly. But Tina was thoroughly exhausted by her light exertions. Unable to walk, she was carried home in her father's arms, and remained for a long time in a state of semi-consciousness.

After the first night's performance a pantomime is not again rehearsed. This was fortunate for Tina. She lay almost motionless the whole of that next day, with wan cheeks and lustreless eyes, that bespoke her utter prostration. Yet, as evening drew near, she roused herself with a strong effort, and rose cheerfully, and said she was better, and ready to go to the theatre.

"Are you able, my darling?" asked her mother, sadly.

"I *must* be *able,* mother dear; for they have no substitute, and the pantomime can't go on without the Fairy Queen."

The little girl went through her part with minute carefulness; but her actions were all mechanical, and bore little resemblance to her former fresh and spirited delineations. Her fatigue was not so great as on the previous evening; to use a theatrical expression, she was "getting back into the traces."

The pantomime "ran" thirty nights, and every night the heroic child conquered her languor, and went through her duties without a murmur. But she faded visibly; her attenuated form seemed the lightest, most transparent fleshly temple that could enshrine an immortal soul.

The pantomime was announced for the last time. Tina found herself scarcely able to totter through the first scene. She struggled,—struggled desperately,—the words died away unuttered on her parched and powerless lips. Then she smiled mournfully, and shook her head; those who were acting with her comprehended the signal; they no longer waited for their *cues*, but spoke when she was unable to proceed.

Mr. Gildersleaf stood watching her at the wing. From her earliest infancy she had entwined herself closely about his honest heart. He now left his post, and hurried to the back of the stage, behind the scenes. There stood the bed used for Juliet's chamber. With thoughtful kindness, he took the small mattress, and carried it to the old property-room. As Tina staggered from the stage into her mother's arms, the good man lifted her up gently, and carried her to the couch he had prepared. And there she lay, in that same "property-room," where, nearly seven years ago, she had lain an unconscious infant, about to be launched upon the life of weariness and toil which seemed her heritage. There, in the selfsame corner, stood the old cradle, somewhat hacked and scratched, in which she had been placed as Dot's baby. And there was the young mother kneeling beside her, even as she had knelt upon that memorable night; and now, as then, hopes and fears were struggling for mastery in that fond maternal heart. But hopes seemed then victorious; fears had now gained the vantage-ground.

"You cannot finish the part, my child,— it is impossible," said Susan.

"I must try, mother, I must try; it is only to-night; and this will be the last night of the pantomime,— the last night of——" She saw her mother's look of anguish, and did not finish the sentence.

Restoratives were administered, and the child gradually revived. One after another the members of the company stole in to catch a glimpse of the general favorite. She spoke to them in turn, but in such a strange, solemn manner that some thought her mind was wandering; and to every one she bade a last, tender farewell.

Even Mr. Higgins made his way to the property-room.

"Come, little music-shell, we must get you well again before long. We shall have to put another little girl into Prince Arthur to-morrow night, and she can't hold a candle to you; but your father says it 's not possible for you to attempt the part. What do *you* think?"

How could Mr. Higgins have asked that question of the almost lifeless child? The dominant passion was never silent! The voice of *interest* was stronger within his breast than the pleadings of humanity; he would have encouraged the public's darling to make a mad attempt for his benefit, at the obvious risk of her very life.

"I fear not, sir; I wish I could get through it, but I fear I shall never act again."

"Nonsense, nonsense! Don't talk so! You 're only a little low-spirited and worn out. We 'll soon have you as bright as a button, stirring up the people until they almost drive the old roof off the house with their clapping. Never fear,—we 'll soon set you to rights."

"But if not—if—if I am going away, as I think I am,—if I never see you again, don't forget what I now beg. Be kind to my poor father, my dear mother; they will miss *me* so much!"

"Miss you? We should all miss you, the sweetest music-shell, and 'the noblest Roman of them all.' But we 're not going to miss you; we won't consent to anything of the kind."

"We must all consent to the will of God!" replied Tina, in a tone so full of grave humility that even this ungodly man could not frame a reply. There was something shining in his hard eyes as he gazed at her. It could scarcely be called a tear, but it was the first moisture those eyes had known for years.

The call-boy stood at the door,—"Fairy Queen called."

Tina rose with difficulty, and Susan, who seemed too much exhausted herself to remonstrate in Mr. Higgins' presence, reädjusted the light wings, and smoothed the spangled dress. Mr. Higgins—a wonderful condescension on his part—took the child's hand and led her to the wing. How she went through the scenes that remained was a matter of wonder to herself. Strength seemed imparted according to her need, and she resolutely roused herself to make one last effort.

The pantomime was over; Tina's stage-clothes had been thrown aside for the last time; she was at home again, and Dr. Welldon standing beside her couch.

"It may be temporary exhaustion,—she may revive," were his comforting words to the parents.

Robin knew better, Susan knew better, but neither gave voice to their fears.

The next morning it appeared as though the doctor might be right, for she rallied wonderfully; yet Robin was not deceived.

The play that night was King John, and the poor prompter, with his thoughts full of his dying child, was forced to prompt a play replete with passages that rent his soul. Every word uttered by the new Prince Arthur brought back Tina's tones, her looks, her pretty actions, the bursts of applause that they had evoked. Robin could hardly keep his seat. But, when Queen Constance broke forth in her frantic lamentation,

> "Grief fills the room up of my absent child,
> Lies in his bed, walks up and down with me;
> Puts on his pretty looks, repeats his words,
> Remembers me of all his gracious parts,
> Stuffs out his vacant garments with his form;
> Then have I reason to be fond of grief!"

the wretched prompter dropped his head upon the book, and wept uncontrollably. When that book was used, long years afterwards, who that saw those blistered pages divined with what tears they had been scalded?

On his return home, he found Tina and her mother lying side by side, talking cheerfully. It was so pleasant to have a night of rest away from the exciting sights and sounds that appertain to a theatre! Robin stooped down to receive their united caresses, and for a moment he forgot the menacing clouds about to burst on his head.

Henry the Eighth was the tragedy selected for the ensuing night. Susan was cast as Patience, the attendant of Queen Katharine. In act third Patience sings to the queen when "her soul grows sad with troubles," and in act fourth she sings the hymn which precedes Queen Katharine's death; a hymn introduced on the stage, though, according to the Shakespearian text, solemn music is played, and a sort of spirit dance mutely enacted.

The character of Patience was not of sufficient consequence for Miss Mellen to be persuaded to undertake its personation, and there was no one else in the theatre but Susan to whom the music could be intrusted.

And she must leave her child, the child whose earthly hours she feared would be so few, to appear upon the stage — to sing!

Never had inexorable duty made a harder requirement. There was no appeal from its stern demands; she prepared to depart. Instead of dressing at the theatre, according to her usual custom, she hurriedly arrayed herself at home. No mirror reflected her form as she donned the flowing white robe and graceful drapery suited to the queen's handmaiden. She stood at the foot of the little bed, gazing upon the child, while her unsteady fingers fastened the bands, clasped the girdle, and looped the long pendent sleeves. Miss Amory entered when the task was nearly completed. With instinctive kindness she offered to assist Susan, and the latter did not refuse her services. It was a singular sight, the young Sunday-school teacher, who regarded a theatre with horror, helping to attire the actress for her part. Singular, but, in thy angelic light, heaven-born Charity, how beautiful!

"I shall be back soon, though it will seem long," said Susan, pressing her feverish lips to her child's chilly brow.

"Go, mother! Miss Lucy will stay with me! Go, dear mother, and don't think of me any more than you can help."

Susan opened the door, but twice returned for one more parting kiss, then tore herself away.

An actress of high distinction personated Queen Katharine. The queen's death is one of the most touchingly eloquent scenes upon the stage. Who cannot picture to themselves Susan's emotion, as she sang, to Handel's solemn, awe-inspiring music, the words:

> "Angels, ever bright and fair,
> Take, O, take her to your care;
> Speed to your own courts her flight,
> Clad in robes of virgin white!"

Queen Katharine wakes at the close of the strain, exclaiming,

> "Spirits of peace, where are ye? Are ye all gone?
> And leave me here in wretchedness behind ye?
> * * * * * * * *
> Saw you not, even now, a blessed troop
> Invite me to a banquet; whose bright faces
> Cast thousand beams upon me, like the sun?
> They promised me eternal happiness;

And brought me garlands, Griffith, which I feel
I am not worthy yet to wear ; I shall
Assuredly."

Queen Katharine dies. Her death takes place in the fourth act of the play, and Patience appears no more. Susan neither waited for an escort nor to change her dress, but, wrapping herself in a mantle, hastily bade Robin adieu, and ran home as swiftly as her strength permitted.

There was a fifth act, and a short after-piece, and Robin could not leave until these were over.

As Susan entered the room, Miss Amory took leave; her carriage had been waiting some time.

Tina's eyes shone with supernatural light as they rested on her mother.

"Ah! mother, you are back! I see you again — you will not leave me any more? It seemed so long, and I am so cold; sometimes the room grows dark, then it is suddenly lighted up. I wanted you, my mother, wanted to see you *once* more! Will father be here soon?" The words were gasped out with difficulty, for her breath came rapidly and unevenly.

"O, my child! my child!"

"Don't weep, mother, — you know *it must be!* Don't weep, or perhaps in that other world I shall think of your tears, and not rejoice enough that the Lord has called me. Mother, that heavenly world! All day I have been seeing in my mind those lovely Kew Gardens, the most beautiful sight I ever saw; and that world must be even more beautiful! And you will meet me there, mother!"

"O, I trust so! — soon, very soon; and in time

your father will come, too!" Susan had ceased to weep.

"Now I love to see you, mother, you are so calm — so like yourself. The pain is all passing from me; my heart is so light! Mother, sing me the hymn you sang to-night to Queen Katharine before she died."

Susan's voice was firmer and clearer than it had been on the stage as she sang to her dying child:

"Angels, ever bright and fair,
Take, O, take her to your care;
Speed to your own courts her flight,
Clad in robes of virgin white!"

A portion of the strain is repeated many times, and the music is majestically slow. When the last notes died away, Susan and her child both seemed rapt in holy meditation, — a species of heavenly trance, which remained unbroken until Robin opened the door.

"O, father, father! you are come!" and Tina rose up, and almost leaped into his extended arms.

"My mother, sing to me now once more! Sing the hymn we heard last Sabbath, and which we all love so well; and, father, you will sing to me, too, will you not?"

Susan sang, and Robin's manly voice joined in, unfalteringly.

"Happy soul, secure from harm,
Guarded by thy Shepherd's arm,
Who thy quiet can molest?
Who can violate thy rest?
Jesus doth thy spirit bear,
Far remove each anxious care.

"Shepherd, with thy tenderest love,
Guide me to the fold above!
Let me hear thy gentle voice;
More and more in thee rejoice;
From thy fulness grace receive,
Ever in thy spirit live!

"Filled by thee, my cup o'erflows,
For thy love no limit knows;
Guardian angels, ever nigh,
Lead and draw my soul on high;
Constant to my latest end,
Thou my footsteps wilt attend.

"Jesus, with thy presence blest,
Death is life, and labor rest;
Guide me while I draw my breath,
Guard me through the gate of death;
And, at last, O, may I stand
With the sheep at thy right hand!"

While they still sang, a change passed over the child's countenance; paler it could not grow, but its pallor became transparent. The limbs quivered slightly, and then were extended to their utmost length; the eyes opened wide, as though they saw something invisible to others; she smiled seraphically, and then her features gradually assumed a marble-like rigidity; there was a gurgling, rattling sound in her throat, which the music did not wholly drown; the hands clasped upon her bosom slowly relaxed,—all was very still.

Father and mother saw all, heard all. But they sang on; they feared to disturb the parting spirit by a word of anguish, a rebellious look; they sang on, and neither wept. The hymn ended. They knew that the angel of death had borne away their child before its close. Susan fell upon her husband's breast, and was folded to his heart in one long embrace. Then she calmly turned to the child, and kissed the icy lips many times, and motioned Robin to do the same. They stood side by side, gazing on the angelic countenance, but it was not until kind Mrs. Gildersleaf entered the room that either found utterance.

Then Susan closed the glazing eyes, bound up the falling chin, and, in spite of Mrs. Gildersleaf's remonstrances, insisted on performing the last offices. She had not once thought of herself, or even cast aside her stage attire. She robed the pure limbs in white vesture, smoothed the bright hair for the last time, wound its soft rings around her fingers, folded the tiny, transparent hands upon the cold breast, and fastened them together with a white ribbon. But, when all was over, when there was no more that *could* be done for her child, her unnatural strength gave way with a sudden shock, and she was seized with violent convulsions.

"I knew it! O, I knew it! Thou hast taken thy flight, my *birdie*, and she will follow thee!" groaned Robin, as he gently chafed the clenched hands.

The convulsions lasted several hours, and when they ceased the seal of death was on her dewy brow. She faintly returned the clasp of Robin's hand.

"How hard, how hard for *you!*" she said; "you will be so desolate; for — I — am going — too!"

"Going to be with her,— going to our child! Going to receive the rich reward of all your gentle goodness! No, no; I will not, I *do not* wish it otherwise. Don't think of me; it is wise so, best so! You will suffer no more, will labor no more; you will be happy! I am content! I yield you up, my wife, my heart's love, as I did her! I bless the Lord for the strength he gives me to yield up *both*, my life's sole treasures, to his will!"

Susan could not reply. Again a convulsive spasm distorted her features. The struggle was short, but violent. When it ceased, her face was calm as that of the child, which appeared to be slumbering on its own little bed, her limbs as composed, her frame as pulseless. Mother and child were reünited!

For thee, poor hunchbacked prompter, with thy great, upright soul, not bowed to earth, but lifted heavenward by thy mighty sorrows, go on thy way unmurmuring! Toil! suffer! struggle! plod through thy thankless duties day by day, night by night! Let the bigot revile thy calling, the self-righteous "pass by on the other side," the ignorant stigmatize thee,—what matters it? Thou hast taken up thy cross, and borne it manfully! Thine was the true heroism of self-renunciation! Thine the heaven-descended love, that preferred the joy of those beloved to thine own, that willingly accepted misery as the purchase of their felicity! Thine will be the crown of glory, worn in eternal youth, when that deforming hump shall be shaken off with thy "mortal coil"! The Lord hath taken all from thee but to pay thee back a thousand-fold.

"'God bless all our *gains*,' say we;
But 'God bless all our *losses*'
Better suits with our degree!"

THE

UNKNOWN TRAGEDIAN.

O, I could tell you—
But let it be. Horatio, I am dead;
Thou liv'st; report me and my cause aright
To the unsatisfied. HAMLET.

THE UNKNOWN TRAGEDIAN.

O, I could tell you —
But let it be. Horatio, I am dead ;
Thou liv'st ; report me and my cause aright
To the unsatisfied. — HAMLET.

CHAPTER I.

A Medical Decision. — An Aged Pair. — Singular Fact in Dramatic History. — Mr. and Mrs. Ruthven. — The Stage Villain and First Old Woman of the Theatre. — Elma. — Filial Devotion. — The Unknown Tragedian. — Correspondence. — Mysterious Eccentricities. — Attachment. — The Arrival. — Rehearsal of the Valedictory. — Mortimer's Powers of Captivation. — Interview with Elma. — Painful Position of the Young Girl. — Farewell Benefit of the Aged Actress. — Peculiarities of a Dublin Audience. — Damon and Pythias. — Acting of the Great Tragedian. — Elma's Scenic Talents. — Exotics and Violets. — A Suspicion. — The Venerable Actress as Mrs. Malaprop. — Incidents. — An Expiring Flame. —The Unspoken Adieu. — Touching Close of a Long Career. — The Curtain and Pall.

"WILL you give me your candid opinion ?"

"It 's little short of suicide — you have it."

"But," returned the aged man who had demanded that rarest of commodities, a *candid opinion,* and who, having received it, was ready, after the fashion of the world, to question its truth, — "but you do not know how immovably her mind is fixed on this farewell. You are not an actor — you can have no adequate conception of the reluctance with which we lay down our dramatic mantle, even when our shoulders are too feeble to carry it longer; — how fiercely we wrestle against the infirmities of age, which admonish us that our hour of scenic triumph is nearly expended. You sneer; — that 's natural, for none but an actor can comprehend what the stage is to those whose hairs, as my wife's and mine, have grown gray in the blaze of the foot-lights. She made her dèbût when she was so young that she cannot even remember the occasion; and now she is seventy, just seven years my junior. How, then, am I to forbid this leave-taking of a public in whose presence her life has ebbed away, upon whose favor she has existed?"

"If science may be trusted, her disease must end fatally," coolly replied phlegmatic Dr. Duff; "the exertion of a last effort on the stage will shorten her days. But, on the other hand, the agitation consequent upon thwarting her wishes may produce the same result. I leave *you* to choose between the evils."

"Then, my choice is made," said Mr. Ruthven. "She shall appear. This farewell to her is the rendering up an account of her public stewardship, before she resigns her office forever. If it be true that I must lose her, though I cannot think it, let me not be haunted by the recollection that I denied her last wishes."

Mr. Ruthven rose, and, followed by the physician, entered the adjoining apartment.

In an arm-chair, propped up by pillows, sat Mrs. Ruthven. Even a close observer would not have pronounced that she had, by many years, reached the age which her husband had just declared.

Is there some invisible Medea that waits upon the steps of actors, and, when the frosty hand of age is laid upon them to congeal their blood, who pours into their shrunken veins (as did the niece of Circe into those of old Æson) the juices of precious herbs, which renew their youth? It is a singular fact in dramatic history, that, in spite of late hours, endless exposures, incessant fatigue, constant excitement, and systematically irregular habits, performers preserve a rare degree of personal freshness and intellectual vigor until nature reaches "the very verge of her confine." Whence comes the talisman with which they, despite

"of Age's fiat,
Resist decay"?

This lingering of youth in age is, perhaps, attributable to the daily mental and physical exercise of all their faculties. It is through disuse or disease, rather than by nature's law, that the powers of men are early impaired.

The traces of severe suffering were apparent on Mrs. Ruthven's countenance, but they had not wholly dethroned and banished the beauty for which it once was famed. The rose of youth had not dropped *all* its leaves. Fever lent its repairing glow to the faded cheeks, its delusive light to the once brilliant eyes. These, and a bright, animated expression, concealed the thefts of time.

Mrs. Ruthven was the daughter of an Edinburgh manager. Before she reached her thirtieth year she was distinguished for her consummate skill in the personation of "comic and pathetic old women." This was the "line" which she preferred. No petty, unartistic vanity marred the fidelity of her delineations. Her personal attractions were unconcernedly obscured beneath a series of well-executed disguises. She was perfect mistress of the effects produced by elaborately-painted wrinkles, snowy locks "the dowry of a second head," antiquated costume, and a tottering gait. It was, however, somewhat strange that in her youth she assumed with alacrity all venerable rôles, but after her years numbered half a century she evinced a strong preference for the most juvenile heroines in her repertoire.

Mr. Ruthven was one of the leading members of her father's company, the representative of all the heartless, remorseless, hideous stage villains; for a "good villain" (if we may be excused for the joining of opposites which theatrical parlance unites to convey its meaning) is one of the necessary concomitants of a successful play.

Mr. Ruthven became such an adept in portraying the different shades of knavery, that the audience constantly confounded the man with the characters he assumed. It cordially detested him, and not unfrequently visited the unoffending actor with signal marks of disapprobation; but the hiss bestowed on the villain is a demonstration very nearly as complimentary as applause lavished on the hero.

Mr. Ruthven wooed and won the manager's daughter. Their positions in her father's theatre remained unaltered by this union until his death. Mr. and Mrs. Ruthven then travelled in the provinces for a few seasons, and finally crossed the channel and settled in Dublin. They had now been members of the Dublin Theatre Royal for fifteen years.

Husband and wife were alike enamored of their profession. Though no longer spurred to its pursuance by "necessity's sharp pinch," it possessed allurements to their minds which few considerations could have compelled them to resist.

Upon them both the infirmities of age had crept very slowly. These were chiefly apparent in diminished physical strength and impaired memory. Loss of memory it could not be termed, — for the language of numberless characters which they had enacted in their youth could be recalled without effort, — but to commit the context of recent productions now became a Sisyphus-like labor, ever frustrated the instant it seemed accomplished. Every page in memory's huge volume appeared to be filled. The aged pair were forced to "wing" (as it is called) all new parts; that is, con them at the wings until summoned to appear upon the stage, and resume the study at every exit. Even this drawback could not render their profession less fascinating.

They resided in a handsome but unostentatious mansion in Merrion-square. The smiles of five children had brightened their hearth for a short space, and then the homes of four were exchanged for a heavenlier abode, — one daughter remained.

Elma — her name was a compound of Elizabeth

and Mary, the respective appellations of her mother and grandmother — had just completed her twenty-second year Her infant feet had trodden the boards for the first ten years of her life ; the ensuing ten were passed in the studious seclusion of a justly-celebrated London seminary. Her twentieth birthday brought her back to the paternal roof.

That she should become an actress was certainly not a matter of necessity, but to the minds of her parents it was a matter of course. They regarded the stage as her legitimate and most desirable destination.

Elma did not inherit their attachment for the theatrical profession, nor could a fondness for dramatic representations be engrafted upon her mind by stage triumphs. She shrank from the display of her talents for the entertainment of an incongruous crowd. She felt humiliated when she reflected that the privilege of gazing upon her face, and passing judgment upon her endowments, could be *purchased.* Such thoughts never disturb the brain of the genuine and enthusiastic *artist,* who wholly separates *herself* from her *vocation* — divides her actual life from her stage existence ; but Elma had not been gifted with this faculty.

There is a certain affectation very prevalent among performers, which induces the larger portion to affirm that they detest the stage, they hate acting, they can't abide plays. This assumed contempt is looked upon as a mark of theatrical aristocracy.

When Elma communicated to her parents her repugnance towards the career they designed for her, they imagined that she had adopted the *cant* of the theatre, and laughed at her declaration. She perceived how deeply they would have been wounded, how seriously disappointed, had they believed her distaste unfeigned; and submitted without further argument.

Filial devotion was one of the most strongly-developed attributes of her nature. To suffer in silence was less painful than to oppose the wishes of her parents. Had they not called her the "balm of their age," the sole "thread of their own lives"? That balm should not, by her self-will, be turned to gall; nor that tender thread be changed to an iron band, tightening around and eating into the hearts that cherished her. Thus she became an actress.

She made a successful débût at the Dublin Theatre Royal. For two years she discharged the duties of leading lady of the company.

But to return to Mrs. Ruthven. As her husband and physician entered her chamber, she asked, in a cheerful tone, "Well, doctor, do you intend to humor me?"

"I have left the decision with Mr. Ruthven."

"And, as Arthur is not in the habit of denying me anything, we may look upon the farewell question as settled. Is it not so, Arthur?"

"Dr. Duff thinks there is danger, Mary," replied her husband, as he carefully arranged the pillows that supported her, and seated himself by her side.

"Danger? — the bow is bent and drawn, the shaft must fly! That he has already intimated," answered Mrs. Ruthven; "and I have said 'amen' if it must be, and only ask that you will not refuse to let me bid my friends adieu."

At that moment a young girl entered the chamber.

Her exquisitely-rounded form was several inches above the Medici's height. Her half-stately bearing, her queen-like tread, the classic *pose* of her head on her shoulders, the chiselled regularity of her features, befitted a Juno. But the face itself was more suited to a Madonna — if the arbitrary old masters would allow us to imagine a Madonna with a rich olive complexion, and shining dark hair wound in coronet shape around a broad, low brow.

She bowed to the doctor, quietly removed her bonnet, drew a chair to the invalid, and fixed upon her countenance a pair of soft brown eyes, "sweet, earnest eyes of grace," with an unspoken inquiry. Elma's silence had always a tongue as eloquent as though her thoughts had been made vocal.

The mother replied to her daughter's look. "Yes, I am better, darling, a great deal better; for they will let me have my own way — the farewell is settled upon."

"O no, my mother, my father — you will not consent! Doctor, you surely will not permit this, in my mother's state!" pleaded Elma.

"Elma—" exclaimed Mrs. Ruthven, in a troubled tone; but her husband interrupted her.

"Elma, do not disturb your mother's serenity; you cannot comprehend her feelings. Her earnest desire *shall* be gratified."

Mrs. Ruthven was holding her husband's hand in one of hers, and her daughter's in the other. She drew both fondly to her bosom. The remonstrance that rose to Elma's lips remained unuttered.

"Mr. Ruthven says you expect the great tragedian. Do you really think he will be here for your farewell?" asked Dr. Duff. "Mr. Mortimer is so uncertain, so eccentric, that he can never be depended upon."

"The rest of the world may have no cause to rely upon him," said Mrs. Ruthven, "but we have,— for 'here is metal more attractive' than the whole world can offer."

She smiled upon her daughter as she spoke.

But the delicate bloom on Elma's cheek deepened not to crimson, as it is wont to do on maidens' faces at the sound of a name inscribed in the innermost centre of their hearts. Her eyes sought the ground, but their lids veiled a look of pain rather than one of sweet confusion.

"Here is Mortimer's letter in answer to mine; quaint as himself,— read it," continued Mrs. Ruthven, handing a note to the doctor.

He perused aloud:

"*Newcastle on Tyne,*
October 6th, 18—.

"'What so poor a man as Hamlet is may do, to express his love and friending to you, God willing, shall not lack.' GERALD MORTIMER."

Those were the only words the paper contained.

The minds of actors are often so richly stored with poetic lore that their lips borrow the language of the dramatists almost unconsciously. The student of Shakspeare, in particular, finds in his wondrous, teeming treasury every passion, every emotion, every aspiration, almost every situation in which humanity can be thrown, clothed with fitting and forcible expression. Truly has a humbler minstrel sang, that words of power,

> "Flung from Shakspeare's bolder hand,
> Went vibrating through all the land,
> And found in every heart a tone
> That seemed an echo of their own." *

Mortimer was an acknowledged devotee at the shrine of this Apollo of the drama, and constantly sounded notes from his lyre in the strains of every-day life.

The history of Gerald Mortimer was enveloped in impenetrable mystery. Five years previous to the period of which we write, a "star" suddenly burst upon the dramatic firmament of Dublin, and the gazing crowd sank down with involuntary homage.

"Whence came this potent magician?" "What is his history?" "Has he worn the buskin before?" These were questions no one could answer.

Gerald Mortimer took his audience by storm, towered above criticism, and in a single night leapt to the drama's highest eminence.

He was eagerly sought by managers throughout Great Britain. In obeying or declining their summons he appeared to be actuated solely by caprice. His fame reached London. Offers from Drury Lane, Covent Garden, the Haymarket, the Princess', poured in upon him. All solicitations from the metropolis were briefly declined. No reason was vouchsafed.

It was generally acceded that the name of Gerald Mortimer was assumed for stage purposes. There

* William H. Burleigh.

were numberless rumors afloat concerning the tragedian's probable parentage. Many asserted that noble blood flowed in his veins. Others soared higher, and whispered strange tales of the devotion of one of England's kings to an actress.

If a majestic presence, "an eye like Mars, to threaten or command," a brow shadowed by "Hyperion's curls," were insignias of illustrious blood, he bore about him his patent of nobility. Certes his name stood high on *nature's* peerage-roll, if upon no other.

From his earliest acquaintance with Mr. and Mrs. Ruthven, Mortimer entertained for them a venerating esteem. In their presence he often laid aside his grave demeanor, habitual reserve, and laconic intercourse. Their devotion to their art, which he confessedly shared, was, perhaps, the first uniting link of sympathy. A stronger chain was forged when Elma appeared before him. Admiration quickly mellowed into attachment.

Mortimer, before he addressed the young girl, declared his hopes to her approving parents. In that avowal he confided a portion of his own history, enough to remove all scruples from their minds. His confidence was kept sacred even from their daughter. If he were blessed in winning her affections, the veil that obscured his past career would be torn away before he claimed her hand. That promise was all-sufficient.

Mrs. Ruthven earnestly desired that the evening upon which she resigned her stage honors might be commemorated by one of the powerful dramatic efforts of her most valued friend. She had penned him her wishes, and had received by return of mail the brief but expressive reply which Dr. Duff had just perused.

After a consultation with the manager, the farewell benefit (so it was called) was arranged to take place at the close of the ensuing week. Mortimer was duly apprised. His answer was concentrated in two sentences:

"I shall be with you; part, Damon. G. M."

Mrs. Ruthven's forte was comedy. She selected Mrs. Malaprop, in Sheridan's play of The Rivals, for her last assumption.

Mortimer never cast aside the sceptre of tragic state to don the cap and bells. He would appear in the drama of Damon and Pythias, which was to precede the comedy.

The Dublin theatrical world was thrown into a state of high excitement by the announcement of the proposed farewell. The night would be a memorable epoch in dramatic annals.

The morning of the benefit arrived. Rehearsal passed off without Mortimer. But he often dispensed with its ceremonies.

Actors are usually very tenacious about the sides they occupy, and the exeunts and entrances of those who are performing with them. The unexpected change of a situation to which they have been accustomed will sometimes obliterate from their minds the context of the play. But, whenever Mortimer was asked by a member of a company "On which side do you wish me to enter?" his invariable reply was, "Where you like; I shall find you."

On several occasions, when public expectation was raised to an unusual pitch, Mortimer had failed to appear. He never condescended to account for his absence. The manager who ventured to remonstrate was silenced by a haughty request to name his losses. Enormous penalties were paid by the tragedian without discussion.

As the protracted rehearsal drew to a close, the actors whispered their doubts of Mortimer's coming; the manager exhibited his anxiety by unwonted irritability; and even Elma and her father began to be alarmed. Mrs. Ruthven was not present.

After rehearsal, Mr. Ruthven hastened to the hotel where the tragedian usually lodged, to learn if he had arrived. Elma returned home alone.

Her hand was on the door of her mother's sitting-room, when a sound from within arrested her. Those deep, rich tones could belong to no voice but Mortimer's. Her mind was relieved of one anxiety; and yet she hesitated, as though another had usurped its place. The soft brightness of her countenance, which might aptly be likened to the subdued light of the moon, was under an eclipse as she entered.

Mortimer rose eagerly, and the hand she offered was clasped somewhat more warmly than mere friendly courtesy warranted. She released it with a look of distress, rather than of embarrassment, as she said,

"Everybody will be so glad you have come! They feared at the theatre you would not be here."

"And is Elma included in the 'everybody' who is glad that I have come?"

"Of course."

"Your mother had no fears that I would prove faithless to my word. Were you as confident?"

"I hoped — I could not tell; but you must not expect every one to have the unbounded confidence in you that my mother has." Elma concluded her sentence in as sprightly a tone as she could command.

Mortimer resumed his seat without removing his dark, penetrating eyes from her countenance.

"Will your father be here soon, my love?" asked her mother.

"He went to inquire for Mr. Mortimer — but here is my father."

Mr. Ruthven and Mortimer greeted each other heartily.

"Sit down, all of you," said Mrs. Ruthven. "I have one rehearsal more to go through, and that will be the last. Our friends will expect a few parting words to-night. I have just written down my valedictory. Listen, little audience, and I will read to you."

They gathered around her, and she read, in a faint, tremulous voice, from the paper in her hand. She briefly summed up the events of a life which had "in public service flown," from the hour when childhood's lisping tongue first became the interpreter of the poet's language, even to this, when the hand of disease had seized her, and age stood ready to place its paralyzing seal upon her lips. Then gushed forth a torrent of thanks, pent up by an adieu.

Her husband bowed his head and hid his face in his hands. Elma, as she listened,

> "shook
> The holy water from her heavenly eyes."

Mortimer had risen and walked to the window. When he returned, "the many-colored iris round his eye" betrayed that Nature would not be defrauded of her custom, in spite of Manhood's shame.

Mrs. Ruthven fell back exhausted. Then, as she marked the signs of dolor in the little group before her, she rallied her fugitive faculties.

"Come, come, good people, don't weep before the time! No crying at rehearsal, you know! Now, let me lie down. Gerald, give me your arm. Arthur is hardly young enough to support me, for I have grown as old as Sybilla within the last month, and I doubt whether Sybilla was half as decrepid."

With the tenderness of a son the dark-browed tragedian supported the aged actress to her chamber. Elma accompanied them.

"Now, leave me to myself, my — *children*."

The mother gave affectionate emphasis to the last word.

Mortimer turned to depart, but Elma still lingered by her mother's couch. It was not until Mrs. Ruthven, regardless of her daughter's soliciting look, repeated the request, that she returned with Mortimer to the drawing-room. Mr. Ruthven was no longer there. He had retired to "deal with grief alone."

Few men were better fitted to captivate a woman's heart, and compel its deep fountains of devotion to gush forth responsive to his will, than Gerald Mortimer. He possessed that persuasive eloquence which enthralls the ear; that impressive earnestness which fixes every wandering thought; that reverence of manner towards the weaker sex which lures it to forget man's actual superiority, and feel itself the stronger; and — most potent of all — that considerate tenderness which recognizes that womanhood is dowried with sufferings from which he is exempt, to render her existence sacred in the eyes of man.

"Your mother is failing fast, Elma," said he, when they had resumed their seats.

"Very fast; and to-night — how I dread it! But no persuasions could induce her to forego this farewell. She loves her profession so passionately — it is enigmatical!"

"Enigmatical to your mind, Elma, where there is no answering chord; but it quickly translates itself to mine, which has strings to respond to this too earthly music. Yet your unaffected distaste for the stage only commands my admiration."

"It hardly deserves the name of *distaste*. I *have* experienced a *sort* of pleasure in certain personations; but my imagination pictures a more delightful mode of life. I am lamentably deficient in ambition. 'I could be bounded in a nutshell, and count myself a queen of infinite space;' my throne a cheerful hearth-stone, my sceptre too unpoetic a household badge to bear mentioning. A serene seclusion, a holy round of daily duties —" Elma paused abruptly, as though the picture she was painting might reveal too many hidden thoughts.

"An actor's wife need not perforce be an actress!" replied Mortimer, pointedly.

Elma turned away.

"Do not fear, Elma! I will not press my suit until you grant me permission. One single word silences me forever. My happiness could not be purchased by your misery. I am content to know that this 'white wonder' is not promised to any other."

And he took her hand, which was indeed

> "As soft as dove's down, and as white as it."

"It is not promised," she answered; but the hand was withdrawn.

"And your heart, Elma,—that has chosen no lord?"

A blush that had stolen its hue from the sunset sky now suffused her countenance, as she faltered out,

"You question me strangely; you—"

There was a suppressed emotion, a calmness almost terrifying, in Mortimer's tone, as he interrupted her.

"Be frank with me, Elma! Although your words must pierce every sense, enter like daggers in my ears, and cut my heart in twain,—though all my future prove builded on sand, and crumble at your feet,—yet tell me truly, *mercilessly*, if you love another!"

Elma shrank away from his gaze as though she would evade the lightning's scathing.

"What cause have I given you for such a suspicion?"

"No cause, nor have I ever stooped to suspicion. I asked the question inadvertently. I make no complaint of your reserve—your coldness, for perhaps it deserves that name. I can exist upon the assurance that your heart is free."

At this crisis Mr. Ruthven entered the room. Did

Mortimer note Elma's look of relief? Did he remark the alacrity with which she busied herself upon some feminine trifles pertaining to her theatrical wardrobe? Could he fail to lack her presence, when she thought him absorbed in conversation with her father, and softly glided from the apartment?

Elma's upright mind would never have *premeditatedly* allowed her to be placed in her present position towards Mortimer. He had poured out his own wealth of passion, and claimed no return. He was satisfied to woo with Jacob-like patience, if the jewel of his soul enriched no other bosom. Elma had not, therefore, been called upon to fan or extinguish a flame so self-existent. Nor could she have overthrown the cherished hopes of her parents without a pang too severe to be needlessly encountered. Mortimer's high gifts excited her admiration, his magnanimity won her esteem; and, in a nature truly feminine, esteem is ever mingled with some degree of affection; but he had failed to inspire her with an all-engrossing love. And why? She had scarcely acknowledged the impediment to herself.

The performances of the evening commenced with the drama of Damon and Pythias, the clever production of John Banim, a youthful Irish dramatist.

Mortimer enacted Damon, Mr. Ruthven the tyrant Dionysius, and Elma, Calanthe, the betrothed of Pythias.

As Mrs. Ruthven did not appear until the first play was concluded, her husband and daughter were compelled to leave her at an early hour.

The thronged audience overflowed upon the stage. Chairs were ranged to receive them in front of the proscenium, and the entrances behind the scenes were so densely crowded that the performers could scarcely force their way. Not a foot's space throughout the theatre remained unoccupied. Hundreds never even caught a glimpse of the stage.

The impressibility and vivacity of the Irish character are peculiarly inspiring to actors, and call forth their highest powers. No audience ever responded more instantaneously to noble and heroic sentiments, or was more quickly penetrated by touches of genuine pathos, or evinced a keener sense of the humorous.

Mortimer's delineations always excited their wildest enthusiasm. We will not attempt to describe the boisterous exhibition of delight with which he was saluted when he stood before them as Damon. To a looker on it seemed as though their manifestations could only end in the galleries descending upon the stage, and bearing him about on their shoulders. But the tragedian never once bent his stately head while they "vented clamor from their throats." His lips curled with a slight expression of scorn. If ambition had ever made him covet these evidences of popularity, they became worthless in his eyes the moment they were gained.

"Long life to the star of the world!"

"Blessings be on all the bones of his body, and all the hairs of his head!"

"Never was the likes of him seen!"

These, and similar ejaculations, mingled with the uproar.

At the first majestic uplifting of his hand, silence fell upon all around, like the sudden stilling of tempestuous waves. He spoke; the words rolled from his lips in a gush of mellifluous sound, that seemed the mingling of trumpet and bugle tones; they stirred or melted, fired or calmed, the hearers at will.

Mortimer's imposing presence dignified, ennobled, idealized, the most insignificant character he assumed; but to such a rôle as the self-sacrificing, warlike Damon he imparted a heroic grandeur indescribable. At one moment he plunged into the profoundest abysses of passion, and brought their strong workings to view; the next, his melting tenderness struck the rock of stoniest hearts, and sent its waters to the subdued eyes.

Damon's soul-harrowing parting with his wife, his fury with his freedman, his thrilling meeting with Pythias upon the scaffold, were almost terrific in their sublime intensity.

Yet, while the actor seemed to hold the heartstrings of the audience in his hands, while he strained them to agony at pleasure, he either was not or affected not to be moved by his own personation. He compelled those who occupied the stage with him to believe that his most powerfully portrayed emotion was a counterfeit, the

> "painting of a sorrow,
> A face without a heart."

While the spectators cheered until they were hoarse, the stoical tragedian, in a tone of irony, uttered some humorous sarcasm, which excited the uncontrollable merriment of the players,— a mirth which it was often difficult to conceal.

From the same audience who were so clamorous in their demonstrations to the tragedian Elma won a silent respect even more flattering, and to her peculiar temperament far more acceptable. They never broke out into noisy admiration until she had passed from their presence. They never addressed to her an audible criticism, eulogium, or comment.

Calanthe is a subordinate character, yet one that enlists sympathy.

It is difficult to define the exact order of Elma's scenic talents. Her performances lacked vivid coloring. They might have been deemed cold, but it was a marble coldness of statuesque beauty; they were carved, as it were, in alabaster, but sculpture was not dumb.* She never rose out of herself, but she filled her assumed characters with her own inseparable loveliness. If they were narrow, she seemed to compress her nature to enter into their contracted limits, reminding the beholders of a butterfly struggling to force itself into an empty chrysalis-shell, but failing to hide its bright, tinted wings.

She never descended to stage trickeries, nor ever, like Mortimer, courted the applause which she disdained.

The extreme polish of her delivery lent one great charm to her personations. Never was the Saxon tongue more musically syllabled than by her lips. Every word was cut fine and sharp, and invested with a value and a meaning which betokened intellect, though unallied with ardor.

* "Verse ceases to be airy thought,
And sculpture to be dumb."

The much-abused practice of flinging bouquets at the feet of favorite performers had not, in those days, reached a height of absurdity. A floral token might fall upon the stage without awakening the suspicion that this was only a portion of the performance, prepared by the manager, possibly by the receiver. In the first act, while Damon and Pythias were conversing, Calanthe stole in upon them. The instant she appeared, a couple of bouquets dropped upon the stage. The one was a magnificent collection of exotics; the other, a bunch of woodland violets, the stems of which were confined by a golden arrow.

The representative of Pythias gathered up the flowers, and presented them to Elma. Mortimer's gaze was fastened upon her as she received them. He detected the involuntary direction of her eyes, though the look was as brief as a flash. That glance had sought the stage-box. In the seats nearest to the stage sat young Lord Oranmore, and his relative, Leonard Edmonton. The fiery eyes of the tragedian rested upon the countenance of the nobleman with an expression which might have been interpreted into a wrathful menace. Then he turned them again upon Elma. The bouquets were in her hands, but her face was innocently raised to that of Pythias, who regarded her, saying,

"By the birth
Of Venus when she rose out of the sea,
And with her smile did fill the Grecian isles
With everlasting verdure, she was not,
Fresh from the soft creation of the wave,
More beautiful than thou!"

Mortimer's fierce look gradually changed to one of trustful confidence.

We pass over the stirring action of the play, which abounds in fine situations.

When the curtain fell, Elma found her mother, attired as Mrs. Malaprop, seated in the green-room. Her antiquated attendant, Winifred, stood fanning her. The members of the company crowded around, with welcomes and kind inquiries.

A gleam of the olden light "fired her fading eye." Departed vigor returned to her enfeebled frame, and to the voice, so faint and hollow a few hours before, its clear, far-sounding tone was restored.

The sensations of the aged actress, on the eve of her farewell, were fitly expressed in the touching adieu delivered by John Kemble but a few years previous:

"As the worn war-horse, at the trumpet's sound,
Erects his mane, and neighs, and paws the ground,
Disdains the ease his generous lord assigns,
And longs to rush on the embattled lines,
So I, your plaudits ringing in mine ear,
Can scarce sustain to think our parting near!
To think my scenic hour forever past,
And that these valued plaudits are my last!" *

Elma could only spend a moment at her mother's side. The young actress was allowed but a brief space to exchange her Grecian costume for the modern adornments of Lydia Languish.

As the comedy of "The Rivals" is deficient in a knave, Mr. Ruthven's labors for the night ended with Dionysius. The accomplished stage villain was

* Walter Scott.

metamorphosed into the most worthy and devoted of husbands.

The welcome which the audience bestowed on Mrs. Ruthven might almost have been said to surpass their tornado-like greeting of the half-idolized tragedian. It was not received by her with Mortimer's scornful hauteur.

"Blessings be *wid* ye!"

"The best of luck to ye!"

"Long life to ye!" resounded on every side, at her oft-repeated obeisances.

The Dogberry-like misapplications of Mrs. Malaprop, who asserts that "if she reprehends anything in the world, it is the use of her oracular tongue and a nice derangement of epitaphs," never elicited heartier merriment.

As the play progressed, it became apparent that Mrs. Ruthven's suddenly restored powers were but the bright flashes of life's expiring flame. During the fifth act she could not stand without support. She leaned heavily on the arms of the performers who chanced to be nearest to her; and if the exigences of the play required them to alter their situations, others took their place. Every moment she grew feebler, until her limbs wholly refused their office. She was placed in a chair, and remained seated during the final scene.

The actors, regardless of the parts they were representing, gathered affectionately around her, fanning her, bathing her brow, making her inhale pungent odors.

The comedy was hurried to its conclusion. The curtain fell. The audience had received the impression that their favorite was on the verge of a fainting-fit, produced by fatigue. After a few moments of compassionate silence, the exhausted actress received the usual summons, and the eager crowd awaited her last adieu.

Mr. Ruthven placed the paper upon which the address was inscribed in her hands. She endeavored to rise, but in vain.

"Do not make the attempt," remonstrated Mortimer, who had hastened to her side the instant the curtain fell. "Sit still, just as you are; let the curtain be raised, but do not try to stand."

Mrs. Ruthven smiled consent.

Elma stood beside her mother's chair, as the curtain was slowly lifted to the expectant multitude. One loud peal was followed by a silence so profound that the hard-drawn breath of the suffering actress was distinctly audible. Every ear was strained to catch the last words they might ever hear from those lips by which they had so often been charmed. There was a strange, nervous twitching about the mouth, in its desperate effort to articulate. The eyes, that wandered slowly around the theatre with a long, last look of regret, grew filmy and glassy. The face had become thin, sharp, and ghastly, within a few hours. The paper dropped from the powerless hand. The head drooped slowly to one side, and was caught by Elma, who had fallen upon her knees by her mother's chair.

A voice reached the audience from behind the scenes: "Let fall the curtain; they will never hear her speak again!"

Every one recognized the deep, sonorous tones of Mortimer.

Many and many a sob broke the solemn stillness, as the curtain, like a pall, slowly descended, and shut out mother and daughter; one of them for the last time — for this, her place, would never know her more!

CHAPTER II.

Elma's Attributes. — Divine Providence. — A Trustful Spirit. — The Death-Bed and Betrothal. — The Box of Mementos. — A Confidence Postponed. — Mortimer's Departure. — Withered Violets. — Change in the Stage Villain. — Expiring Faculties.—An Irish Absentee.—Lord Oranmore and Leonard Edmonton. — Their Visit to Elma. — Discussion between the Nobleman and Student of Divinity. — The Portrait. —Elma's Titled Suitor. — An Offer. — Reply of the Actress.

For nearly a week Mrs. Ruthven lay in a semi-stupor.

Elma's filial love proclaimed its strength and depth by her thoughtful, all-anticipating, untiring devotion, as it had never done by words. Her nature was undemonstrative. She ever shunned the display of emotion, however real. Her profoundest, tenderest feelings were always voiceless. Her character had a strong affinity to that of Lear's gentle daughter. Cordelia-like, her love was "richer than her tongue," nor could she "heave her heart into her mouth," and make boast of its pulsations. Even her sorrow recoiled from outward show. She might have said, with Hermione,

> "I am not prone to weeping, as our sex
> Commonly are ; the want of which vain dew
> Perchance shall dry your sympathies ; but I have
> That honorable grief lodged here, that burns
> Worse than tears drown."

Those who beheld her ministering, with unruffled brow, tearless eyes, and tranquil mien, to a dying mother, might have deemed her deficient in that very attribute which she possessed to the highest degree.

Why was it that life's strange or sad mutations stirred not, overcame not her, as they overwhelmed stronger, prouder, more aspiring spirits? Her ægis was heaven-descended, and against it the powers of earth could not prevail. In her perfect trust to the Divine Providence whose invisible agency, like the penetrative atmosphere, pervades all creation; the workings of whose secret springs, hourly made manifest, redeem life's humblest trifles from insignificance; the Providence which watches over "the falling of a sparrow," which "shapes our ends, rough-hew them as we will," — in *that* trust lay her might. She felt that absolute reliance is the *condition* of receiving angelic influences — that they are *attracted by* the *trusting* spirit, can approach and enter in where Faith opens the door, but have no power to pierce the barrier of unbelief; she knew that to live in accordance to the laws of natural and spiritual order is to float on the divine current which bears all upon its tide to a haven of peace. Tossed by the stormiest sea, her eyes ever looked beyond the hour, and beheld the beacon of promise shining in the distance — ay, through the gloom of sorrow's darkest night. The placid, daily beauty of her life could not be ruffled or conquered by *circumstance,* because she ignored the existence of *chance.* Such a being could never become the sport of fate, a

"pipe for Fortune's finger,
To sound what stop she please."

Elma sat musing beside her mother's couch, pondering over such reflections as we have just penned. She looked up, after a long abstraction, and saw the invalid's eyes fixed upon her face. A smile parted the livid lips. It was the first look of intelligence that had lighted her countenance since the hour when she fell into slumberous insensibility. For a few seconds Elma moved not, nor uttered a word. Mother and child spoke to each other's hearts with their eyes alone.

"You know me, my mother?" at length Elma asked, in a low, loving voice.

Mrs. Ruthven was still speechless, nor could she reply by the affirmative motion of her head; but the lids of her dim eyes closed and opened again, and her smile grew brighter; these gave assent.

Elma, without turning her face from her mother, rose, and opened the door of the adjacent apartment. There sat the aged actor and the tragedian.

Mortimer was expected to fulfil an engagement in Liverpool two nights after his appearance at the farewell of Mrs. Ruthven. The following curt epistle conveyed to the infuriated manager a change of plans.

"You will not see me on Monday. Name damages. GERALD MORTIMER."

"My father," said Elma, "will you come in? My mother seems quite conscious again."

Mr. Ruthven and Mortimer hastened into the room.

The filmy eyes of the invalid became clearer as they rested upon them. The old man embraced her with deep emotion, and laid his withered, tear-stained visage on the pillow beside hers.

It was a strange sight to behold the being who had portrayed stern and ruthless villains until he cheated an audience into believing that he had himself no sense of natural ties, no tenderness, no heart, now playing the woman with his aged eyes!

Mortimer had reverently taken the hand of the sufferer, and raised it to his lips. She feebly stretched out her other hand to receive Elma's, then laid the hand of her child in that of Mortimer, clasping both together with a look the import of which was unmistakable. Mortimer sank upon his knees, and drew down Elma beside him. There was a silent benison on the face of the dying woman — the blessing which a mother bestows upon her betrothed children. That expression remained stamped upon her countenance.

The affianced pair still knelt with their united hands yet clasped in hers, as she sank to sleep; yes, to *sleep*, for her breathing stirred a snowy lock of the head that lay beside her. And now the silvery threads moved less and less — now they glittered motionless on the pillow. The hand which grasped that of her daughter and of the son she had chosen became a bond of ice. O, most sad prognostic!

"She is gone!" said Elma, in a solemn whisper. "Support my father!"

"*Our* father, Elma! She has confided you to me, — mine own, mine forever!" answered Mortimer. And Elma, who could not misinterpret her mother's dying wish, recoiled not.

* * * * *

We will not dwell upon the ceremonies that consign the soul's unjewelled casket to its native earth. In spite of reason, they are fraught with bitterest anguish to all mourners, even to those who feel assured that "life's true receptacle" descends not

> "To the dark mould, where sods above it close!"

who do not blindly

> "Confound this mouldering dust
> With the true person — with the inner form
> Which gave the outward all it had of fair;
> Which is no kindred of the worm,
> No warrant for despair."*

Mortimer had taken his place beside the bereaved husband as an acknowledged son.

Elma's countenance wore throughout a serene mournfulness; her grief never once found vent in loud lamentation.

A week passed on.

Elma sat poring over a box of treasured mementos which she had gathered up from her childhood.

"I have come to say farewell," said Mortimer, entering the room.

She closed down the lid with unusual abruptness.

"You did not tell us that you were about to leave," she remarked.

"I was not aware of it myself. You know I am a creature of impulse, and often cannot attempt to account for my own sudden fancies. I start for Liverpool in an hour, and shall try to satisfy Wilcox by acting a night or two for him."

Perhaps Mortimer did not peruse Elma's counte-

* Epes Sargent.

nance aright, but he imagined that she looked, at that moment, more cheerful than of late.

"Elma, dearest, this is no fitting season to talk to you of my joy in the promised possession of the hand your dying mother placed in mine —"

Elma looked at him with such deprecating eyes that he checked himself; then added: "I will not talk to you of plans for the future; but, Elma, there is one subject to which I am bound to allude; I ought not to leave you without. You divine the topic, do you not?"

"Yes."

"A man has no right to conceal what nearly concerns himself from his affianced bride; yet it must cost me dear to repeat the history to which your mother listened — with which she was content; for, after hearing it, she bestowed her child upon me."

"I do not ask to hear that which it will pain you to relate."

"Generous Elma! I thank you for this confidence. I may postpone the hour, then? You will be satisfied with the assurance that there is no blemish upon the name which I ask you to share, and which I have only renounced for a season. The one I now bear is assumed. My own befitted not a profession to which I was not born. I do not mean that I was destined for any other. Idleness was one of my inheritances — the one of which I grew most weary. In my early youth a teaching of that immortal bard who can inform the world struck deep root in my mind. The words are these:

'What is a man,
If his chief good and market of his time
Be but to sleep and feed ? — A beast, — no more.
Sure he that made us with such large discourses,
Looking before, and after, gave us not
That capability and godlike reason
To rust in us unused !'

Those lines converted a worldling drone into an actor; for I had always that passion for the stage which you cannot comprehend. Need I tell you more ?"

"No more."

"Are you satisfied — quite satisfied, Elma ?"

"With your history ? — Yes. I believe that no blot can attach itself to your fair fame."

"I did not mean that; but our relationship to each other will be a source of joy to you, — our hearts will make no discords ? When time's potent balm has soothed the poignancy of your present sorrow; when I return to claim you — "

"Pray !" —— That single word broke from Elma's lips so supplicatingly that Mortimer ceased.

"Enough; — I am content. 'How poor are they that have not patience !' I was a selfish brute to press this subject upon you at such a moment. Nor should I ask for words or assurances from such a woman as you are. You bear too strong a likeness to her of whom the brave, blunt old Kent declared

'Nor are those empty-hearted whose low sound
Reverbs no hollowness.'

Farewell !"

He stooped over her, his lips lightly touched her smooth forehead; and, without another word, he departed.

Why did not the maidenly blood mount in confusion to the brow which received that unwonted impress? Why did it become paler than before, as though the ruby current had retreated at the touch? And, now that he is gone, why does Elma clasp her hands so tightly together, and why does that deep, agonizing groan break from her lips?

She turns again to the box, which she hastily closed when he entered. She has taken out a bunch of withered violets, confined by a golden arrow. She gazes on them sorrowfully for a while, then stoops her head involuntarily, as if she would press them to her lips; but no,— she drops the faded token with a shudder, as though she had been tempted to commit some deadly sin, shuts down the lid, and resolutely walks away.

After the death of his beloved partner, Mr. Ruthven grew rapidly infirm. A deep melancholy settled on his spirit. At times he seemed on the verge of dotage. The only relief he could find lay in his profession. But his scenic powers seemed to have departed. His *villains* had become tame, meek, and pathetic. They lacked the diabolical element. His memory failed. The prompter's voice could not reach his age-dulled ears. Parts with which he had long been familiar he was forced to have copied in large characters, and the pages on which they were inscribed hung upon the wings, out of sight of the audience. The old man constantly wandered from his situation on the stage to consult these suspended documents.

Sometimes he painted a speech that played the fugitive in his mind upon the palms of his hands, or wrote a few of the most important words on his nails, erasing one impression and substituting another whenever he made his exit. Elma was seldom absent from his side. He grew restless and fretful when he missed her.

In her deportment there was a marked and touching change. Her reserved manner invited no sympathy; she never descanted upon "*afflictions*" which were too heavy to be borne; but there was an alarmed, troubled expression on her countenance, as though some constant dread were ever present to her thoughts, some inevitable calamity ever menacing her. But for the mild submission that softened that look it would have become one of settled despair.

She had received no visitors since her mother's decease. One morning her father entered her boudoir most unexpectedly, accompanied by Lord Oranmore and Mr. Edmonton. Mr. Ruthven had encountered them on his return from rehearsal, and invited them to his house, where they were in the habit of visiting.

The father of Lord Oranmore was an Irish nobleman, who, at an early age, abandoned his estates, and took up his residence in London. In that metropolis one son and three daughters were born and educated.

It was through the representations of his relative, the Rev. Erastus Edmonton, that the self-exiled lord had been gradually convinced of the wrong and injustice of an absentee towards his tenantry. He hearkened, at length, to the wailing cry sent up by England's sister country, and remembered that it was his own. Two years previous to the period of which we write, he returned to his extensive estate on the outskirts of Dublin.

The Rev. Mr. Edmonton, who was now a widower, and in declining health, was induced to exchange his pastorate for the lighter duties of private chaplain at the castle. The living thus left vacant was promised to his son.

Leonard Edmonton had been educated with young Lord Oranmore, who, being an only son, lacked companionship. The youthful nobleman and his father had used their best endeavors to induce Leonard to enter the army. He resisted all entreaty, and became, by choice, a student of divinity. But when the season for his ordination arrived, with unaccountable capriciousness he postponed the ceremony, assigning no cause.

Elma greeted Lord Oranmore with dignified cordiality, then bowed to Mr. Edmonton without offering her hand, without lifting her eyes to his face.

Here was a striking difference in her salutation of the young men. A casual observer would have said that the florid, fair-haired, dashing young nobleman so wholly absorbed her attention that she had not a glance to bestow upon the chaplain's son. Yet the fine oval of that mild, thoughtful countenance, that open brow from which the raven locks waved back and gave its loftiness to perfect view, those singularly-dark eyebrows arched over deep blue eyes, those bland, delicately-curved lips, were not unworthy a fair lady's note.

Leonard Edmonton lacked Lord Oranmore's buoyant, precipitate manners, but a polished ease took their place.

The vivacious nobleman very nearly rendered the conversation a monologue. Mr. Edmonton addressed Elma but twice, and drew from her only monosyllabic replies. The visit of the young men was necessarily brief.

As they left the house, Lord Oranmore said to his companion, "What a cold-blooded fellow you are, Edmonton, — a perfect north-pole icicle! Even this charming creature cannot thaw you. And yet, it's odd, when she was acting you never missed one of her nights at the theatre. There you sat this morning like a stock, actually letting her forget that you were present!"

"A feat you never once performed yourself, I believe!" returned Edmonton. His laugh but half concealed that he winced at the random thrust.

"No, indeed; I force her to think of me, because I can't help thinking of her. You are always accusing me of hunting after new fancies, but I have been constant to this ever since I first saw Elma Ruthven; — one whole year! I then became infatuated with her personations; but *herself* is far more charming than all the poetic and dramatic angels she assumes. *Now* it is the woman that I am over head and ears in love with."

"*In love with!*" Edmonton ejaculated those words in a tone of horror. "And your *intentions are* —"

"Well, really, I never ask myself what they are.

I do not know that I have any fixed intentions at all. I leave the future to bring forth what it will."

"But if you should find that Elma Ruthven returns your affection?"

"I shall be deeply indebted to her, shall feel highly complimented, greatly delighted, and — as I said before, let the future bring forth whatever it has in store. I suppose a man may be pardoned for a little vanity, if he discover himself to be an object of consideration to this divine creature, whom destiny has rendered an actress."

"Elma Ruthven, in her chaste loveliness, is not a woman whose name should be irreverently uttered. Nor can her character be lightly estimated by any one who has been granted the privilege of knowing her in private. The man who is crowned with her love will become the monarch of a heavenly realm, and may well be proud; but that her preference should excite *vanity*, in the sense which you seem to imply, is a thought as humiliating to her as it is unworthy of you."

"Hey day, Edmonton! have you just waked up? I never heard you launch out in her praise before. Why, you are not in love with her yourself, are you? I shall begin to think it is this actress who is keeping that living vacant, and has postponed a certain ordination for which you were duly prepared. You were afraid of disgracing your cloth, — is that it? What has fired you so suddenly?"

"I believe I was a little warm," returned Edmonton, relapsing into his usual quietude; "but you know what reverence I have for womanhood; I cannot bear to hear the name of such a woman as Elma

Ruthven lightly used, or the rich gift of her affections (which can only be bestowed accompanied by her hand) rated so carelessly. That is my excuse."

"No harm done, Leonard; only don't grow sanctimonious before the time. No offence in talking of an actress as though she were flesh and blood, is there?"

"Don't separate the flesh and blood from the spirit that animates and gives them life, which makes the pulses temperately beat in response to all noble aspirations, making such holy music as Elma's—— but here comes your groom. At what a furious rate he is driving those horses!"

"Like their master, they object to the curb, even though the bridle be held by a friendly hand," replied Lord Oranmore, laughing. "Are you going directly to the castle?"

Edmonton answered in the affirmative.

"Then jump in the phaëton, and spend a little of your judicious whip and bridling upon the horses yourself. Your lessons will do them good. Wish I could say as much for their master! Terence, I shall not dine at home. Bring the horses to the club by ten to-night."

The chaplain's son drove off, evincing no little skill as he curbed the fiery steeds.

Lord Oranmore turned his steps to the principal bookseller's shop in Dublin.

"I must have some pretext for the visit," he said to himself, as he entered.

He tossed over a number of richly-bound annuals, and at last selected and purchased a volume of standard plays, which contained a portrait of Mrs. Ruthven as the Widow Rackett. The clerk was ordered to follow him with the book, as he purposed to deliver it in person.

It was conveyed into Elma's presence. She was alone. Lord Oranmore pointed out the portrait; said that he met with it accidentally; that he found the likeness of Mrs. Ruthven so very striking he could not refrain from bringing it himself, that he might witness her daughter's pleasure. He begged that the volume might be left for her father's acceptance.

Lord Oranmore was very sorry, he added, not to find Mr. Ruthven at home; no, he corrected himself, he would be frank, and say that he was rejoiced; for there was a subject upon which he wished to converse with Elma. Time, he declared, had dragged very heavily with him during the four weeks in which he had not beheld her. What was life out of her presence? Would that his life could be passed at her side! Existence would be elysium. And could not this be? Would she not give him hope that it might be?

Elma made a fruitless attempt to check him. In spite of her chilling mien, his ardent temperament hurried him on.

There was a touch of regal scorn in the look which she turned upon him, as she replied:

"Is it because I bear the name of an *actress*, my lord, that you have ventured to address me thus? What in my conduct has ever given you the right? I have only to request that you will leave me to the privacy upon which you have intruded."

Lord Oranmore in an instant saw his error, and at

that moment she became more dear than ever. He would not lose her thus.

"Miss Ruthven, — beautiful Elma! How you have misunderstood me! You could not, for a second, imagine me capable of insulting you! How often has the stage given up its heroines, that coronets might gain additional lustre by encircling their brows! I ask to place one upon yours,

'Where partial nature hath already bound
A brighter circlet, radiant Beauty's own.'

Let me rob the public to enrich myself. You have no love for the stage; will you not abandon it for my sake?"

"No."

"Why is your manner so frigid? Have I unconsciously offended beyond pardon?"

"No woman has the right to be offended by the honorable addresses of an honorable man. But your offer is one that I cannot accept. I should not, were I free; I *cannot*, for my hand is already promised." The last words Elma uttered with a violent effort.

Lord Oranmore started up in dismay.

Elma silenced the remonstrance on his lips. "It was the wish of my dying mother,— that must be sacred. My lord, you will excuse me if I put an end to this interview." She moved towards the door.

"One moment, Elma. I cannot yield up all hope —" But Elma had passed from the room.

"I will not relinquish her!" exclaimed the impetuous young nobleman, as he darted out of the house.

CHAPTER III.

Lord Oranmore's Startling Communication to Leonard.—Rage of the Noble Father at the Proposed Alliance of his Son.—The Unwilling Ambassador.—The Chaplain's Visit to the Actress.—A Disappointment.—Elma's Declaration.—Mr. Ruthven's Chosen Son.—Unwavering Trust.—Mortimer's Return to Dublin.—Enthusiastic Attachment of the Company.—Singular Traits.—Lavish Charities.—Mr. Ruthven's Disclosure to Mortimer.—A Vision of Elma's Future.—Performance of Gisippus.—Mental Anguish of the Tragedian.—The Frantic Improvisation.—Lord Oranmore in the Boxes.—Mortimer's Exit from the Theatre.—Sudden Disappearance.

Ingenuous and reckless by nature, Lord Oranmore made no concealment of his feelings and intentions. That evening he gave Edmonton an animated account of his second interview with Elma. They were sitting in the theatre at the time. The play represented was Sheridan Knowles' tragedy of The Wife. Elma was to make her first appearance since the death of her mother. Edmonton's attention seemed rivetted upon the performance. But when Lord Oranmore repeated Elma's declaration that her hand was promised, his friend gave a violent start. Amazement—what else could it be?—lent to the eyes which he fixed upon the speaker a strange, lurid glare. The words "Not possible!" issued involuntarily from his ashy lips.

"She told me so herself," replied Lord Oranmore

"But that does not alter my resolves; it has only given them a new impetus. A woman worth winning and wearing is worth pursuing. Notwithstanding this prior engagement, I believe in my ultimate success."

Edmonton was again, to all appearance, engrossed in the play. For the rest of the evening, Lord Oranmore found it impossible to conquer his companion's taciturnity.

On the morrow, the young lord, with characteristic frankness, — we might say *daring*, — made known his matrimonial intentions to his stately father. The astonishment and wrath of the latter could hardly exceed his son's anticipations. An angry discussion ended as arguments between enraged parents and self-willed sons generally conclude. The father threatened to disinherit him as far as possible (an entailed estate limited the paternal power); the son intimated his willingness to accept this penalty as the price of following his own inclinations.

Lord Oranmore looked upon Elma's rejection of his son as one of the coquettish wiles by which she purposed more firmly to ensnare him. At first the indignant nobleman was strongly tempted to call upon her himself. Then he reflected that his chaplain would be a more suitable person.

This gracious, aged man, a benign and charity-loving Christian, evinced great reluctance to undertake the mission. In vain he protested that he was not qualified to act in such matters. The excited father would receive no denial. Mr. Edmonton must paint to the young girl the discord and misery which would be brought into the family by her forced admission; must obtain from her a promise that she would decline all further communication with Lord Oranmore.

Elma was at rehearsal when the unwilling ambassador called at her father's house. The clergyman announced his intention of waiting, and was ushered into the drawing-room.

Elma, when she entered, was not aware that the apartment was occupied. She stood directly in front of the venerable man, who had ample time to scan her person before she was conscious of his presence.

He rose and mentioned his name. What a flood of radiance seemed poured upon her face and shone from her eyes in "a thousand dewy rays"! There was not a trace of the usual cold reserve in her greeting, as she seated herself with unsuspicious confidence by his side. Her dignified simplicity and quiet grace made a deep impression upon her guest.

"This visit no doubt surprises you, Miss Ruthven? And yet some of your friends, I believe, now and then exchange our fireside for yours."

"Yes. Lord Oranmore has been quite a frequent visitor, and also your — your son, Mr. Edmonton."

"My son? Yes, I believe I have heard him say so; but I was not thinking of him."

"Not thinking of him?"

Elma echoed the words internally with painful surprise. What, then, was the object of his father's visit? The dancing, sparkling lights that illumined her countenance grew dimmer and dimmer as she mused, and then were wholly extinguished.

Her reverend guest noticed without comprehending the change. After an embarrassing pause, with much delicacy he disclosed his errand.

To the father of Lord Oranmore, to any one in the world save the man who sat before her, Elma would have replied haughtily. But there was a subdued sorrow in her tone which hardly accorded with the language of her reply.

"His lordship has nothing to fear from me. Unwelcomed I could never enter any family. In regard to Lord Oranmore, I would not unite my fate to his were his father and all his kin humbly to sue to me. I have never even entertained a passing preference for him."

"I believe you, my dear young lady. There is an air of truth about you which no one could doubt. My report will wholly calm the fears of Lord Oranmore, for I see you are not a woman who could be guilty of trifling. He did you wrong in supposing that your rejection of his son was a coquettish lure to enslave him."

"Great wrong. I am as proud as his lordship, though perhaps in a different way."

Mr. Edmonton gladly dropped the subject. Though his mission was accomplished, he experienced a strong inclination to extend his visit. He introduced other topics, and Elma conversed freely. He found how richly her mind was stored, how nobly her actions were guided, and wondered not at Lord Oranmore's infatuation, or only marvelled that the hair-brained youth had planted his hitherto fluctuating affections upon so worthy a foundation.

At length the clergyman rose to depart. He laid

his hand tenderly on the head of the young girl, with a fervent "God bless you, my child!"

Elma knew not that the face she raised to his beamed with reverential affection. The old man pondered for some time afterwards on that involuntary look. It gave his imagination the rein.

When Elma informed her father of Mr. Edmonton's visit, she also communicated to him Lord Oranmore's offer, made on the day previous, and her rejection.

Mr. Ruthven would have been indignant at the messenger sent to his child by the imperious nobleman, had he not experienced a proud satisfaction in Elma's decisive refusal. He was flattered that a man of illustrious birth had "rivalled for his daughter;" but he would not have allowed her to enter a noble family. That would be to separate her from himself, to wholly lose her. No! he greatly preferred to behold her the wife of an eminent actor,— above all others, of Gerald Mortimer! He told her this, in emphatic language.

Elma replied: "It is my chief happiness to please you, my father; but let us not talk of marriage. That I should marry yet is not an inevitable necessity. Let us put off all thoughts of it at present."

"I did not mean to urge you, or to *hurry* you, child; but it would be a joy to have Mortimer always with us,—we are so sad and lonely since your mother went, and Mortimer's presence is always exciting, inspiring. I need a son's aid. No, we won't *urge* you; but the sooner the day comes, the better, and no doubt so Mortimer thinks. He has been gone three weeks, and now he writes to apprise me that he will be in Dublin next Monday, and will commence an engagement. Here is a note enclosed for you."

Elma had, perhaps, been overcome by her interview with Mr. Edmonton, for her head swam, she grasped a chair for support, then tottered rather than walked to the window. Her father threw it open.

"You are not as strong as you were. Your mother's death has broken down both of us. Lean out; the air will revive you. But you have not taken Mortimer's note. There should be a restorative in that. Break the seal at once; I will leave you to enjoy the contents uninterrupted."

Though her father left the room, Elma sat in pensive meditation, with the note lying unheeded on her lap. At last she glanced over the brief lines, and laid them aside with a deep sigh. After that, she went steadily on her way as before, ever hoping that the patient discharge of daily duties would bring repose to her troubled mind. She was passing through a valley of shadows, groping in darkness for a season, but she never doubted that light shone in the unseen distance. To fulfil the task that Heaven assigned her, was to attract its rays to her obscured pathway.

"If all were ours *unearned*, what need of action?
If God no problem set for our unfolding,
Where were the joy, the power, the benefaction,
Of toil, and faith, and prayer, our spirits moulding?" *

Lord Oranmore sought Elma again, but was denied admission to her presence. He appealed to Mr. Ruthven, and learned that his daughter was affianced

* Epes Sargent.

to Mortimer. The nobleman was not discomfited. He could not place his suit on an equality with that of an actor ; he remained confident that Elma might be won.

A storm delayed the arrival of the steamer on the morning that Mortimer was to reach the Irish shores. It was near midday before the passengers disembarked at Kingston, and entered the railway carriages that conveyed them to Dublin.

The play for that evening was Gisippus, the youthful production of Gerald Griffin, a highly-gifted Irish novelist, who, in spite of the allurements of a brilliant literary career, grew weary of the world, and entered a monastery in Cork. There he died, at the age of thirty-five, in the second year of his novitiate.

Gisippus was one of Mortimer's most wonderful delineations.

Rehearsal had been called at a much later hour than ordinary, in anticipation of the tragedian's delay on the channel. He was, however, so regardless of stage observances, that his presence at the theatre in the morning was scarcely expected. It was an agreeable surprise to the manager when Mortimer, soon after rehearsal commenced, walked upon the stage. He was warmly welcomed by the whole company; perhaps we ought to except Elma, but she was never demonstrative. Mortimer was a rare instance of a dramatic favorite enthusiastically beloved by the players themselves. His manner was wholly free from the overbearing tyranny which tragic heroes are accustomed to assume towards their inferiors. He treated the subordinates of the theatre with manly courtesy, and an acknowledging remembrance that the feelings of the humblest were entitled to some consideration.

It was singular that, while he totally disregarded the clamorous approval of the audience, an unstudied expression of delight falling from the lips of a "bearer of banners," or a "general utility," imparted a thrill of pleasure. He often declared that actors were the only judges of acting — the only true critics. The panegyrics with which the journals teemed he never read. He scorned the "quirks of blazoning pens," which, to display the critic's own wisdom, manufactured beauties, or "shaped faults that are not," at random.

Mortimer dispensed charities with lavish hand. It was currently reported that the enormous proceeds of his nightly exertions were distributed among the suffering members of the profession. He had freed many from the galling bondage of the stage, and established them in more congenial employment. Did space permit, we might relate not a few touching histories of the objects of his bounty.

Upon this day, in particular, he listened with ready ear to tales of grief and want, and brightened the dim eyes of poverty with the reflected glitter of gold. He was happy, and true happiness yearns to share its joyful throbs with others, to double, treble them, by that communion.

Mortimer's manner was unusually buoyant during rehearsal. At its conclusion, he accompanied Mr. Ruthven and his daughter to their home. Elma had some needful preparations to make for the evening, and absented herself for a short time.

Left alone with Mortimer, Mr. Ruthven, with paternal pride, made known the flattering addresses of Lord Oranmore, and Elma's rejection of his hand.

Every word struck on Mortimer's ears as the poisonous dart of serpent tongues. He called to mind the last night that he stood upon the stage with Elma, the direction of her eyes when the bouquets were placed in her hands; — they had turned to the stage-box where Lord Oranmore sat. Heart-searing, crushing, was the conviction that took strong possession of his mind. Elma loved this frivolous, sycophantic young nobleman!

Yes, it must be so; and her troth to Mortimer had compelled her to refuse her lordly suitor. She loved him, and Mortimer must yield her up! Lord Oranmore would snatch her from the throne before which he had knelt with the worshipping crowd — would strip from her brow its crown, from her hand its sceptre, to discover that with them she had lost the charms of which he was enamored! He would transplant her to a petty conventional sphere of fashionable frivolities, where she must play a cold and narrow part upon a stage where there is more acting than in the play-house. How terrible would be her fate!

Mortimer dwelt more upon her probable misery than upon his certain wretchedness. For love seeks the felicity of the object beloved, rather than its own joy. From the heart where it dwells in pristine purity the demon Selfishness is wholly cast out.

Elma had no cause to reënter the room so timidly; she needed not to fear being left alone with her lover, nor to dread an outpouring of his passionate devotion.

Mr. Ruthven considerately withdrew.

Elma bent over her embroidery, counting the stitches with as much earnestness as though there were no more interesting occupation in life. Mortimer watched her for a short time in silence; when he spoke it was upon indifferent subjects. Very soon he abruptly took his leave.

Elma did not see him again until they met at night upon the stage.

She represented Sophronia, the Athenian maiden betrothed to Gisippus, who secretly loves Fulvius.

On the very morning of their bridal a doubt of Sophronia's affection springs up in the mind of the noble Gisippus. His magnanimity of soul points out but one course. He will learn the truth, and return to Sophronia her freedom, if he discover that she is about to place in his an unwilling hand. Gisippus thus addresses her:

"Lay your heart before me,
Naked as it appears to your own thoughts,
With all its aspirations. You may find
That I can act as worthy and as free
A part, as if I ne'er had stooped so low,
To win the love that hath, at last, deceived me.
For, though my heart doth witness, I do prize
That love beyond the life-blood that flows through it,
I would not weigh it 'gainst your happiness,
The throbbing of one pulse — now believe and trust me.
Sophronia. You are too noble!
Gisippus. No — no!
Do not think that, Sophronia;
Nor let your generous fear to wound a heart
Too sensitive affect your confidence.
The rigid schools in which my youth was formed
Have taught my soul the virtue that consists

In mastering all its selfish impulses !
And, could I bring content into your bosom,
And bid that care that pines your delicate cheek,
And pales its hue of bloom (fit paradise
For the revelry of smiles), resign his throne there,
My heart without a pang could lose ye ! (*Aside.*) How
It burns, while I belie it !
Soph. I have heard you
With wonder, that forbids my gratitude.
How have you humbled me ! O, Gisippus,
I will deceive you yet — for you shall find,
Although I cannot practise, yet I know
What greatness is, and can respect it truly ;
I would requite your generosity,
And what I can, I will. Do not distrust me
From any seeming ! *I have plight my promise,*
And it shall be fulfilled.
Gis. My fears were just, then ?
Soph. Let them be banished now ! My noble monitor,
When I shall make advantage of your goodness,
Virtue forswear me ! You have waked my heart
To duty and to honor. They shall find
An earnest votary in it ! "

The audience might have deemed it "excellent dissembling," but there was no acting in the deep intensity with which these passages were delivered.

The confidence of Gisippus is restored, and he departs to hasten the preparations for his nuptials. Fulvius enters, and upbraids Sophronia. Gisippus unexpectedly returns, and hears their converse.

"*Soph.* Pray you, Fulvius,
Resolve me this.
Fulv. What is 't you ask ?
Soph. Suppose —
(I do but dream now while I speak of this) —

But say that it were possible our loves
Might yet be favored !
Fulv. Ha !
Soph. Beware, young Roman !
I speak this as a dreamer. But, suppose —
Gisippus, you know, is worthy,
And loves you as a friend —
Fulv. Alas, I 've proved that,
But ill requited him !
Soph. I pray you hear me.
Suppose your friend should give me back the promise
That I have plighted — (O, most unwillingly !)—
And leave me free to make my own election,
Wrong or dishonor set apart !
Fulv. I hear ye.
Soph. How would my freedom move ye ?
Fulv. (*Rapturously.*) As my life
Restored beneath the lifted axe !
Soph. We should rejoice, then !
Fulv. We should pale the front,
The Afric front of night, with revel lights,
And tire her echoes with our laughter !
Soph. Ay !
And Gisippus would laugh, too.
Fulv. Ha !
Soph. He 'd be
The loudest reveller amongst us ! Ay,
We should be famed in story, too. The best
The truest friends — self-sacrificers ! — O !
Our monuments should be the memories
Of every virtuous breast, — while Gisippus
Might find his own dark tomb, and die forgotten."

By this dialogue the noble Athenian learns that his affianced bride weds him from a sense of honor, though her affections, in spite of herself, belong to another. Gisippus suddenly comes forward, and confronts the lovers. They are overwhelmed with confusion; but he, with glorious self-abnegation, resigns Sophronia, and bestows her upon the chosen of her heart.

Mortimer's eyes had sought the stage-box as he spoke. Lord Oranmore and Leonard Edmonton sat in their customary seats, the former bending forward with eager interest. The anguish and despair of the tragedian became all-puissant, and burst forth in a wild strain of improvised eloquence. He called down the most appalling maledictions upon the one for whom he yielded up his heart's best treasure, if sorrow ever crushed her spirit or tears scalded her furrowless cheeks, and ended with a prayer for her whose weal he had shipwrecked all his hopes to secure.

Actors and audience were alike taken by storm. Never had his magical sway over their emotions been so entire. The theatre rose *en masse*, with waving hats and handkerchiefs, and a whirlwind of acclamations.

Elma stood petrified.

A calmness as sudden as his violence now sank upon Mortimer's perturbed spirit. He returned to the language of the author, but even through that colder channel his agony found vent. Fulvius and Sophronia depart together, and Gisippus, left alone, cries out, in sorrow's last extremity:

"Gone! Alone!
How my head whirls, and my limbs shake and totter,
As if I had done a crime! I have — I 've lied
Against my heart. What think ye now, wise world?
How shows this action in your eyes? My sight
Is thick and misty, and my ears are filled
With sounds of hooting and of scorn —

What should I fear? I will meet scorn with scorn!
It is a glorious deed that I have done.
I will maintain it 'gainst the wide world's slight,
And the upbraiding of my own racked heart!
O! there I'm conquered!"

He sinks despondingly upon a rude bench, lifts from his brow the nuptial garland, and drops it at his feet.

The remaining acts of the play were unmarked by any extraordinary incident.

As Mortimer passed out of the theatre he had to force his way through a dense crowd of men, women, and children, assembled around the stage-door. Men who cheered, children who clung to his garments, women who held up their infants begging that he would bestow one look upon the "poor craythurs," just for good luck's sake. His hands were seized and kissed repeatedly, and it was with some difficulty that he could disengage them. When they were free, he drew a handful of silver from his pocket, and scattered it among the crowd. As the delighted mob scrambled for the coin, he leaped into his coach.

Mortimer had hurried from the theatre without bidding good-night to Elma or her father.

The next day the tragedian did not appear at rehearsal. This awakened no surprise. He did not call upon Elma. Night arrived — the hour for the rising of the curtain — and still Mortimer came not. A messenger was sent to his lodgings. The answer spread consternation throughout the theatre. After returning home, on the night previous, he had walked out, and had not been heard of since!

The play was suddenly changed.

Elma's mind was full of presageful fears. That frantic burst of eloquence had disclosed his belief that she loved Lord Oranmore. What consequences might not the fatal error bring forth! She dared not picture them.

CHAPTER IV.

Displeasure of the Audience. — Illness of Mr. Ruthven. — Maid of Mariendorpt.— The Tragedian's Return.— Singular State. — Elma's Joy. — Mr. Ruthven's Delight. — General Rejoicing. — Mortimer's Protestations. — Contract between Elma and Mortimer. — The Willing Signature. — The Father's Project. — Elma's Unexpected Consent. — Restoration of the Invalid.— Departure of the Tragedian, Elma, and her Father, upon a Provincial Tour.

Four days dragged wearily on. No tidings came from Mortimer. His mysterious absence threw an additional weight upon Elma's already oppressed spirits. Mr. Ruthven, after struggling upon the stage for two nights, called down the displeasure of the audience by his imperfect assumption of his favorite villains, fell ill, and was confined to his bed.

His constant query was, "Has Gerald come yet? Has Gerald been heard from?" And, when the same sad answer was repeated, he would ask, for the fiftieth time, in an upbraiding tone, "Elma, did you say anything to distress him? Did you — *could you* ill-treat Mortimer?"

Her assurances satisfied him only for the moment.

"Nature's foster-nurse, Repose," fled from him. No sweet oblivion closed his straining, restless eyes. Grief had outstripped time, in deadening all his faculties. He became helpless, petulant, and childish.

He could not endure Elma to be absent from his

side, yet he would not allow her to relinquish the arduous professional duties, which unavoidably separated her from him during a portion of the morning and the whole of the evening.

The Maid of Mariendorpt was the play represented on the fourth night after Mortimer's sudden disappearance. The filial devotion of the heroine stirred a deep spring in Elma's bosom. She could not but think of her suffering, perhaps dying, father. Her acting won a supremacy over the minds of her audience never before attained.

The play was over. She was passing to her chamber to disrobe, and hasten home, when she beheld in the obscure distance a familiar form.

"How like Mortimer!" she ejaculated, internally. The figure drew nearer. An exclamation of joy broke from her lips. She rushed towards it, and seized the cold, nerveless hand.

"You have returned! Is it you, indeed? No ill has befallen you? Heaven be praised, a thousand and a thousand times!"

There was no possibility of mistaking the rapture that betrayed itself in her tone, her mien, her glowing countenance. Those rare, delicious auguries shed their melting warmth on Mortimer's chilled heart.

The dress of the tragedian was travel-stained and disordered. His boots were pierced in many places, as though he had walked over rough roads for a long distance; his hair hung matted and entangled about his bloodless face; his lack-lustre eyes had the peculiar dreamy look of recent awakening from a somnambulic trance.

"Tell me where you have been?" questioned Elma, with anxious interest.

"I do not know,—walking—through woods—I believe,—I cannot tell where!"

"Walking all this time, without shelter, without food, without sleep? Impossible!"

"How long is it, then?" he asked, abstractedly.

"Four days since you left us."

Mortimer seemed to be reflecting, trying to calculate the time; but he could or would give no further explanation.

Several of the company had caught sight of him, and they gathered around with joyful welcomes.

Elma had placed her arm in his. She was confident that his presence at her father's bedside would possess a remediate influence.

"You will continue your engagement? You will appear to-morrow night?" inquired the calculating manager.

Elma's voice joined in. "Do consent; you must not leave us yet; your absence has terribly distressed my father,—he is very ill!"

"Ill? Indeed! Let us go to him directly," returned Mortimer, with emotion.

"But your engagement,—surely you will conclude it? I must have posters put out immediately. Let me entreat you—" persisted Mr. Villars.

"I had no intention of breaking it," replied Mortimer.

Elma's stage raiment was quickly exchanged for her ordinary garments, and, accompanied by Mortimer and old Winifred, in a few moments she was on her way home.

Her father was anxiously awaiting her return, counting the very minutes of her absence. He accosted her peevishly with:

"Is it you, at last? The play must have been over half an hour ago. Elma, why do you neglect me so? Why did you not come sooner?"

"I was detained, my dear father; shall I bring in my apology? Do not be too much rejoiced, for I am going to offer it in the person of a valued friend, whose presence you have missed even more than you did mine."

Mr. Ruthven raised himself upon his elbow.

"Has he come? Has he come?"

"Mr. Mortimer—" cried Elma.

Mortimer entered at the summons.

The aged actor's delight bordered on the precincts of pain. He could not ask where Mortimer had been,—why he had gone; he cared not to know. It was enough that he had returned. All the questions his tongue could frame were swallowed up in the entreaty: "*You will not leave us again?* I am an old man now. Gerald, you will leave us no more? Say yes to that."

Mortimer turned to Elma; the eyes of her father followed the direction.

"Yes, yes; I know what that means. She is a girl of few words, yet she also will bid you stay,—will you not, my daughter!"

"Yes," replied Elma, promptly.

Mortimer as readily, but with marked solemnity, answered, "I will never leave you until she bid me."

The pain-contracted, wrinkled features of the old man relaxed into a childlike calm. He lay gazing upon the two beloved beings until slumber, so long a fugitive, gently rocked his spirit, and with her balmy breathing closed his eyes.

Elma feared that some sudden movement might disturb him. She softly rose, and led the way to the boudoir adjoining, closing the door as she passed out.

"Elma," said Mortimer, when they were alone together, "have I deceived myself? Was the joy you exhibited at my return all for your father's sake?"

Elma, while she sat by her father's couch, had nerved herself for this interview.

"I did not rejoice for my father's sake *alone.* Your unaccountable absence has given me great uneasiness, much pain."

"How shall I explain it?" returned Mortimer. "Your father told me of Lord Oranmore's suit, and of your rejection. An accidental occurrence caused me to believe that you loved him. With that conviction my heart seemed turned to stone. I might truly have said, with the tortured Moor, 'I strike it, and it hurts my hand;' for I carried in my bosom a thing of marble coldness and of iron weight. I fear to tell you to what desperate deed I was tempted as I wandered. Stretched on the rack of doubt, I thought I could not longer face the ills of this harsh world. But my better angel stood beside me, and held back my rash hand. I know not how long, or whither, I strayed, or what chanced, until a voice whispered, soothingly, that I was the dupe of my own phantom-like fears. I had not learned from

Elma's lips that she loved this brainless lord; that voice sent me back to ask the question."

"I do *not* love Lord Oranmore, never have loved him, never could love him," answered Elma, firmly.

"Those words fall like the healing nucta-drop upon the pestilence in my soul, and calm and purify its troubled, tainted atmosphere. If you *had* loved him, Elma, do not think that I could have thrust myself as a hideous barrier between you and happiness. Had you made such a choice, I must have trembled for your future, I would have prayed you to reflect; but, though my soul is so enfettered to your love, I would have broken the chain with resolute hand when I found that it hung heavily upon you. But this is not so; you do *not* love him; you have said it. I may pray you to listen to me while I tell you all you have been to me, all you are, all you can be! When I tell you how you may make or unmake — "

Though Elma did not interrupt him, though she sat with folded hands, and half-bowed form, and eyes bent down, until the long, silky lashes cast a deep shadow on her cheek, Mortimer paused. Elma, actress as she was, could not banish from her countenance an expression of intense suffering.

"Your look renders me dumb. Elma, I implore you, let me not deceive myself again. There is something I cannot comprehend. Give language to your thoughts,— even to those which could pain me most. I entreat you, do not keep me a stranger to them. What shadow is this upon your sweet countenance? You do not love Lord Oranmore; you would not marry him; surely there is no other ——"

In an instant Elma regained the self-possession which had forsaken her. She prevented his concluding the sentence.

"I—it is that I—I do not desire to marry." Then, as she caught his searching eye, she added, "Not while I feel as I do at this moment."

For a brief space the tragedian sat pondering.

"God forgive me if I commit an ungenerous action!" he said. "Many men have been guilty of such deeds when passion gained the mastery over their judgment, and they could accept no other guidance. I fear myself!"

After a longer silence, he added: "Elma, I will but ask one sacrifice from you—one which, perhaps, I have no right to demand; for, though your mother joined our hands, I must relinquish you, if your heart does not ratify that solemn compact. I fear the effect upon my own mind, were I to give you *wholly* up. I ask but one promise from you; I would pray you to attach your name to a contract which my eyes can look upon and drink in comfort from, when I feel something dangerous battling within me; when I have cause to fear that

> 'My blood begins my safer guides to rule,
> And passion, having my best judgment collied,
> Assays to lead the way.'

Will you promise me never to give your hand, while I live, without my consent?"

"Yes, gladly," replied Elma, without hesitation.

She rose and placed upon the table materials for writing. Mortimer dashed off a few lines, and handed her the paper; she perused it, subscribed her name, and returned it with a bright smile.

A sound from the inner chamber sent Elma to her father's bedside. He was awake. His first inquiry was for Mortimer, who immediately answered in person.

Mr. Ruthven begged his daughter to retire. Mortimer asked permission to watch beside his friend all night; the proposition was received with grateful acquiescence.

Elma sank to rest with a lighter heart than had throbbed in her bosom since the death of her mother. She was spared the utterance of lip-vows unechoed by her soul; she was saved from the commission of that legal sin which daily stains the lives of thousands. She asked not that the yearnings of her spirit might be accomplished; their fulfilment lay with the Great Ruler of events. Whatever was best for the perfecting of her spiritual state, whatever would promote its healthfulness here and progression hereafter, that would surely be. In this confidence she was content.

When she reëntered her father's chamber, at an early hour the next morning, she found him conversing in a cheerful tone with Mortimer.

"Behold my physician, and the effects of his mystical power," was Mr. Ruthven's greeting, as he pointed to Mortimer.

With an affectionate frankness which she had never evinced towards him before, Elma placed her hand in that of the tragedian, and looked in his face with tender gratitude.

"Our project,—tell her our project, Gerald, while I spare speech," said Mr. Ruthven, hilariously.

"We only wait for your consent, Elma; but the plan is your father's. He says that Dublin and familiar scenes recall old memories, which have grown painful to him since your mother left us; that his health is broken; that he desires to travel, but he is too feeble to travel without—a—a *friend.*"

"A son—a son—*a dear son!*" interrupted the old man, warmly.

"True, a son,—at least, one who will ever delight in performing a son's duties. He proposes a round of engagements in England and Scotland, for you, Elma, and myself."

"Assisted—assisted by me, when I have strength, as I will have," added the invalid.

"Of course, assisted by your father, when his health permits. We will travel through the British provinces—"

"Perhaps go to London; no fear of Elma's not being appreciated there. Gerald has had so many solicitations from London managers, and it would be of such an advantage to you, child!"

Mortimer's countenance fell. He was unwilling to thwart the old man's whims or wishes. He had invariably declined all overtures from the metropolis.

"Time enough to decide about that, my dear father," said Elma, for she saw that it gave Mortimer pain to utter a denial.

"Then you consent, my child?"

"Willingly, if we can obtain the permission of Mr. Villars; we are under contract to him for the rest of the season."

"I have a *douceur* to make him yield up his claims," replied Mortimer. "Trust me, that matter can be arranged."

And it was arranged, though not without some difficulty, for Elma had become of sterling value to the theatre. But Mortimer conducted the transaction with the manager, and what arguments he used did not transpire.

Mortimer's engagement had commenced on Monday; he had absented himself four nights,—Saturday evening alone remained. Upon that night he appeared with Elma. More than once he fancied that her eyes strayed to the box where, as usual, Lord Oranmore sat, but he was now fully convinced that their direction was accidental.

On Monday, Gerald Mortimer, with Mr. Ruthven and his daughter, started for a provincial tour.

CHAPTER V.

Provincial Engagements. — Mr. Ruthven's Dissertations on Represented Villany. — Unpaid Performances in the Boxes of the Theatre. — The Surprise. — Lord Oranmore and Mr. Edmonton. — Painful Effects of her Father's Intelligence upon Elma. — Mortimer's Solicitation for her Confidence.— Gloom of the Tragedian. — Elma's Disturbed Equanimity. — Leonard Edmonton's Visit. — His Character and Views. — A Betrayal. — The Forgotten Contract. — Happiness Renounced.

We do not purpose step by step to follow Mortimer and Elma's career in the provinces. They were everywhere received with enthusiasm. To these audiences the tragedian was already familiar. He brought Elma before them with exultant pride.

Mortimer's habitual eccentricity ceased to be painfully manifested. The erratic comet now moved in a fixed orbit. She was the sun around which he revolved with steady light. Managers, whom he had hitherto kept in a constant state of doubt and fear, rejoiced, and sat beneath their (painted) vineyards and fig-trees in peace.

No word of love ever fell from Mortimer's lips, no allusion to the contract he held, no half-breathed hope for the future. The blissful present filled life's goblet to the brim, and mirrored in its sparkling juices but the day and the hour.

Mr. Ruthven's eager desire once more to tread

the boards remained unabated, but ungratified. His voice had grown feeble and piping, his gait tottering, his form bowed, his mind infirm; and yet his profession could not lose its strong fascination. He strolled about nightly behind the scenes until the play commenced, and then took his seat with the audience, listening with entranced ears to the eulogiums drawn forth by Mortimer's vivid delineations, or Elma's sculpture-like embodiments.

Not unfrequently it was the aged actor who "started the applause" at some delicate point, which would have escaped the uninitiated audience.

The personators of the *villains* invariably excited his ire, they "imitated humanity so abominably;" so, at least, he declared to his accidental neighbors. Between the acts, his learned dissertations upon the true mode of "making up" and depicting a genuine rogue, and his illustration of the effects of crime upon the facial muscles, nightly drew around him a group of wondering auditors. Impelled by love for his art, he indulged them with a small, unsalaried performance of his own, which certainly combined *instruction* with entertainment.

It was two months since the travellers left Dublin. They were now performing in Glasgow. Mr. Ruthven, according to his custom, sat in front of the theatre. He was too much interested in Mortimer's "Gamester," and his daughter's Mrs. Beverly, to observe who occupied the seat adjoining his. When the curtain fell, at the close of the first act, a familiar voice saluted him with,

"Ruthven, how are you? Glad to see you looking so well!" and his neighbor warmly grasped his hand.

"Bless my heart and soul! You don't say so? I had n't the least idea of seeing you here, my lord. Very glad, I assure you. Is that Mr. Edmonton by your side? Exceedingly glad, sir, to meet you again, — most unexpected rencontre, I declare! When did you leave Dublin?"

"Only three days since, — arrived in Glasgow this morning, — are making a brief tour of pleasure. I need not ask after Miss Ruthven's health. I never saw her look more charming, and she has gained dramatic power. We may expect a fine performance to-night."

What father is not gratified by encomiums bestowed upon his child? If any such there be, Mr. Ruthven was not of the number. He conversed freely with the young men of Elma, until the individual who assumed that "double-distilled villain," Stukely, awakened his wrath; for the rest of the evening he could only discourse, with the garrulity of age, upon his favorite theme.

When the play ended, Lord Oranmore, courteously ignoring the past, expressed a desire to pay his respects to Miss Ruthven. The father assured both gentlemen that they would be welcome.

Mr. Ruthven rejoined his daughter, to conduct her home. She was standing near the green-room door, beside Mortimer. He was consulting her upon the best selection of a play for his benefit-night.

"Do you know that you have been acting for some Hibernian friends?" asked Mr. Ruthven, gayly.

"No!" replied Elma.

"No! who are they?" asked Mortimer.

"Lord Oranmore and Mr. Edmonton. Mercy on me! what's the matter with Elma?"

As her father gave utterance to those names, a deadly pallor spread over her face, her eyes half closed, her head sank back, her pulses stopped. But only for a second — she recovered herself almost before he had ceased speaking, and made an effort to reässure him by a forced smile.

"Are you very weary? Has Mrs. Beverly overcome you?" asked her father.

Elma was the soul of truth; she could not have stooped to subterfuge; she answered, though with an unsteady voice, "No, — I was not, — I am not more fatigued than usual."

Mr. Ruthven looked puzzled, as he conducted her to the carriage, followed by Mortimer.

When they returned to the hotel, the latter seized an opportunity while her father was at the supper-table to say: "Elma, confide in me, I implore you; disclose to me your heart. The pen-stroke upon that paper binds you to nothing but *confidence* in me. What have you to fear, Elma? What would I not sacrifice for you? Life itself is but a breath I would gladly yield up, were your happiness to be secured thereby. Only confide in me freely."

"I have nothing — there is nothing I can confide," replied Elma; but her eyes were not raised to his with their wonted ingenuous clearness.

"Strange!" said Mortimer, sadly, and rising as he spoke, "that I have so seldom failed in reading hearts, — hearts that were indifferent to me, — and I have no power to scan yours, which is dearer than my own!" and he left the room.

"Read my heart?" Elma slowly repeated. "How should he, when I dare not turn my eyes inward and view it myself?"

The mist-like gloom that for two months had melted from Mortimer's brow regathered in a night. When they met the next morning, Elma perceived the ominous cloud; but she had no power to strike it with sunshine, and dispel its darkness.

Some invisible hand had troubled the calm-gliding, heaven-reflecting stream of her own life. She was no longer queen over herself, all her emotions in subjection to her will. Every time the door opened, her eyes turned that way; the sound of a knock caused her to bound from her seat; her color varied at every approaching step.

During rehearsal she was strangely *distraite*. She made several unaccountable blunders, forgot her entrances, took wrong situations, grew confused, and could not conceal that her wandering thoughts refused to be chained down to that charmless locality.

Rehearsal was but half over, when Mortimer suddenly forsook the stage. The call-boy searched for him in vain. At last word was brought that the door-keeper had seen him leave the theatre.

"How vexatious!" exclaimed Mr. Busby, the stage-manager. "Everything has gone so smoothly through this engagement! He has conducted himself, for once, like an ordinary mortal. I was just congratulating myself. Now, I'll answer for it, we shall have some fresh eccentricity. No more rehearsals, I warrant! I suppose something has vexed him; ten to one if he will make his appearance to-night!"

Elma, on her return home, found upon her drawing-room table Lord Oranmore's card, with pencilled regrets at her absence. It was still in her hand, when the door was thrown open, and a servant announced Mr. Edmonton.

Where was all Elma's wonted equanimity and self-control? It had fled, beyond her recalling, at the sound of a name. In her agitation, her fruitless struggles for composure, how could Leonard Edmonton help perusing that page of her heart which was most precious to the eyes of a lover?—for that he was a lover the reader need hardly be told.

When Lord Oranmore proposed to make the tour of England and Scotland, his sole object was to behold Elma once more. Edmonton had been the associate of his former travels, and was again solicited to bear him company. It was *possible*—we might say *probable*—that Leonard's ready acquiescence sprang from the same hope that animated the bosom of his noble friend.

The characters of these two young men were in striking contrast to each other, though their affections centred upon the same object. Lord Oranmore was thoughtless, flippant, worldly,—a titled coxcomb. By him Elma was the more highly prized because a gaping multitude bowed down before her. To Edmonton that very circumstance would have made her less dear, had he not known that she carried an antidote in her heart which rendered harmless the subtle poison of popular adulation.

In his pure and lofty mind the false and the hollow

found no echoes. Yet his expansive heart unfolded itself genially, and embraced all that Heaven created. The harsh judgments, that shot with withering condemnation from self-righteous tongues, never sullied his lips.

He had become a student of divinity, against strong opposition, because he preferred to be a messenger of peace, a bearer of balm to wounded, broken spirits, rather than to hold the highest office which the power of man could bestow.

He was too liberal, too well-informed, too deeply imbued with Christian charity, to suppose that evil necessarily intermingled with the represented history which takes the name of the drama. He thought it no shame to love such a woman as Elma, though she chanced to bear the title of an actress; though she was the daughter, and the granddaughter, and the great-granddaughter, of actors.

The lights which shone upon her life had been struck from sparks that Leonard first kindled. It was he who had taught her to seek the kingdom of heaven and its righteousness, believing that all things needful would be added unto her, — all things which regarded her *actual* good, — not her mere transient prosperity in time, but her unperishing, ineffable, ever-increasing felicity in eternity. From this source sprang her unrebellious patience, her never-failing trust.

Leonard Edmonton was on the eve of declaring his attachment to Elma, when he was thunderstruck by the information that Lord Oranmore had sought her hand; that he had been rejected; that she was already betrothed.

Her image was interwoven with every fibre of his heart, yet he must pluck it thence. It was a hard disjunction, a cruel severing. For a time the flood swept over him, and the Ararat of his existence disappeared.

When Lord Oranmore proposed the visit to Scotland, Edmonton found it impossible to trample out a hope which still flickered in his breast. He would see Elma once more, make "assurance doubly sure," and part with her, if needs must be, forever.

And when he came, Elma, as we have already seen, forgot for the moment her interview with his father, her bond to Mortimer,—everything but the joy of standing in his presence, beholding him, listening to him once again. Her manner awakened a thousand delicious hopes, and emboldened Edmonton to give them utterance. The answer at which his heart throbbed tumultuously was not syllabled in language, nor conveyed in any form that could be coldly transcribed upon paper.

But when Edmonton strove to break the spell of her eloquent, trembling silence, and implored her to tell him that he had not been wholly banished from her thoughts,—that she had cherished some memory of him during their separation,—she raised the lid of a box which stood on the table, took from an inner drawer a small packet, and laid it in his hand.

He opened the paper. Within was the bunch of violets, fastened by a golden arrow, which had fallen at her feet on the night of her mother's farewell.

But Elma checked his exclamation of rapture.

"Selfish and thoughtless! what have I done?" she cried. "How totally I have forgotten all that—

O, there is so much that I have yet to tell you! That bond —"

"A bond? Do not say that you are not free, Elma!" he exclaimed, in a tone of consternation.

"Free? Yes, I am; and yet not wholly free. There is my father crossing the street, — it is not possible now to tell you all. O, forget these few moments of happiness! I can promise you nothing."

"Do not keep me in cruel suspense, Elma! When am I to see you again? Let it be to-day, — let me know the worst to-day."

"To-day! how is that possible? The day is nearly over."

Mr. Ruthven, whom Elma had seen from the window, now entered the room.

Edmonton lingered as long as politeness would permit; then took his leave, without obtaining another word of explanation from Elma.

Mr. Ruthven was in a disturbed, querulous state, because Gerald could not be found; because Elma could not account for his sudden departure from rehearsal.

Well might her heart sink as she reflected how necessary Mortimer was to her father's happiness!

Her self-possession once restored, her resolution was quickly taken. She would not cause her aged parent sorrow; she would not render Mortimer miserable. She closed her eyes upon the vision of that calm and holy future which had risen up before her. She would seek the earliest opportunity to confide everything to Edmonton. He was too noble-minded to endeavor to change her purpose.

CHAPTER VI.

A Lover's Perplexity. — Edmonton behind the Scenes. — Elma's Confession. — Sudden Appearance of the Tragedian. — Parting of the Lovers. — Mortimer's Inexplicable Conduct.— Conversation with Elma. — Reciprocal Generosity. — The Father's Misinterpretation.

Leonard Edmonton's interview with Elma had lifted him for a moment to the highest pinnacle of felicity, then plunged him into an abyss of doubt. Certain and inevitable evil he could have encountered with calmness; but these perplexing, bewildering hopes and fears put to flight his wonted self-control. Delay became intolerable; he must see Elma that very evening, and entreat her full confidence.

At the theatre in Glasgow access behind the scenes was not attended with difficulty. A quarter of an hour before the rising of the curtain, Edmonton presented himself at the stage entrance, and requested to see Miss Ruthven. Without comment or question, the door-keeper gave him admission. No guide was vouchsafed. Leonard entered and wandered about until he reached the back of the stage, behind the "flats." Here a couple of carpenters were constructing a throne (King Lear was the tragedy to be represented that evening). The intruder was unnoticed until he accosted them. He had written a few words on his card, and wished to send it to Miss Ruthven. One of the men, without interrupting his occupation, shouted to Jock, the call-boy. A sandy-haired lad answered the summons, received the card, and walked off, deliberately perusing the pencilled lines as he went.

A few moments afterwards, Elma, in her Cordelia attire, appeared before her lover.

The carpenters had completed their royal elevation, and now bore it away.

Elma and Leonard stood alone in the dim light. She was no longer the blushing, trembling girl, who had been surprised into the betrayal of her heart's dearest secret. She had advanced towards Leonard with a firm step, an air of sad composure, a look of steady resolve.

"I fear I have committed an impropriety in presenting myself here, Elma; but I could not endure the state of torturing uncertainty in which I parted from you."

"I am glad that you have come," replied Elma, very quietly; "I have blamed myself severely for the false hopes I gave you this morning."

"False hopes, Elma? Was I wrong, then, in believing what your looks told me in such thrilling language? Must I doubt — "

"Spare me!" supplicated Elma. "Do not try my strength! My heart may prove weaker than my judgment — my resolution!" Then she added, in a quicker, more excited tone: "But why need I make any concealment from you, who are worthy of all trust? I should not blush to admit that Heaven could not bless me more than by exchanging my uncongenial *present* for a *future* by your side."

"Elma, what words of — "

Elma interrupted him. "Let me tell you all while I can. My parents chose for me a husband; — one whom they loved, one for whom I have the profoundest esteem. My dying mother placed my hand in his; my father clings to him with the devotion of a parent. I could not, *would not* rob that infirm and grief-worn father of this chosen staff of his age."

"But, dearest, if his consent could be obtained —"

"It is *not possible!* But, if it were, an insuperable barrier still divides us. He to whom I was betrothed, Gerald Mortimer, as he is called, loves me with all the uncontrollable ardor of his strong nature. There is a mystery attached to him that I have not endeavored to penetrate; he will unfold it himself in good time. But sometimes I have fancied that there must be hereditary insanity in the family to which he belongs. All painful excitements appear to unsettle his mind. *I* have exerted a calming influence over him which no one else seems to possess. Think you I could now purchase my happiness at the price, perhaps, of his reason?"

"You are then engaged to him? I thought you told me you were free!"

"I *was* engaged to him, but, the moment he had cause to doubt my affection he generously released me. He now holds my written promise that I will never bestow my hand, while he lives, unsanctioned by him. His consent I well know would be granted at a single word of mine; but that word, which must seal his misery, will never pass my lips! Be content with the confession I have so frankly made, that you are dearer to me than all else upon this earth; though I will not wring my father's heart,

I will not wreck Mortimer's happiness, by becoming your wife — never! never!"

At this moment a groan, so full of mortal anguish that it seemed the severing of a soul from its earthly tenement, reached their ears.

They turned. Elma recognized the kingly robes of Lear. No face was visible, for the clenched hands were pressed upon the brow. The figure passed silently on its way to the green-room.

"It is Mortimer!" exclaimed Elma, in accents of consternation. "He must have heard my words! Leave me, I pray you! Let me go to him at once, else some terrible consequence may ensue."

"One word more, Elma! I honor, yes, with my whole soul, I reverence your motives. I will not, even in thought, seek to alter your heroic resolution. I would be unworthy of you, if I could do so. Only grant me the privilege of sometimes seeing you still as the dearest of friends. But, come what may, even if we never behold each other again upon this earth, there is a realm where we *must* meet; and, until the day of that blessed reünion, be sure that my heart is true to yours."

"As mine will ever be!" answered Elma, in a scarcely audible tone.

With one confiding clasp of their hands they parted.

Elma sought Mortimer in vain. She feared that, in the rash madness of the moment, he had rushed from the theatre.

Just as the curtain rose, to her great relief, he joined the group who stood ready to take their situations on the stage in King Lear's hall of audience.

His mien was placid, his thoughts were apparently engrossed in his part.

When the act concluded, Elma approached, and addressed him. He answered mildly. His manner was even calmer than usual.

Elma began to doubt that he had overheard her words; but she could not rest without assuring herself, and timidly asked,

"Was it not you whom I saw, a few moments ago, when I was conversing with — with Mr. Edmonton?"

Mortimer regarded her in amazement; then answered, with forced composure:

"Probably; I was near you for a few seconds. O, Elma! Elma! why is it so hard for me to say

'Yield up, O love, thy crown and hearted throne'?

Why are you so dear that the strength of a giant will cannot tear you from my thoughts? But do not fear; do not look so troubled. You have nothing to dread from me."

"I know it, Gerald."

"You have made a noble choice, Elma. His love is not a mere 'toy in the blood,' as was the fanciful passion of Lord Oranmore. I have heard the praises of Leonard Edmonton from tongues that delight only in censure."

Could Elma prevent the dawning smile that unconsciously stole over her countenance? Could Mortimer help the icy pang that smile shot through his heart?

"Do not say 'my choice,'" replied Elma, recovering herself. "Mr. Edmonton is aware — expects nothing from me."

Mortimer made no rejoinder, and Elma was at a loss in what manner to continue the conversation, or to construe his silence.

Lear was called to the stage.

When the play concluded, Mortimer returned with Elma and Mr. Ruthven to their hotel.

Elma could trace nothing unusual in the tragedian's conduct; no changeful fits and starts, no evidences of the great convulsion of spirit which she had cause to anticipate.

When they parted, there was so much tenderness in his adieu, so much confiding affection in hers, that the aged parent, who sat contentedly gazing upon them, drew happy auguries from their mutual cordiality.

As he pressed his lips on Elma's forehead, and bestowed his nightly benediction, he said:

"Best of daughters! what a source of unmingled joy you have ever been to me! a joy that is ever increasing. You leave none of my wishes unfulfilled. It makes me glad at heart when I see you so kind to Gerald. You will not keep him much longer in suspense; even these old eyes can see that plainly."

"My father! my father!" exclaimed Elma, in a tone of deep anguish, as she clung to him, and hid her face upon his shoulder.

"What does that mean, Elma?"

"God only knows the future!" she answered, as she released her hold, and, with slow steps, retired to her chamber.

CHAPTER VII.

The Tragedy of Bertram. — Rehearsal.— Elma's Astrologer.— An Enigma.— Performance of Bertram.— A Rash Deed and Terrible Reality.— The Contract Annulled. — The Tragedian's Closing Scene.— Mystery that remains Unsolved. — A Year Later. — Farewell of an Actress. — Picture in a Parish Church.

The tragedy of Bertram, by the Rev. Charles Maturin, of St. Peter's, Dublin, was the play selected for representation on the ensuing evening. The thrilling personations of Edmund Kean first imparted to this highly-wrought drama a decided but transient popularity. The more fastidious taste of audiences at the present day rarely demands its performance.

Mortimer and Elma met as usual at rehearsal. The anxious, questioning eyes she raised to his countenance were withdrawn with an expression of grateful content. Mortimer's face was unruffled, as on the night previous. It was fixed, almost rigid, in its placidity.

While a scene in which she was not concerned was rehearsed, Elma sat beside the prompter's table, her head leaning upon her hands, her eyes half-closed. She was thinking of her father, and of the stormy grief and displeasure which would be conjured up by the knowledge that she could never become the wife of Mortimer. She was asking herself whether waywardness and selfishness were not largely intermingled with her affection for Edmonton. She was hearkening to reproaches that cried out in her heart with clamorous, accusing tongues, and drowned love's low-voiced, timorous defence

Mortimer stood contemplating her for a brief space. Then he drew near, and said,

"Elma, I cannot bear to see a shadow upon that dear countenance. Look up, and smile; for the darkness is passing away. Listen, while I play the astrologer, and tell you of the fortunate star that shines over your head. It gleams through a cloudless sky, and rests above an earthly abode of peace and love, where Elma will dwell. Do not cast the poor prophet of to-day quite out of your thoughts when you stand on the rose-twined threshold of that home, and look up to that star."

"You speak in riddles," said Elma, trying to laugh; "and I am the very dullest of diviners."

"Time will solve the enigma. When it does, waste a thought upon one who will not be by to remind you —"

"What do you mean?" asked Elma, in a startled tone. "You are not going away? You do not intend to leave us?"

"No — yes,— I cannot tell."

"Do not, I entreat you! Think of my father, of his happiness —"

"I have thought of his, and of yours. I would secure his with yours, and through yours."

"Bertram and Imogine called!" cried Jock, saucily thrusting himself between the pair, and widely grinning with delight at breaking up the conversation of supposed lovers.

Mortimer did not again approach Elma while rehearsal lasted, nor did they meet during the rest of the day.

Bertram does not appear until the second act. In Act I., Scene 5th, Imogine is discovered sitting at a table, with a miniature in her hand.

The character of Imogine, the Lady of St. Aldobrand, was not faithfully interpreted by Elma's chaste and unimpassioned delineation.

As she made her first exit at right, she passed by Mortimer, who had stationed himself where he could survey the audience.

"He is there!" he murmured, in a strange, unnatural tone.

Not an atom of coquetry was infused in Elma's nature. She did not ask "who," as other women might have done; nor did she affect surprise. She had not once turned her eyes in the direction where Edmonton sat; yet she was instinctively, magnetically, conscious of his presence.

That night Mortimer surpassed all his grandest efforts in the depiction of fierce, frantic, startling, and appalling passions.

In the last act Imogine dies in the arms of Bertram. Mortimer, during this scene, in particular, appeared wrought up to frenzy. Cold drops poured from his brow, his face was livid, his whole frame quivered with strong emotion.

After the death of Imogine, instead of snatching a sword from one of the knights (according to stage direction), he drew a dagger from his own girdle. The steel glittered for an instant, as he pronounced the words,

"Bertram has but one fatal foe on earth,
And he is *here!*"

then was violently plunged into his breast. He sank upon the ground, exclaiming, in an exultant tone,

"Lift up your holy hands in charity!
I died no felon death —
A warrior's weapon freed a warrior's soul!"

Elma's eyes were closed as she lay upon the stage. She marked not the red current that flowed upon the ground, even till it reached her white raiment. The actors beheld it, and looked aghast. The audience saw it with mute horror.

Mortimer lay motionless, weltering in blood. The curtain fell. His companions stooped to raise him.

"Gently! gently!" he groaned; "you are — carrying — a — dying — man!"

They bore him to the green-room, and laid him upon the sofa.

"Is he fatally injured?" "How came he by a sharp dagger?" "Was it an accident?" were the whispered queries of pallid lips on every side.

Elma knelt by the couch, and with firm and skilful hands essayed to bind up the wound.

He shook his head, as he regarded her, and said, hoarsely, "Past all surgery!" Then, with a painful effort, he lifted his hand, felt in his bosom, took thence a stained and crumpled paper, and thrust it into her hands.

His voice was so faint that she could scarcely distinguish his words (so she bore testimony afterwards), but she thought they were, "It is annulled;

let the sacrifice not be in vain! Pardon, O, my God! Pardon, for her sake!"

A portion of the audience had rushed behind the scenes, and now thronged the apartment. From their midst Mr. Ruthven pressed forward, with tottering limbs and horror-stricken countenance. When he saw Elma bending over Mortimer, with crimsoned hands and garments, he would have fallen, had not a manly arm supported him. It was that of Edmonton.

Mortimer's glazing eyes turned to his aged friend, and to him by whose arm he was sustained. He motioned them to draw near. The old man appeared stupefied by grief. He seemed incapable of obeying Mortimer's gesture. It supplicated him to bend down, that he might catch the words the dying man could with difficulty articulate. But Edmonton bowed his head close to the pale and stiffening lips.

When he raised his face again, Mortimer had expired.

Whether the fatal blow had been deliberately given, whether it was purely accidental, whether it had been inflicted in a state of uncontrollable excitement, produced by his portrayal of Bertram's stormy passions, none knew to a certainty. If it were a deed of wilful crime, God alone could judge him, — God alone beheld the maddening throes of his loving, yet renouncing, clinging, yet despairing, spirit.

The history of Gerald Mortimer remained unrevealed. If Mr. Ruthven possessed a clue by which it could have been traced, this last shock had so far impaired his memory that the questions of the coroner failed to discover the missing thread.

* * * * * *

One year after that night of tragic horror, a thronged audience were collected in the Dublin Theatre Royal. They had assembled to receive the adieu of one who was dear to them for her mother's sake, and honored for her own.

Elma would have glided unmarked from a profession which she had never loved, — "the world forgetting, by the world forgot," — but for her reverence to the wishes of her father, who was obstinately punctilious in all professional and public observances. "The unruly waywardness that infirm and choleric years bring with them" rendered even his daughter's entreaties powerless ; he would not allow her to dispense with this formal farewell.

Since Mortimer's tragical death Mr. Ruthven's mind was gradually weaned from its fondness for the stage. He had slowly consented to Elma's casting off the glittering chain that had long pressed heavily on her unambitious, unworldly heart.

Elma had personated the Maid of Mariendorpt, one of the few characters which she loved to represent, for the last time. The curtain had fallen. When it rose again, she was standing where, less than two years before, her mother had sat hearkening to farewell plaudits, which sounded musical even to her dying ears. They had no such melody for those of her child.

A serene joy lighted Elma's countenance, as, with quiet, courteous dignity, she bowed her adieu. No accents passed her lips. What had she to say? She had done her duty, they had rewarded her, she thanked them. That was conveyed without words.

The injudicious few were not content, and demanded a vocal farewell. Elma met the request with a smile that softened her denial, but gave no hope of compliance, and silenced entreaty.

The descending curtain shut out that gay throng forever, and Elma rejoiced. She was no longer an actress!

She turned to her former associates, her fellow-laborers, and gave her hand to every one in turn, and spoke a few gentle words even to the humblest. They gathered around her, uttering tearful adieus, and blessings, and thanks for past kindnesses. Then her father led her away, and proudly told her she had done all things well.

Scarcely had they passed their own threshold when she was folded to a heart as true as ever beat in mortal breast, and her own leaped joyfully at the fervent whisper, "The world's no longer! Mine wholly, mine forever!"

The voice was that of Leonard Edmonton, her affianced bridegroom.

* * * * * *

In a parish church, near Dublin, a youthful pastor was preaching his first sermon to the little flock intrusted to his care. Heaven had gifted him with wondrous eloquence. Oratory was applied to its highest, holiest use.

> "Persuasion's golden flood,
> Gushing from depth of heart and brain,
> Rolled o'er the sluggish multitude
> In turbid wave on wave amain!" *

The messenger had chosen for his text, "Behold, I bring you good tidings of great joy."

* John Locke.

As manna divine dropped from his lips, his face shone almost "as the face of an angel;" or, rather, as though the angelic host who inspired his thoughts had shed upon his the reflection of their own radiant countenances.

His listeners grew light of heart as they hearkened. Darkly despairing minds received a ray of hope. The sad were comforted, the faint-hearted grew strong, the struggling were touched with peace, the true laborers tasted of the precious grapes that grew in the vineyard of their Lord.

There were but three occupants in the pew nearest to the chancel. At the further end sat an aged man with face upraised, in rapt attention, gratefully welcoming these "good tidings," which had only come to him after the snows of eighty years had fallen upon his head. Could this be the "stage villain," at whose portraitures of crime men once had trembled?

His venerable companion, at the opposite extremity of the pew, was some ten years younger. Few and pleasant were the lines that time had traced upon his benignant countenance. Those "good tidings" had been inscribed upon *his* heart in youth, yet were they ever new. More than once he turned from the preacher to gaze fondly upon one who sat between him and the other occupant of the pew. It was that young pastor's wife, the old man's newly-bestowed daughter. He watched every change of her soft and lovely visage, as

> "Now and then an ample tear trilled down
> Her delicate cheek,"

while the peaceful smile upon her lips seemed indeed

"not to know
What guests were in her eyes, which parted thence
As pearls from diamonds drôpped!"

Was Elma happy? Had she made a rich exchange? The answer was written upon her countenance in characters so luminous that even the blinded eyes of erring mortals could not misinterpret them.

FINIS.

BOSTON, 135 WASHINGTON STREET,
NOVEMBER, 1855.

NEW BOOKS AND NEW EDITIONS

PUBLISHED BY

TICKNOR AND FIELDS.

CHARLES READE.

PEG WOFFINGTON. A NOVEL. Price 75 cents.
CHRISTIE JOHNSTONE. A NOVEL. Price 75 cents.
CLOUDS AND SUNSHINE. A NOVEL. Price 75 cents.
SUSAN MERTON. A NOVEL. (Nearly ready.)

WILLIAM HOWITT.

LAND, LABOR AND GOLD. 2 vols. Price $2.00.
A BOY'S ADVENTURES IN AUSTRALIA. Price 75 cents.

THOMAS DE QUINCEY'S WRITINGS.

CONFESSIONS OF AN ENGLISH OPIUM-EATER, AND SUSPIRIA DE PROFUNDIS. With Portrait. Price 75 cents.
BIOGRAPHICAL ESSAYS. Price 75 cents.
MISCELLANEOUS ESSAYS. Price 75 cents.
THE CÆSARS. Price 75 cents.
LITERARY REMINISCENCES. 2 Vols. Price $1.50.
NARRATIVE AND MISCELLANEOUS PAPERS. 2 Vols. Price $1.50.
ESSAYS ON THE POETS, &c. 1 vol. 16mo. 75 cents.
HISTORICAL AND CRITICAL ESSAYS. 2 vols. $1.50.
AUTOBIOGRAPHIC SKETCHES. 1 vol. Price 75 cents.
ESSAYS ON PHILOSOPHICAL WRITERS, &c. 2 vols. 16mo. $1.50.
LETTERS TO A YOUNG MAN, AND OTHER PAPERS. 1 vol. Price 75 cents.
THEOLOGICAL ESSAYS AND OTHER PAPERS. 2 vols. Price $1.50.
THE NOTE BOOK. 1 vol. Price 75 cents.

HENRY W. LONGFELLOW'S WRITINGS.

THE SONG OF HIAWATHA. Price $1.00.

THE GOLDEN LEGEND. A Poem. Price $1.00.

POETICAL WORKS. This edition contains the six volumes mentioned below. In two volumes. 16 mo. Boards $2.00.

In Separate Volumes, each 75 cents.

VOICES OF THE NIGHT.
BALLADS AND OTHER POEMS.
SPANISH STUDENT; A PLAY IN THREE ACTS.
BELFRY OF BRUGES, AND OTHER POEMS.
EVANGELINE; A TALE OF ACADIE.
THE SEASIDE AND THE FIRESIDE.
THE WAIF. A Collection of Poems. Edited by Longfellow.
THE ESTRAY. A Collection of Poems. Edited by Longfellow.

MR. LONGFELLOW'S PROSE WORKS.

HYPERION. A ROMANCE. Price $1.00.
OUTRE-MER. A PILGRIMAGE. Price $1.00.
KAVANAGH. A TALE. Price 75 cents.

Illustrated editions of EVANGELINE, POEMS, HYPERION, and THE GOLDEN LEGEND.

ALFRED TENNYSON'S WRITINGS.

POETICAL WORKS. With Portrait. 2 vols. Cloth. $1.50.
THE PRINCESS. Cloth. Price 50 cents.
IN MEMORIAM. Cloth. Price 75 cents.
MAUD, AND OTHER POEMS. Cloth. Price 50 cents.

OLIVER WENDELL HOLMES'S WRITINGS.

POETICAL WORKS. With fine Portrait. Boards. $1.00.
ASTRÆA. Fancy paper. Price 25 cents.

NATHANIEL HAWTHORNE'S WRITINGS.

TWICE-TOLD TALES. Two volumes. Price $1.50.

THE SCARLET LETTER. Price 75 cents.

THE HOUSE OF THE SEVEN GABLES. Price $1.00.

THE SNOW IMAGE, AND OTHER TWICE-TOLD TALES. Price 75 cents.

THE BLITHEDALE ROMANCE. Price 75 cents.

MOSSES FROM AN OLD MANSE. New Edition. 2 vols. Price $1.50.

TRUE STORIES FROM HISTORY AND BIOGRAPHY. With four fine Engravings. Price 75 cents.

A WONDER-BOOK FOR GIRLS AND BOYS. With seven fine Engravings. Price 75 cents.

TANGLEWOOD TALES. Another 'Wonder-Book.' With Engravings. Price 88 cents.

BARRY CORNWALL'S WRITINGS.

ENGLISH SONGS AND OTHER SMALL POEMS. Enlarged Edition. Price $1.00.

ESSAYS AND TALES IN PROSE. 2 vols. Price $1.50.

JAMES RUSSELL LOWELL'S WRITINGS.

COMPLETE POETICAL WORKS. Revised, with Additions. two volumes, 16mo. Cloth. Price $1.50.

SIR LAUNFAL. New Edition. Price 25 cents.

A FABLE FOR CRITICS. New Edition. Price 50 cents.

THE BIGLOW PAPERS. A New Edition. Price 63 cents.

CHARLES KINGSLEY.

AMYAS LEIGH. A Novel. Price $1.25.
GLAUCUS; OR, THE WONDERS OF THE SHORE. 50 cents.
POETICAL WORKS. (In Press.)
A CHRISTMAS BOOK. (In Press.)

CHARLES SUMNER.

ORATIONS AND SPEECHES. 2 vols. $2.50.
A NEW VOLUME. (In Press.)

JOHN G. WHITTIER'S WRITINGS.

OLD PORTRAITS AND MODERN SKETCHES. 75 cents.
MARGARET SMITH'S JOURNAL. Price 75 cents.
SONGS OF LABOR, AND OTHER POEMS. Boards. 50 cents.
THE CHAPEL OF THE HERMITS. Cloth. 50 cents.
LITERARY RECREATIONS AND MISCELLANIES. Cloth. $1.00.

EDWIN P. WHIPPLE'S WRITINGS.

ESSAYS AND REVIEWS. 2 vols. Price $2.00.
LECTURES ON SUBJECTS CONNECTED WITH LITERATURE AND LIFE. Price 63 cents.
WASHINGTON AND THE REVOLUTION. Price 20 cents.

GEORGE S. HILLARD'S WRITINGS.

SIX MONTHS IN ITALY. 1 vol. 16mo. Price $1.50.
DANGERS AND DUTIES OF THE MERCANTILE PROFESSION. Price 25 cents.
SELECTIONS FROM THE WRITINGS OF WALTER SAVAGE LANDOR.

HENRY GILES'S WRITINGS.

LECTURES, ESSAYS, AND MISCELLANEOUS WRITINGS. 2 vols. Price $1.50.

DISCOURSES ON LIFE. Price 75 cents.

ILLUSTRATIONS OF GENIUS. Cloth. $1.00.

BAYARD TAYLOR'S WRITINGS.

POEMS OF HOME AND TRAVEL. Cloth. Price 75 cents.

POEMS OF THE ORIENT. Cloth. 75 cents.

WILLIAM MOTHERWELL'S WRITINGS.

POEMS, NARRATIVE AND LYRICAL. New Ed. $1.25.

POSTHUMOUS POEMS. Boards. Price 50 cents.

MINSTRELSY, ANC. AND MOD. 2 vols. Boards. $1.50.

ROBERT BROWNING.

POETICAL WORKS. 2 vols. $2.00.

MEN AND WOMEN. 1 vol. Price $1.00.

CAPT. MAYNE REID'S JUVENILE BOOKS.

THE DESERT HOME: OR, THE ADVENTURES OF A LOST FAMILY IN THE WILDERNESS. With fine Plates, $1.00.

THE BOY HUNTERS. With fine Plates. Just published. Price 75 cents.

THE YOUNG VOYAGEURS: OR, THE BOY HUNTERS IN THE NORTH. With Plates. Price 75 cents.

THE FOREST EXILES. With fine Plates. 75 cents.

a *

GOETHE'S WRITINGS.

WILHELM MEISTER. Translated by THOMAS CARLYLE. 2 vols. Price $2.50.

GOETHE'S FAUST. Translated by HAYWARD. Price 75 cents.

R. H. STODDARD'S WRITINGS.

POEMS. Cloth. Price 63 cents.

ADVENTURES IN FAIRY LAND. Price 75 cents.

REV. CHARLES LOWELL, D. D.

PRACTICAL SERMONS. 1 vol. 12mo. $1.25.

OCCASIONAL SERMONS. With fine Portrait. $1.25.

GEORGE LUNT.

LYRIC POEMS, &c. Cloth. 63 cents.

JULIA. A Poem. 50 cents.

PHILIP JAMES BAILEY.

THE MYSTIC, AND OTHER POEMS. 50 cents.

THE ANGEL WORLD, &c. 50 cents.

ANNA MARY HOWITT.

AN ART STUDENT IN MUNICH. Price $1.25.

A SCHOOL OF LIFE. A Story. Price 75 cents.

MARY RUSSELL MITFORD'S WRITINGS.

OUR VILLAGE. Illustrated. 2 vols. 16mo. Price $2.50.

ATHERTON, AND OTHER STORIES. 1 vol. 16mo. $1.25.

MRS. CROSLAND'S WRITINGS.

LYDIA: A WOMAN'S BOOK. Cloth. Price 75 cents.

ENGLISH TALES AND SKETCHES. Cloth. $1.00.

MEMORABLE WOMEN. Illustrated. $1.00.

GRACE GREENWOOD'S WRITINGS.

GREENWOOD LEAVES. 1st & 2d Series. $1.25 each.

POETICAL WORKS. With fine Portrait. Price 75 cents.

HISTORY OF MY PETS. With six fine Engravings. Scarlet cloth. Price 50 cents.

RECOLLECTIONS OF MY CHILDHOOD. With six fine Engravings. Scarlet cloth. Price 50 cents.

HAPS AND MISHAPS OF A TOUR IN EUROPE. Price $1.25.

MERRIE ENGLAND. A new Juvenile. Price 75 cents.

A FOREST TRAGEDY, AND OTHER TALES. (In Press.)

A NEW JUVENILE. (In Press.)

MRS. MOWATT.

AUTOBIOGRAPHY OF AN ACTRESS. Price $1.25.

PLAYS. ARMAND AND FASHION. Price 50 cents.

MIMIC LIFE. 1 vol. Price $1.25.

ALICE CARY.

POEMS. 1 vol. 16mo. Price $1.00.
CLOVERNOOK CHILDREN. With Plates. 75 cents.

MRS. TAPPAN.

RAINBOWS FOR CHILDREN. Illustrated. 75 cents.
THE MAGICIAN'S SHOW BOX. Illustrated. 75 cents.

MRS. ELIZA LEE.

MEMOIR OF THE BUCKMINSTERS. $1.25.
FLORENCE, The Parish Orphan. 50 cents.

MRS. JUDSON'S WRITINGS.

ALDERBROOK. By Fanny Forrester. 2 vols. Price $1.75.
THE KATHAYAN SLAVE, AND OTHER PAPERS. 1 vol. Price 63 cents.
MY TWO SISTERS: A Sketch from Memory. Price 50 cents.

POETRY.

ALEXANDER SMITH'S POEMS. 1 vol. 16mo. Cloth. Price 50 cents.
CHARLES MACKAY'S POEMS. 1 vol. Cloth. Price $1.00.
HENRY ALFORD'S POEMS. Just out. Price $1.25.
RICHARD MONCKTON MILNES. Poems of Many Years. Boards. Price 75 cents.

CHARLES SPRAGUE. POETICAL AND PROSE WRITINGS. With fine Portrait. Boards. Price 75 cents.

GERMAN LYRICS. Translated by CHARLES T. BROOKS. 1 vol. 16mo. Cloth. Price $1.00.

THOMAS W. PARSONS. POEMS. Price $1.00.

LYTERIA: A DRAMATIC POEM. BY J. P. QUINCY. Price 50 cents.

JOHN G. SAXE. POEMS. With Portrait. Boards, 63 cents. Cloth, 75 cents.

HENRY T. TUCKERMAN. POEMS. Cloth. Price 75 cents.

BOWRING'S MATINS AND VESPERS. Price 50 cents.

YRIARTE'S FABLES. Translated by G. H. DEVEREUX. Price 63 cents.

MEMORY AND HOPE. A BOOK OF POEMS, REFERRING TO CHILDHOOD. Cloth. Price $2.00.

THALATTA: A BOOK FOR THE SEA-SIDE. 1 vol. 16mo. Cloth. Price 75 cents.

PASSION-FLOWERS. By Mrs. HOWE. Price 75 cents.

PHŒBE CARY. POEMS AND PARODIES. 75 cents.

MISCELLANEOUS.

G. H. LEWES. THE LIFE AND WORKS OF GOETHE. 2 vols. 16mo.

OAKFIELD. A Novel. BY LIEUT. ARNOLD. Price $1.00.

ESSAYS ON THE FORMATION OF OPINIONS AND THE PURSUIT OF TRUTH. 1 vol. 16mo. Price $1.00.

WALDEN: OR, LIFE IN THE WOODS. By HENRY D. THOREAU. 1 vol. 16mo. Price $1.00.

LIGHT ON THE DARK RIVER: OR, MEMOIRS OF MRS. HAMLIN. 1 vol. 16mo. Cloth. Price $1.00.

WILLIAM MOUNTFORD. THORPE: A QUIET ENGLISH TOWN, AND HUMAN LIFE THEREIN. 16mo. Price $1.00.

NOTES FROM LIFE. By HENRY TAYLOR, author of 'Philip Van Artevelde.' 1 vol. 16mo. Cloth. Price 63 cents.

REJECTED ADDRESSES. By HORACE and JAMES SMITH. Boards, Price 50 cents. Cloth, 63 cents.

WARRENIANA. A Companion to the 'Rejected Addresses.' Price 63 cents.

WILLIAM WORDSWORTH'S BIOGRAPHY. 2 vols. $2.50.

ART OF PROLONGING LIFE. By HUFELAND. Edited by ERASMUS WILSON, F. R. S. 1 vol. 16mo. Price 75 cents.

JOSEPH T. BUCKINGHAM'S PERSONAL MEMOIRS AND RECOLLECTIONS OF EDITORIAL LIFE. With Portrait. 2 vols. 16mo. Price $1.50.

VILLAGE LIFE IN EGYPT. By the Author of 'Purple Tints of Paris.' 2 vols. 16mo. Price $1.25.

DR. JOHN C. WARREN. THE PRESERVATION OF HEALTH, &c. 1 vol. Price 38 cents.

PRIOR'S LIFE OF EDMUND BURKE. 2 vols. $2.00.

NATURE IN DISEASE. By DR. JACOB BIGELOW. 1 vol. 16mo. Price $1.50.

WENSLEY: A STORY WITHOUT A MORAL. Price 75 cents.

GOLDSMITH. THE VICAR OF WAKEFIELD. Illustrated Edition. Price $3.00.

PALISSY THE POTTER. By the Author of 'How to make Home Unhealthy.' 2 vols. 16mo. Price $1.50.

THE BARCLAYS OF BOSTON. By MRS. H. G. OTIS. 1 vol. 12mo. $1.25.

HORACE MANN. Thoughts for a Young Man. 25 cents.

F. W. P. GREENWOOD. Sermons of Consolation. $1.00.

THE BOSTON BOOK. Price $1.25.

ANGEL-VOICES. Price 38 cents.

SIR ROGER DE COVERLEY. From the 'Spectator.' 75 cents.

S. T. WALLIS. Spain, her Institutions, Politics, and Pub lic Men. Price $1.00.

MEMOIR OF ROBERT WHEATON. 1 vol. Price $1.00.

LABOR AND LOVE: A Tale of English Life. 50 cents.

Mrs. PUTNAM'S RECEIPT BOOK; An Assistant to Housekeepers. 1 vol. 16mo. Price 50 cents.

Mrs. A. C. LOWELL. Education of Girls. Price 25 cents.

THE SOLITARY OF JUAN FERNANDEZ. By the Author of Picciola. Price 50 cents.

RUTH. A New Novel by the Author of 'Mary Barton.' Cheap Edition. Price 38 cents.

EACH OF THE ABOVE POEMS AND PROSE WRITINGS, MAY BE HAD IN VARIOUS STYLES OF HANDSOME BINDING.

☞ Any book published by Ticknor & Fields, will be sent by mail, postage free, on receipt of publication price.

Their stock of Miscellaneous Books is very complete, and they respectfully solicit orders from CITY AND COUNTRY LIBRARIES.

ILLUSTRATED

JUVENILE BOOKS.

CURIOUS STORIES ABOUT FAIRIES. 75 cents.
KIT BAM'S ADVENTURES. 75 cents.
THE FOREST EXILES. 75 cents.
THE DESERT HOME. $1.00.
THE BOY HUNTERS. 75 cents.
THE YOUNG VOYAGEURS. 75 cents.
A BOY'S ADVENTURES IN AUSTRALIA. 75 cents.
RAINBOWS FOR CHILDREN. 75 cents.
THF MAGICIAN'S SHOW BOX. 75 cents.
TANGLEWOOD TALES. 75 cents.
A WONDER BOOK FOR GIRLS AND BOYS. 75 cents.
TRUE STORIES FROM HISTORY AND BIOGRAPAY. 75 cts.
MERRIE ENGLAND. By Grace Greenwood. 75 cents.
CLOVERNOOK CHLIDREN. 75 cents.
ADVENTURES IN FAIRY LAND. 75 cents.
HISTORY OF MY PETS. By Grace Greenwood. 50 cents.
RECOLLECTIONS OF MY CHILDHOOD. 50 cents.
FLORENCE, THE PARISH ORPHAN. 50 cents.
MEMOIRS OF A LONDON DOLL. 50 cents.
THE DOLL AND HER FRIENDS. 50 cents.
TALES FROM CATLAND. 50 cents.
AUNT EFFIE'S RHYMES FOR LITTLE CHILDREN. 75 cents.
THE STORY OF AN APPLE. 50 cents.
THE GOOD NATURED BEAR. 75 cents.
PETER PARLEY'S SHORT STORIES FOR LONG NIGHTS. 50 cents.
THE HISTORY OF THE AMERICAN REVOLUTION. 38 cents.
THE HISTORY OF THE NEW ENGLAND STATES. 38 cents.
THE HISTORY OF THE MIDDLE STATES. 38 cents.
THE HISTORY OF THE SOUTHERN STATES. 38 cents.
THE HISTORY OF THE WESTERN STATES. 38 cents.
THE SOLITARY OF JUAN FERNANDEZ. 50 cents.
JACK HALLIARD'S VOYAGES. 38 cents.
THE INDESTRUCTIBLE BOOKS FOR CHILDREN. Each 15 cents.

www.ingramcontent.com/pod-product-compliance
Lightning Source LLC
LaVergne TN
LVHW021144110826
845150LV00005B/1122
9781425547639